Employment Skills for Office Careers

Employment Skills
for Office Careers

Grady Kimbrell
Educational Consultant
Santa Barbara, California

Charles Francis Barrett
Automated Office Occupations Instructor
Regional Occupational Program (ROP)
Daly City, California

West Publishing Company
Minneapolis/St. Paul   New York   Los Angeles   San Francisco

Copy Editor: Allen Gooch
Composition: Parkwood Composition Services, Inc.

West's Commitment to the Environment

In 1906, West Publishing Company began recycling materials left over from the production of books. This began a tradition of efficient and responsible use of resources. Today, up to 95 percent of our legal books and 70 percent of our college and school texts are printed on recycled, acid-free stock. West also recycles nearly 22 million pounds of scrap paper annually—the equivalent of 181,717 trees. Since the 1960s, West has devised ways to capture and recycle waste inks, solvents, oils, and vapors created in the printing process. We also recycle plastics of all kinds, wood, glass, corrugated cardboard, and batteries, and have eliminated the use of Styrofoam book packaging. We at West are proud of the longevity and the scope of our commitment to the environment.

Production, Prepress, Printing and Binding by West Publishing Company.

 TEXT IS PRINTED ON 10% POST CONSUMER RECYCLED PAPER  PRINTED WITH SOY INK

British Library Cataloguing-in-Publication Data. A catalogue record for this book is available from the British Library.

COPYRIGHT © 1995 By WEST PUBLISHING COMPANY
                610 Opperman Drive
                P.O. Box 64526
                St. Paul, MN 55164-0526

Library of Congress Cataloging-in-Publication Data

Kimbrell, Grady.
   Employment skills for office careers / Grady Kimbrell, Charles
Francis Barrett.
     p.   cm.
   Includes index.
   ISBN 0-314-02246-5 (soft)
   1. Office practice—Vocational guidance. 2. Vocational guidance.
I. Barrett, Charles Francis. II. Title.
HF5547.5.K478 1995
651′.023′73—dc20   94-22666
                                          CIP

Photo credits follow the Index.

Contents in Brief

Contents

■ Chapter 5   On the Job: What to Expect   166

■ Chapter 6   Getting Along with People   204

■ Chapter 7   Moving Ahead toward Your Career Goal   248

Preface

Employment Skills for Office Careers was written to emphasize "people skills" and thus better prepare students for the job market and for success in the office environment. *Employment Skills for Office Careers* also provides career information and introduces the students to the vast array of job opportunities and the most effective methods for pursuing those opportunities.

Employment Skills for Office Careers is interesting as well as informative. In addition to using an easy to understand, lively, conversational writing style, the authors have developed an abundance of high-interest features to capture and hold the student's attention.

- Each chapter of *Employment Skills for Office Careers* opens with "Before You Begin" questions to help spark student interest. These questions are completed as "In Conclusion" questions at the end of the chapters so that students can see how their knowledge and opinions have changed as a result of studying the chapter.
- Special features within each chapter such as "Making Office Decisions," "What's Your Attitude?" and "Human Relations" emphasize the importance of these topics to the use of real-life scenarios.
- The "Industry Focus" feature provides perspectives of managers from corporations.
- The marginal "Office Tips" offer practical suggestions.
- "Large Office/Small Office" compares the tasks and environments in large and small offices, thus giving students help in evaluating their personal career interests and objectives.
- At the end of each chapter is a comprehensive section of study aids.

■ A quiz and activities close each chapter. The activities allow the students to apply what they learn from the textbook, therefore bridging the gap between classroom and office careers.

Employment Skills for Office Careers contains much valuable practical information, interesting features, and activities. The authors believe that this approach will ensure content comprehension and thoroughly prepare students as professionals to move successfully toward their ultimate career goals.

About the Authors

Grady Kimbrell has been involved in business and career education for more than twenty years. He began as a business education teacher in Kansas and California, supervising his students on the job who were part of a school-sponsored work-experience program. Later he served as District Coordinator for Work-Experience Education in Santa Barbara, California.

An interest in research and computers led to Grady serving as Director of Research in Santa Barbara Schools. This experience, in turn, led to a variety of consultancy opportunities both in schools and private businesses.

Grady's first business and career publications were motivated by the apparent lack of realistic goals voiced by students in California schools. Those early efforts were well received and provided encouragement for developing new programs and more than a dozen books dealing with business and career education.

Grady holds degrees in business administration, educational psychology, and business education.

Charles Francis Barrett received his Bachelor of Science degree from Stonehill College and his Master of Arts degree from San Francisco State University. For over 20 years he has been a business education instructor for the San Mateo County Office of Education's Regional Occupational Program (ROP). In addition, he has been a Supervisor of the ROP's Evening and Saturday Division. He is also a Teacher/Trainer for the California State Department of Education's Designated Subjects Credential Program. He is the author of various articles for state and national publications. His accomplishments include San Mateo County ROP Teacher of the Year, and his program was recognized as one of the most outstanding vocational programs in the country by the U.S. Department of Education. For many years Charles has been an active member of the California Business Education Association of which he has been a section officer and held statewide committee chairs. He has kept current in his teaching by working as a word processor/secretary for private industries.

Introduction

Consider for a moment the word *work*. It's as sturdy a sounding word as we have in our language. It has weight and importance. It sounds like what it is.

Work was undoubtedly the earliest of human endeavors because it literally meant survival. Work can be anything from making sandwiches to programming the flight of the space shuttle. The person who delivers your newspaper works. The president of the United States works. What Rembrandt did was work.

Work is many things to those who work. It is necessary, meaningful, interesting, challenging, and honorable. It can be as fulfilling an experience as any we will undertake in our lives if we are doing what we want to do.

If you are reading this book, you are preparing to enter the world of work. You are laying the foundation of your career. *Employment Skills for Office Careers* will guide you as you build on that foundation. Think of it as your blueprint for success.

Chapter 1 will introduce you to the nature of work and why people work. There's a lot more to it than you may have realized. The importance of the right attitude will be discussed and stressed. And stressed again. You will learn how to evaluate and adjust your own attitude. Your success in the world of work depends on it.

Chapter 1 will also introduce new terms such as self-concept and positive affirmation. As in all chapters, there will be exercises and problems to solve as well as chapter reviews.

Chapter 2 will present the occupational outlook through the year 2005. This will give you a general idea of office employment opportunities. You will also learn about specific job classifications.

Chapter 3 will help you determine the right career for you based on your personal attributes, your choice of life-style, and your interests. It will illustrate the importance of defining your goals and how informed planning leads to goals you can reach. This chapter will provide sources of career information and resources, as well as realistic suggestions on planning your career.

Chapter 4 lays out the reality of the job search for you—a process most people dread, often with good reason. It can be a discouraging and frustrating experience. But preparation is the key to success here, and this chapter will prepare you. It will help you get into the right frame of mind to begin your search and then lead you step-by-step to an offer of employment.

You will learn about networking and following up on leads. You will be provided with sample resumes and job applications. Effective interviewing skills will be discussed. In a competitive job market, you need to distinguish yourself in the eyes of a potential employer.

Chapter 5—All right! You got the job. Now what? In this chapter, you will learn what to expect. The nuts and bolts of employment are discussed here, such as the W-4 form, company policy, paychecks, work schedules, and time cards. Working conditions, orientation, work space, and office equipment are among the things you, as a new employee, will face.

This chapter will also prepare you for your employer's expectations regarding productivity, quality of work, dependability, and absenteeism. You will become aware of unwritten policy, such as dress and personal conduct.

Chapter 6 is an extensive look at interpersonal relationships. Getting along with people is as important as any other office skill. You will be part of a team. You will be expected to operate in a professional manner with enthusiasm and courtesy. You will need to know the difference between aggressiveness and assertiveness and why one is more appropriate than the other.

This chapter also gives a brief supervisor's perspective. Remembering that bosses are human and have good days and bad days like everyone else is to your advantage when dealing with them.

Difficult people also are discussed in this chapter, and some coping strategies are suggested. Receiving and giving criticism is unavoidable, and there is a graceful way to do this. Well-developed interpersonal skills will make you a valuable employee.

Chapter 7 will help you evaluate your progress on the job. You will understand how to work with your supervisor to improve your job performance. You will understand how to enhance your chances for promotion and how to present your case for a salary increase.

Chapter 7 also addresses in detail "the look" of a successful businessperson with attention to grooming, style of dress, and overall presentation. Your appearance is judged, and that is a fact of life whether it seems fair or not. When you have been out in the work world awhile, you cannot help but notice that successful people have "the look."

The recurring theme throughout *Employment Skills* is this: have a positive attitude and do whatever you must to maintain it. It will make your work experience a happy and meaningful one. Now get out there and show the world who you are!

Your Attitude and Work

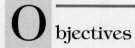

Objectives

After completing this chapter, you will be able to do the following:

1. List and describe at least five reasons people work.
2. Describe the effects on others of a positive versus a negative attitude.
3. Explain how to change a negative attitude into a positive attitude.
4. List five attributes that all employers expect of their employees.

New Office Terms

esteem	self-concept
negative attitude	self-talk
positive affirmation	values
positive attitude	work
self-actualization	work ethic

Before You Begin . . .

Answer the following questions that preview material covered in this chapter:

1. *Why do people who have no need for further income often continue to work?*
2. *What is a self-fulfilling prophecy and what effect does it have?*
3. *How can you change a negative attitude into a positive one?*

Success in the world of work and how satisfied you are with your place in it depend largely on *attitude.* This means not only your attitude toward the work itself, but your attitude toward those with whom you work. This overall *work attitude* will naturally depend on your attitude and feeling about yourself—your *self-concept.* If you enjoy your job and feel that you are doing something worthwhile, you will receive satisfaction from your work. You will look forward to going to the office to start a new project or to complete one.

When you get along well with your co-workers, you will look forward not only to working with them but also to having personal conversations with them during breaks. You may even form friendships that extend beyond the workplace.

Your attitude toward work will significantly affect your overall happiness even when you are not on the job. In fact, your work may become the central activity of your life.

■ WHAT IS WORK?

The Random House Dictionary of the English Language says that work means "exertion or effort directed to produce or accomplish something; labor; toil."

There will be breaks during your working day for relaxing and talking with co-workers.

Ralph Waldo Emerson wrote, "The purpose of life is not to be happy. It is to be useful, to be honorable, to be compassionate, to have it make some difference that you have lived and lived well." But could it follow that happiness is a by-product of being purposefully engaged in work? Feeling good about what you do and how you do it—your work attitude—takes the concept of work to a higher level.

Think of some well-known people today in business, science, and the arts—people such as Microsoft founder Bill Gates, Redken Labs founder and CEO Paula Kent Meehan, Nobel laureate Linus Pauling, astronaut/astrophysicist Sally Ride, or actor/writer/producer Bill Cosby. The dictionary gives us the basic definition of work, but Emerson's philosophy gives us its fullest and truest definition.

When actor Buddy Ebsen was asked during an interview when he intended to quit working, he said never. "Working is my life," he explained. He was in his eighties.

Bette Davis continued making movies after she was eighty and after a severe stroke had left her face partially paralyzed. TV interviewer Barbara Walters asked Davis what kept her going. The actress replied, "Really and truly—what keeps me going is work." The driving force that kept her alive and happy was accomplishing something worthwhile.

Anthropologist Margaret Mead is quoted as saying she might die someday but she would never retire!

Work doesn't have to be an unpleasant activity. If you enjoy what you're doing, it can seem nearly effortless—an important, vital part of your life and your existence as a creative human being.

Work, then, is any useful activity or purposeful, creative endeavor.

■ WHAT MOTIVATES PEOPLE TO WORK?

In the world of work, there is a world of reasons why people work. Money is the motivator most of us are familiar with, but intellectual challenge, creative fulfillment, and the satisfaction of being part of a team add to the value of work.

Money

Money is the primary reason people work. Few of us are in a position to work without pay regardless of how much we enjoy our jobs.

The money you earn by working provides independence, and having money in your pocket makes you feel good. One of your reasons for pursuing your career goals may be to increase your earning power. Perhaps you also have the responsibility of a family. Having enough money to meet the expenses and obligations of a family adds to a sense of security and safety.

Most people enjoy and take pride in having a home, so they spend time and money decorating and repairing their living space. A major part of earnings can be spent on home improvements and furnishings.

Your sense of security will also be enhanced if you are able to earn enough money to establish a regular savings program. Education, unforeseeable medical bills, and traveling are just a few examples of large expenses you may wish to be able to cover from your savings.

People also want money for social and leisure activities. Hobbies, movies, recreation, and consumer goods such as clothing, automobiles, and televisions are only part of an endless list of things on which you might want to spend your money.

In some circles, a person's worth is gauged by how much money he or she earns. Money can bring power and influence. Some people work very hard for years to acquire things and accomplish goals that are materially based simply because it makes them feel important.

Is it important to you to make a lot of money? If so, earning a lot of money will require you to spend long hours on the job at the expense of other things you might do in your leisure time.

Creative Fulfillment

Many people are driven by the need to be creative. Writers, dancers, musicians, and artists work to express their special talents. Mozart, Jane Austen, and Benjamin Franklin are among those historical figures who distinguished themselves through a need for creative fulfillment.

You probably have a special talent or something you do especially well. For example, you may have a wonderful speaking voice that could lead to a career in radio, sales, or customer service. A speaking voice of fine quality will be an asset as you greet others in person or on the telephone.

Creative fulfillment can be achieved when pride and diligence result in a job well done. From a small report, carefully and neatly prepared, to a new automobile design that will shake up the market, creative needs are often fulfilled at work.

Being Part of a Team

You and the people you work with are a team. You have tasks to complete and goals to meet. Successful teamwork is a gratifying experience. Consider the people who work for NASA. You've probably seen some of them on television shaking one another's hands, clapping, patting one another on the back, and hugging after a triumphant shuttle mission. Being part of a team that gets things done and gets them done right is a wonderful experience.

Influence and Responsibility

The more responsibility you are willing to take, the greater influence you will have. This feeling of importance is necessary for some people to have a satisfying work experience. They take initiative and responsibility and are most happy when doing so. They often become leaders.

Many people, though, don't choose to accept much responsibility. Their ambitions may be limited or they may not have the time to invest. Yet they feel important because they fulfill their own particular role on a project.

Intellectual Stimulation

Imagine that you have inherited a lot of money. Would you continue to work? There are people who are financially secure who do have jobs because they find the work interesting and stimulating. Work also adds to their sense of purpose. Often, retired people enjoy doing volunteer work because it keeps them mentally sharp and active and makes them feel needed.

Most people spend time in their off hours doing the things they enjoy with friends they met on the job.

Susan learned to sew when she was very young, making dresses for her dolls. As she grew up, she began to draw pictures of dresses, coats, and outfits for girls to wear. She enjoyed sewing and drawing, but she didn't realize that there might be a career for her associated with what she considered to be only a hobby.

In school, Susan learned word processing and later accepted a job as a word processor in a large office. She found her work interesting, but something was missing from her job. She wasn't sure why, but she knew she wasn't completely happy.

Susan's office was in a large building that also housed a dressmaking firm. The building had a cafeteria where she met and had conversations with some people who worked for the dressmaking company. Susan discovered that a word processing job would soon be available in the dressmaking com-

pany, so she applied for the job and was hired.

Though her duties were essentially the same, Susan was so happy in her new environment that she had a wonderful attitude and looked forward to going to work every day.

Susan eventually learned how to design and create clothing with the computer. Her new office responsibilities incorporated dress designing with her word processing and other computer skills. Now she had an active role in an industry that she loved.

1. What effect did the work environment have on Susan's attitude toward work?
2. If you were Susan, and the building you worked in did not include the dressmaking company, would you continue working at the same job or look for something else?

Some jobs and careers are truly fascinating. They may require research, problem solving, inventiveness, the creation of a product or a system, or some other form of intellectual activity. There are those who work just for this challenge.

Even if your job isn't inherently interesting, you can nearly always make it interesting by being concerned about the people you work with and taking special care to complete the tasks that are assigned to you. Your attitude about what you do can make it either very dull or very interesting.

THE WORK ETHIC

The "American Dream" is a phrase that is familiar to all of us. It basically means "work hard, be rewarded." It is our own cultural twist on the Puritan **work ethic,** which simply stated meant "hard work is good." When we trace the concept of the work ethic to its most primitive, i.e., "you don't work, you don't eat," we can see that a work ethic of some sort has been around since earliest human history.

We can expand the idea of the work ethic from the focus on the individual to the bigger picture—the common good. This is the concept that work should make a contribution to society. Many kinds of organizations serve the common good, such as churches, nonprofit community organizations, and social service agencies. These organizations offer diverse and interesting jobs, including office work of all types.

Your job may not directly serve the community, but everyone who works makes a contribution by providing the goods and services needed for the economic survival of society. If you are working, you are living the work ethic to some extent. And you probably understand that most people work for a combination of reasons. There are as many different kinds of jobs as there are different kinds of people. Finding work that suits your needs and interests is one of life's most satisfying experiences.

R ecall Time

Answer the following questions:

1. What are two definitions of *work?* List and discuss them.
2. People are motivated to work because of their own personal needs. What are four reasons people want or need to work?
3. Some people work for *creative satisfaction.* What does this term mean to you?
4. Briefly, what is meant by the term *work ethic?*

YOUR ATTITUDE

When people feel they have choices about the type of work they do, they demonstrate a better attitude on the job. Those who feel trapped in jobs that don't interest them have a different attitude entirely. You will probably work about two thousand hours a year for about forty years of your life. That's approximately eighty thousand hours. It will seem like an eternity if you resent your job and the people with whom you work. You will feel angry and empty without intellectual stimulation or creative fulfillment. Your sense of worth and importance will not thrive and you will feel like a failure.

It will always be to your advantage to have the best attitude you can toward working. Attitude influences not only your emotional and physical health, but your chances for success and happiness as well.

Negative Attitude

What is commonly called a bad attitude is more properly called a **negative attitude,** and it can take many forms. Workers with negative attitudes are unpleasant, indifferent, and rarely smile. They seldom greet their co-workers or have a good word for their associates. They may never offer assistance to anyone.

Do you know someone with a negative attitude? People with negative attitudes usually have low self-esteem and blame others for their own mistakes and shortcomings. They seem unable to appreciate a point of view that is not their own and are overbearing with their opinions. Their own well-being comes first, even if it is secured at the expense of others.

You've seen these people in action. They complain constantly. They complain about supervisors, co-workers, office conditions, their salaries, the weather—anything and everything. They point out problems, but don't offer solutions. They find fault, but never offer praise. Workers with negative attitudes are dark clouds in the atmosphere of the workplace, and their co-workers will make a point of avoiding them.

How is your attitude? Any room for improvement? Attitude adjustment is within everyone's reach and the benefits of an improved attitude will serve you well on the job and throughout your life.

Positive Attitude

You know it when you see it. It is energetic, helpful, productive, and optimistic. People with a **positive attitude** generally have high levels of self-esteem, are pleasant to be around, and have lots of friends and interests. They smile easily, offer their assistance, are considerate of their co-workers, and they know how to compromise.

People with positive attitudes seem even tempered and able to meet adversity with enviable inner strength. They rarely complain and will take responsibility for their mistakes and shortcomings. They don't blame anyone else for their failures.

You will rarely hear people with a positive attitude criticize co-workers or supervisors. They understand loyalty and respect the opinions of others.

Examine your overall attitude, listing both negative and positive traits. Pay special attention to the negative traits and plan how you will go about making them positive traits.

■ FIGURE 1–1
Examples of positive and negative attitude traits

POSITIVE ATTITUDE TRAITS	NEGATIVE ATTITUDE TRAITS
■ Shows consideration for others	■ Thinks only of self
■ Respects other opinions	■ Forces own opinions on others
■ Smiles often and with ease	■ Almost never smiles
■ Complains very little	■ Complains all the time
■ Admits making own mistakes	■ Blames others for own mistakes
■ Helps to solve problems	■ Expects everything to go wrong
■ Looks other people in the eyes during conversations	■ Avoids eye contact during conversations
■ Almost never criticizes others	■ Frequently criticizes others
■ Accepts change or suggestions from others	■ Unwilling to make changes
■ Has many interests	■ Has few interests

O F F I C E   T I P

If your mental energy peaks early in the day, schedule your difficult tasks then.

Molly Lopez
Executive Secretary
The Clorox Company

Q: Mrs. Lopez, how important is a good attitude for an office worker?

A: A positive attitude in an office environment is probably one of the most important characteristics an employee can possess. A positive attitude simply means going into a job with an open mind. Allow yourself to grow with the job; accept the good and the not-so-good aspect of any given task. Offer ideas and suggestions on how to make it a better place in which to work, but do not be disappointed if they are not readily accepted.

Q: Have you seen any examples of workers being promoted because of a great attitude?

A: Yes, two employees were candidates for a promotional opportunity in the Executive Offices. Both had excellent skills. One, however, goes the "extra mile" in everything she does. She, of course, received the promotion.

Q: Have you seen any examples of workers who have been terminated because of a poor attitude?

A: Yes, there was a man with impeccable technical skills. His work was of the highest quality. His negative attitude, however, was felt by the entire office. Within a year of his employment, his "I was looking for a job when I found this one" attitude resulted in his termination.

■ YOUR RESPONSIBILITIES

One important aspect of any job is responsibility. Even if your job doesn't require you to accept total responsibility for the outcome of a project, you will be responsible for your portion of it and for your personal conduct. Your attitude will be reflected in your willingness to meet your responsibilities.

Your employer will have certain expectations of you, and it will be your responsibility to fulfill these expectations. There will probably be times when you aren't sure what your employer wants you to do. When you feel unsure, ask what he or she expects of you.

Cooperation

Your employer will expect you to be cooperative. You will probably not be working alone, so it will be important for you to cooperate with other

Helping out with tasks that might not be part of your job description shows you've got the right attitude!

workers. Some people feel their responsibilities are limited to an established set of tasks. Usually this is not the case, and the work of different people may overlap from day to day. Sometimes other workers will need your assistance. When is it your obligation to help them? In most instances, you should be willing to help unless it prevents you from completing your own assignments. If such a conflict arises regularly, ask your supervisor for guidance.

In addition, sometimes you will be given an assignment that you feel is not part of your job—a task that doesn't fit your job description. Whether you see the request as a regular part of your job or not, you will be expected to take on the assignment willingly, without complaining. You may be asked to do some jobs you just don't like, but your supervisor will see it as your responsibility to be cooperative in doing these jobs willingly and with a positive attitude.

Honesty

Businesses lose huge sums of money every year to theft by their employees. It is your responsibility to understand what is yours and what belongs to the company. Some people think it's all right to take home stationery, pens, postage stamps, pencils, or paper clips. Some act as if these are perks (benefits) of the job. This is not usually the case. In fact, taking such items is usually considered grounds for dismissal. If it is not clearly stated that you are entitled to help yourself to office supplies, then all supplies should stay in the office to be used for official business.

On full-time jobs, your employer is paying you for a full day's work. Standing around the watercooler is not working. Talking on the company telephone to family and friends is not working. Give your employer an honest day's work—that is what you are paid to do.

Your supervisor will expect you to be honest when asked about different aspects of your work. Don't make up stories and excuses for things that are being questioned. Just tell the truth. Your supervisors will appreciate and respect you for it.

Honesty is your responsibility and an obligation you have to your employer.

Dependability

You are dependable if you are on the job every day and on time. Continual tardiness can be grounds for dismissal. If you are ill and cannot report for work, call your supervisor as early as possible. That way, someone can be found to cover your responsibilities for the day.

Missing a day of work without a legitimate reason or not calling in is also grounds for dismissal. Some people just decide to sleep in and don't bother to call. This is irresponsible behavior and reflects a negative attitude.

You are dependable if you can be counted on to complete your work to the best of your ability. You are dependable if you can be relied upon by your co-workers. Dependability means follow-through. It means doing what you say you'll do. Your family and friends want to count on you. Your employer and co-workers will expect to.

Mary Ann was hired as a front desk clerk in the office at the Young Men's Christian Association (YMCA). She was interested in physical fitness and was delighted to get the job. She was efficient and did all that was required of her neatly and on time. She basically liked her job, came to work on time each day, and left at quitting time.

However, Mary Ann rarely smiled and did not seem to have fun with her co-workers and the YMCA members. This gave people the impression that she was indifferent and did not care about her work. The YMCA is a place where people go to relax and have a pleasant time in their leisure. Even though Mary Ann was good at her job, people complained about her attitude.

Actually, Mary Ann was a conscientious young woman, and she wanted to do her best. She was unaware that she had an unpleasant manner. When it was time for her performance review, her supervisor explained that members were unhappy about her behavior. Mary Ann was eager to know how to improve the situation, and her supervisor gave her some ideas about how to behave more pleasantly.

First, her supervisor suggested that Mary Ann smile more often. Second, she suggested that Mary Ann make sure she understood what the members wanted. Third, she asked Mary Ann to try to meet the members' needs by acting interested in their concerns.

Mary Ann's behavior improved, and her co-workers complimented her on her efforts. Several members spent more time with her and seemed to like her much better. Although she had been unaware of her problem, her willingness to change demonstrated a positive attitude—and she was even happier with her job.

1. What would have happened if Mary Ann's supervisor had not explained her effect on co-workers and others?
2. What if Mary Ann's supervisor had been negative in her criticism?
3. What if Mary Ann had not been willing to change?

Willingness to Learn

When you accept a position with a company, you are required to learn that job inside out. You may be learning something new every day for months. You may feel pressure, a little frustration, or some anxiety, but that is the challenge of the new and unfamiliar. You have assured your employer that you will learn this job, and your willingness to take directions will help immensely. And don't underestimate the impact of taking initiative. Learn more than you have to, and you increase your chances for advancement.

You will also be expected to listen to constructive criticism from your supervisor about how you are performing your job. This may not always be comfortable, but it will be to your advantage. Remember Mary Ann and her job at the YMCA? She willingly took suggestions from her supervisor about her behavior. Mary Ann was not aware of her problem. But when her supervisor pointed it out, she willingly listened and made some changes.

Acceptable Personal Conduct

Anything less than a businesslike manner will not be acceptable in the office or workplace. You must dress appropriately, be clean and well

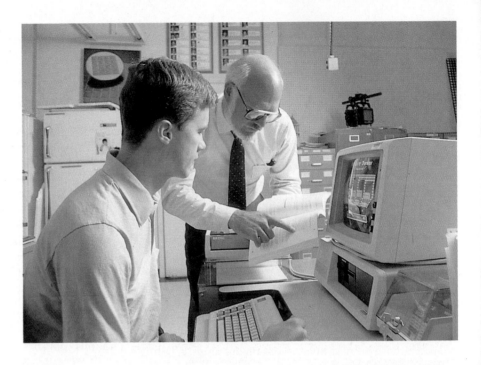

groomed, and refrain from using foul language and loud talk, carrying
food around, and using other bad manners around customers and co-
workers.

Every office has rules. Know them and follow them. Don't assume
you can eat at your desk or smoke in the break room. Use common
sense and practice thoughtfulness and consideration of others. If you
are unsure of yourself or the rules are unclear to you, talk with your
supervisor.

If you have a personal problem such as alcohol or drug abuse, family
dysfunction, or emotional difficulties, it is your responsibility to seek
help. Personal problems sooner or later undermine job performance.
Larger companies may have an industrial nurse or psychologist with
whom you can discuss problems. This will be confidential. A professional counselor can make it easier for you to get the help you need. If
your company doesn't offer counseling services, your county department of health, your church, or other community support group may
be the best alternative.

Some positions require special off-the-job conduct. For example, if
you work in the office of a public figure, such as a politician, you will
be expected to be a model citizen at all times. If you are employed by
a school system, your conduct must be above reproach because of your
contact with children. Can you think of any other jobs with special off-
the-job conduct requirements?

You will always be accountable for your behavior whether as a student or as an employee. Know what is expected of you and maintain
an appropriate level of personal conduct.

Recall Time

Answer the following questions:

1. What are four characteristics of a negative attitude?
2. What are four characteristics of a positive attitude?
3. When you accept a job, you accept responsibility. What might an employer expect from you as an employee?
4. An employee is responsible for his or her personal conduct. What does this statement mean?

ATTITUDES AND SELF-CONCEPT

Psychologists study human behavior in an effort to understand it and then explain it to the rest of us. They examine behavior and the influence attitude has on behavior. And they trace our attitudes to our **self-concept**—how we feel about ourselves.

Did we please or disappoint our parents? Many psychologists believe that attitudes develop according to that experience. Did our parents have expectations we were unable to meet? Were their expectations vague or inconsistent? The messages we got as children shaped our attitudes and they shaped our self-concepts.

When presented with a challenge, do you say "Let me at it!" or "I'll never be able to do this"? Your attitude sets the tone of your life. Your self-concept sets you up for success or failure.

What can you do if your self-concept has kept you from success? Can a self-concept be changed?

Self-talk is the accumulation of all positive and negative thoughts we store in our subconscious that, in turn, affect our behavior. In a popular book called *The Self-Talk Solution*, author Shad Helmstetter, Ph.D., discusses how we can change negative ideas about ourselves by changing the things we say to ourselves. The idea is that when you feel a negative idea coming on, you can quickly change it to a positive one.

Positive affirmation is a term that may be familiar to you. It brings the concept of self-talk into the 1990s. It is a pep talk you give yourself in the form of a repetitive phrase or phrases such as "I'm smart, I'm prepared, I can do this!" Some people like to look in the mirror when they do a positive affirmation.

Another concept, related to self-talk, is called a *self-fulfilling prophecy.* This means that what you say about your chances of success or failure influences the outcome. When you believe certain things about yourself—about your abilities and personal characteristics—you tend to become the person you believe you are. Example: A woman sees an ad for an accounting clerk job. She is very interested, but her self-concept creates an obstacle. She tells herself she could never compete with all the other people who surely will apply for the job. But she would be halfway to being hired if she would declare her qualifications in a positive affirmation.

Is this person sending a positive message about her attitude to the job?

Self-confidence is not only an appealing trait, it is a necessary one if a person is to live life to the fullest. Self-confident people have positive attitudes, and positive attitudes help clear the path to success.

Esteem

Esteem is the favorable opinion you hold of yourself and others. To be held in esteem by your colleagues means you are highly regarded and your contributions are valued.

The need for esteem is one reason people work. Through work, you receive the recognition you deserve for diligence, talent, and accomplishment. Your self-esteem is honestly earned and that provides you with a sense of well-being.

Self-Actualization

Self-actualization is a psychological term that means individual potential fully realized. It means that you have become what you have aspired to become. You are your best possible self.

Self-actualization is difficult to attain, but those who reach this pinnacle of personal development often do it through meaningful work. Self-actualization is built on a foundation of self-concept, values, and self-esteem.

Values

Values are the beliefs or principles that guide our lives. Your values are a system of beliefs that define your character. For many of us, our personal values take shape in childhood and are firmly set when we reach adulthood.

Many of your personal values will be the same ones employers look for in an employee. Some may not. Employers place a premium on honesty, integrity, ambition, diligence, and respect for others. If these are your values, your employability is enhanced. If your values don't include one or more of these, they can be developed.

R ecall Time

Answer the following questions:

1. Self-concept means how we see ourselves. What are some ways our self-concept is developed?
2. Self-talk is a way to redirect negative thinking about ourselves. Give an example of positive self-talk, also known as a positive affirmation.
3. We all have beliefs, or values, that are important to us. What are your values?
4. What values are prized by employers?

▮ SUMMARY

People are motivated to work for many reasons. The need to earn a living is foremost. We must provide shelter, food, and clothing for ourselves and those who depend on us. We save for emergencies, a new car, or perhaps a house. People work to establish financial security and independence.

People also work for creative fulfillment. They enjoy putting their talents and skills to practical use. There are those for whom teamwork is a satisfying experience. They thrive on reaching a common goal as part of a hard-working, problem-solving group.

People work to feel useful, to feel important, and to feel needed. Some people are driven by ambition—the desire to be the best at something and be recognized for it. Some people must have constant intellectual stimulation. Some must have more money than they'll ever need or use. Most of us work for a combination of reasons.

The work ethic has always been a part of the human experience from the days when people literally had to hunt for or pick their own food. The Puritan work ethic simply meant hard work is good for you. The "American Dream" presents a work ethic most of us relate to—work hard, be rewarded. The work ethic also means that you do your share or make your contribution.

Everyone who works has a perceptible attitude whether positive or negative. A positive attitude is characterized by a smile, an optimistic outlook, a willingness to be helpful, and an eagerness to learn. People who have positive attitudes make friends easily and have many interests. They enjoy life.

A negative attitude is characterized by a pessimistic outlook, a complaining nature, and a tendency to blame others for one's own errors or shortcomings. People with negative attitudes often create tension and unpleasantness in the workplace. They are unable to understand or appreciate anyone else's point of view and are not usually sought after as friends.

Observe your co-workers and notice how attitude influences job performance. Notice who accepts responsibility with enthusiasm and who accepts it grudgingly. Those with the best attitudes get the most satisfaction from work.

Acceptable personal conduct is expected on every job. Good manners, appropriate language and dress, and respect for co-workers are obligations you must meet when you accept employment.

Self-concept refers to how we see ourselves. How you see yourself influences your attitude. Your self-concept is a complex development of experience and genetic predisposition. Often how we felt about ourselves as children carries over into adulthood. If your self-concept is holding you back from what you want to be, then practice self-talk or positive affirmations.

Values are the beliefs or principles we use to guide us through life. There are specific values employers find as important as specific skills. If honesty, dependability, and integrity are among your values, you are highly desirable as an employee.

Most people will spend a large portion of their lives working—about forty years. It can be an emotionally and financially rewarding experience or it can seem like a life sentence. Let this chapter be your guide to a satisfying work experience. If you feel an attitude adjustment is due, answer the following questions:

1. Do I like the job I am doing?
2. What are the reasons I want to work?
3. Would I work if I did not receive money for it?
4. Do I demonstrate a positive attitude?
5. Do I demonstrate a negative attitude?
6. Am I taking responsibility for the activities and events in my life, such as family, job, and other relationships.
7. How do I talk to myself, with positive or negative messages?
8. What things do I consider important in my life? What are my values?

In Conclusion . . .

When you have completed this chapter, answer the following questions:

1. *Why do people who have no need of further income often continue to work?*
2. *What is the effect of a self-fulfilling prophecy and what is the reason for this effect?*
3. *How can you change a negative attitude into a positive attitude?*

Review and Application

REVIEW YOUR VOCABULARY

Match the following by writing the letter of each vocabulary word in the space to the left of its description.

___ 1. esteem at its highest level
___ 2. mental position or emotional posture resulting in behavior that is unpleasant, indifferent, rarely smiling
___ 3. all the negative and positive thoughts we have about ourselves
___ 4. concept implying that you are valued by yourself and others
___ 5. mental position resulting in behavior that is pleasant, interested in others, often smiling
___ 6. what we believe about ourselves
___ 7. idea that everyone should do his or her share and make a contribution to society through working
___ 8. things a person believes are important
___ 9. a repetitive phrase or phrases used as a pep talk to change one's self-concept

a. esteem
b. negative attitude
c. positive attitude
d. self-concept
e. self-actualization
f. self-talk
g. values
h. positive affirmation
i. work ethic

DISCUSS AND ANALYZE AN OFFICE SITUATION

1. Barry has a job as a computer operator in a busy office. He likes his job and is punctual, honest, willing to learn new things, and in other ways responsible. But Barry spends weekends drinking with his friends, and some Monday mornings he finds it difficult to get to work on time. A nondrinking friend suggests that perhaps Barry's drinking is becoming excessive and a problem, even though Barry is generally functioning well on the job. What should Barry do?

2. Susan is a private branch exchange (PBX) operator for a large corporation. She likes her job and generally demonstrates a high level of competency and an excellent attitude. However, problems arise when people speak to her about her work. She becomes defensive and argumentative, making it difficult for her supervisor to approach her with any suggestions.

Susan's supervisor takes Susan aside to discuss these problems with her. The supervisor discovers that Susan comes from a family in which her mother was disapproving and complained to Susan for the smallest mistakes, causing Susan to develop a negative self-concept.

How might Susan begin to fix her negative self-concept?

PRACTICE BASIC SKILLS

Math

1. Jerry is searching for a job that matches the computer skills he learned while in school. The job he thought he would like doing doesn't pay as much as some of the others. To help him make his decision, he creates a monthly budget for himself to clarify what he needs to earn to help his family the way he wishes.

Create a monthly budget for Jerry with some of the following categories:

■ rent
■ utilities
■ gasoline
■ auto insurance
■ lunches
■ other food
■ clothing

What other items will Jerry need to purchase or pay for? If you have a checking account, review your own check register to recall how you have recently spent money. Fill in the figures for Jerry's budget, and add them up.

English

1. To maintain a high level of self-esteem and therefore improve your attitude, you must speak and write Standard English. In the following paragraph, underline non-Standard English.

   I can type real good. And phone answering is my top thing. If you decide I'm a hire, I'll asset your office. I get on good with people, too, and don't mind working OT. Thanks much for this interview.

Proofreading

1. In your office job, you may be asked to do some minor editing for your supervisor. You will want to respond to this request with a positive attitude. Edit the following letter, underlining the misspelled words and nonstandard language and correcting the punctuation.

   Dear Mr. Brown:
      I'd like to take this opportunity to speek to you about a business mater in our last shipmat we received several more peaces than we had ordered. We wood hope that you would be willing to adjust our billing of May 3 deducting the cost of the merchandise, a list of the items we didnt order is atached.
      Thank you.

   Yurs truely,

   Mr. John Green

1. Make a list of the kinds of things you might say to yourself if you were practicing positive self-talk. Try saying these to yourself for a few days, then write about the results.
2. It is important that you become aware of negative ideas and attitudes that you may be demonstrating. Make a list of the negative attitudes you suspect in yourself. Then ask your friends for candid ideas about how you could improve your negative attitudes. List them and attempt to put them into practice.

QUIZ

*Write a **T** if the statement is true or an **F** if the statement is false.*

_____ 1. People with a negative attitude are more likely to advance to super-visory jobs because they are good at criticizing others.

_____ 2. Most people are motivated to work by more than a high salary and good fringe benefits.

_____ 3. If you have self-esteem, you are likely to be conceited and unfriendly.

_____ 4. The friends you make at work are usually people you will see only at work.

_____ 5. Taking pens home from the office is not dishonest because everyone does it.

_____ 6. It's a good idea to try to figure out ways to solve problems in the workplace on your own, without going to a supervisor.

_____ 7. People who have a good sense of humor are desired by most employers.

_____ 8. It is possible to talk yourself into having a negative attitude about something.

_____ 9. A self-fulfilling prophecy comes true because you believe it will.

_____ 10. Taking responsibility for your actions means being accountable to others for the things that you do.

_____ 11. There are people who would work just for the creative satisfaction they get from their work, even if they weren't paid.

_____ 12. Taking suggestions from others is evidence that you are easy to push around and probably will not succeed.

_____ 13. The work ethic teaches that everyone has a duty to work for the common good.

_____ 14. The way people speak to one another on the job doesn't vary much from one workplace to another.

Attitude Self-Survey

A positive attitude is important for success in the world of work. Workers may lose their jobs if they have negative attitudes. Completing the following attitude inventory will help you to see if you have a positive or negative attitude and if you need to improve your attitude.

Read each statement below. To the left of each statement, write the number that most accurately describes your response.

5 = yes   2 = usually no
4 = usually yes 1 = no
3 = undecided

After you have completed the inventory, total your score. Rate your attitude according to the scale at the end of this activity.

__4__ 1. Do you make friends easily?
__5__ 2. Do you like to help others?
__3__ 3. Do you try not to complain, even if you are unhappy?
__5 4__ 4. Can you admit your mistakes?
__5__ 5. Can you do a good job without boasting or bragging?
__4__ 6. Do you usually see the good in other people's ideas?
__5__ 7. Are you a good loser?
__5__ 8. Are you willing to take risks?
__5__ 9. Are you a good listener?
__4__ 10. Do you compliment others readily?
__5__ 11. Can you direct a situation without being bossy?
__4__ 12. Do you speak well of other people?
__5__ 13. Are you courteous?
__4__ 14. Are you able to disagree politely?
__4__ 15. Do you show enthusiasm for other people's successes?
__5__ 16. Do you try to avoid feeling sorry for yourself?
__5__ 17. Are you cooperative?
__4__ 18. Do you try to avoid being prejudiced?
__4__ 19. Are you able to control your temper?
__5__ 20. Do you respect other people's opinions?
__5 4__ 21. Do you generally smile and appear pleasant?
__4__ 22. Do you accept compliments graciously?
__5__ 23. Do you like people of all different ages?
__5__ 24. Are you considerate of other people's time?
__5__ 25. Do you keep your work well organized?

119

Use this scale to rate your attitude.

112–125 Your positive attitude has you on the road to success!
90–111 You have a good attitude.
70–89 You need to work on improving your attitude.
25–69 You need to spend a considerable amount of time looking at your attitude and finding ways to improve it.

Attitudes and Self-Concept

Examining your attitudes and their roots will help you understand how to be more successful in your work. As you read the following case studies, try to determine how each individual's self-concept affected his or her behavior. Think about your own attitudes as you answer the questions.

Peter is one of several file clerks in a large hospital. One day at work, the supervisor questioned Peter and the other file clerks about a batch of missing files. Even though Peter had not handled the missing files, he became very defensive about being questioned and threatened to quit if the boss was going to accuse him.

■ Do you think Peter's response was reasonable? If you were his supervisor, how would his response affect you?

No, Peter's response was not reasonable.
If I was his supervisor his defensiveness would
have made him look guilty and his threatening to quit
seems like he's not too concerned about his job, so I'd
probably fire him.

Elise was a clerk in a hospital pharmacy. She did her work well and required little supervision. Her boss was a very quiet man who seldom spoke with her except about work. Elise felt uncomfortable asking him questions. She assumed he did not like her since he was so quiet. She worried that he was going to fire her and find someone else to do the job.

■ Explain Elise's attitude. Suggest some things she could do to help change this attitude.

Elise seems kind of paranoid. There are probably many
reasons why her boss is so quite and none of
them probably have to do with her. She has low
self-confidence & it's affecting her attitude. She
could be more confident w/ herself & try to talk to her boss more.

Joel was beginning his first day on the job as a law clerk. He was pleased to have the job but felt certain there must have been other candidates who had better qualifications. He tried to listen carefully as his supervisor explained his responsibilities. He was very nervous and was beginning to wonder if he could handle the job. His nervousness made it difficult for him to concentrate.

(Continued on next page)

■ If you were in Joel's situation, what could you do to help yourself feel more confident?

Realize that I was the one who got the job, so I'm obviously the one that the company thinks is most qualified. I would tell myself that I can do this job + I will do the best I can.

■ How is Joel's lack of confidence apt to affect his job performance?

He might not perform as well as he could on the job. The quality of his work + the quality of how he performs on the job may suffer negatively.

Karen worked for a very demanding supervisor who always managed to find fault with Karen's work. Karen listened carefully to her supervisor's criticisms and readily made any changes her supervisor wanted. In spite of her difficult supervisor, Karen found her work interesting and rewarding. She felt good about her ability to handle the situation, and she was proud of her work.

■ How can you explain Karen's positive attitude in spite of her supervisor's criticisms?

Karen has good confidence + a good sense of self-worth. Since she makes the changes she needs to make + keeps right on going she is successful + probably is also proud of herself + her actions.

Dean took a data-entry job in a hospital even though the work did not interest him. He needed to earn enough money to pay for his school tuition. He complained about the work and made it known he was quitting as soon as he had enough money. His co-workers found him unpleasant to work with.

■ If you were Dean's supervisor, what would you do?

I would talk to Dave about changing his attitude + tell him that he could risk losing his job w/such a neg. attitude.

Employment Skills for Office Careers

Effects of a Negative Attitude

Below is a description of a situation that might occur on the job. Read this example and then answer the questions that follow. The questions should help you consider how one person's attitude affects the people around him or her.

Josh arrived for work just as the doors to the store were opening. He felt very rushed, particularly as he saw the line of customers waiting to get into the store. He hung up his jacket and hurried to take his place at the cash register. Fortunately, his boss was busy and did not to seem to notice his last-minute arrival. The first customer brought her purchase quickly to the register while Josh was busy arranging the cash drawer and the supplies he would need for the day. He felt as if she were interrupting his work, so he completed the transaction quickly, paying little attention to her comments. The boss overheard the conversation and noted that Josh missed an opportunity to suggest another sale.

Josh realized that in his haste, he had forgotten to bring a supply of charge slips to the cash register with him. He asked Caroline, who was working nearby on a display, to cover for him while he went to the back of the store to pick up the charge slips. While he was in the back of the store, Josh decided to take time for a cup of coffee. He had been too rushed earlier to have breakfast before coming to work.

By the time Josh arrived back at the cash register, Caroline was feeling very frustrated. She was having difficulty operating the cash register, and the customers were becoming impatient. Josh took over the cash register and soon had the situation under control. The ease with which he used the cash register made Caroline feel embarrassed. Josh did not offer to show her what she had done wrong. Neither did he thank her for taking over for him.

Caroline returned to her display work feeling upset and unhappy with herself and Josh. Later in the day, Josh began to complain about the lunch schedule. He wanted to meet a friend for lunch, but his lunch break was scheduled at the wrong time. Josh asked Caroline if she would switch lunch times with him. Caroline agreed. Josh did not clear the schedule change with his boss. His boss had arranged the schedule so that Josh would be working during the busiest time of the lunch period because he could work quickly on the register. When it came time for Caroline to relieve Josh for lunch, she commented that she was nervous about working the cash register during a busy time. Josh just laughed and told her it was easy. During Josh's absence, Caroline had to call the boss several times to help with problems on the cash register. Her boss was displeased with the change in schedule.

When Josh returned, Caroline told him what had happened. Josh was angry at her for getting him into trouble. He accused her of ruining his chances for a promotion. Caroline felt hurt and mistreated, but she didn't say anything.

During the late afternoon, the store was very quiet. Caroline asked Josh if he would help her finish up her display work. Josh replied that display work was not part of his job and that he was trying to take care of closing procedures early so that he could leave work as soon as the store closed. He told Caroline he was meeting a friend right after work and didn't want to have to stay late.

At closing, the boss asked Caroline to stay for a few minutes to talk about the day's work. Caroline felt she was being unfairly singled out. Josh quickly grabbed his jacket and ducked out the door.

(Continued on next page)

1. Describe Josh's attitude.

Josh has a very bad attitude - he only
cares about himself, his time, & his wants
+ needs - he is very selfish, he is also lazy

2. How did Josh's attitude affect Caroline and her work?

Caroline + her work suffered - due
to Josh's attitude Caroline was upset
+ she was also left w/ her work not
done because she did Josh's work.

3. How did Josh's attitude affect the boss and the business?

The boss was upset at the wrong
employee + was mad because work wasn't done
right. The business suffered because
customers got upset + things didn't get done on time.

4. How might Caroline have handled the situation differently?

Caroline might have refused to Switch
schedules w/ Josh or she might have told
the boss about Josh's actions + attitude.

5. What do you think Caroline should say to the boss?

Caroline could tell the boss that she
was doing her best and she was trying
to help Josh.

6. If you were Josh's employer, how would you deal with Josh?

I would explain to Josh that his
attitude + actions were inappropriate +
if he can't change he might lose his job.

Employment Skills for Office Careers

Attitudes and Responsibilities

Fulfilling your employer's expectations is your responsibility on any job. Learning to identify responsibilities will help you to meet these expectations. Read the following case studies and consider how you would handle the situations to meet employer expectations.

> More often than not, Mary Ann arrives a few minutes late to her job as a typist clerk. She also takes frequent breaks from her desk to socialize with the other employees. She takes a few extra minutes for her lunch break and cleans her desk early so she can be sure to leave right at quitting time. She is an excellent typist and always finishes her assignments, so she feels she is entitled to the extra time.

■ Is Mary Ann's behavior honest? Explain.

No, she is using company time wrong. The company is paying her to do her work and to be at her workstation & she's off socializing w/others.

> Jerry's boss left town and gave Jerry a list of projects that needed to be completed. He indicated which needed to be finished first. Jerry got bored working on the first job, so he skipped ahead and completed others he thought were more interesting. When his boss returned, he had completed all the work on the list except the first task. His boss was displeased and asked Jerry to stay late to complete the work. Jerry felt his boss did not appreciate all the work he had completed.

■ Was Jerry's boss justified in asking Jerry to work late? Explain.

Yes, his boss gave him a list & specific order in which to complete the tasks, Jerry chose to ignore this & should now pay the price. It's Jerry's responsibility to fulfill his bosses request & complete the project!

> Bill was a new employee in the accounting department of a clinic. His supervisor trained him to make entries in the accounts. Bill had done this kind of work for many years and preferred another method that he felt was more efficient. He did the work the way he felt was best. Bill's supervisor checked his work and pointed out the error. Bill continued to do the work the way he felt was best. The supervisor recommended that Bill be fired.

(Continued on next page)

■ If Bill's method were better, should he have insisted on using it? Why or why not?

No, because the office had a way the
wanted it done. ⊗ Instead of just using
his method, Bill should have explained it
to the supervisor + maybe would've been able to
do it his way.

■ If you were Bill's supervisor, what would you do?

I would sit Bill down + explain that
we have a certain way of doing things +
would like him to do it that way.

Gayle and Dianne shared a work space in an insurance office. Gayle kept her area neat and organized. Dianne's space was messy. Dianne also brought food to her work area. On occasion, her food spilled onto Gayle's work. Dianne's behavior annoyed Gayle and made it difficult for the two of them to work together. Gayle complained to the office manager. The office manager understood Gayle's complaint, but she valued Dianne's work even though her work habits were messy.

■ If you were the office manager, how would you respond?

I would talk to Dianne about
her habits + encourage her to be
more organized. ⊗ Inform Dianne
that her work habits may be
affecting others and she should
try to be neater.

Employment Skills for Office Careers

Attitude Alert

1. Observe: People responding to instructions given to them by a supervisor.

   Write: Brief descriptions of positive responses and negative responses.

   Positive: "Let's get started," I can have this finished soon.

   Negative: I don't want to do this right now. I can't finish this by that deadline!

2. Observe: How a person with a positive attitude carries out instructions and how a person with a negative attitude does so.

   Write: A brief description of the difference.

   Positive: gets things done quickly, correctly, work hard. Does what they were instructed to do & how they were instructed to do it.

   Negative: Puts off the task, doesn't get work done on time, not quality work, may have to be re-done, does work the way they want to do it - doesn't follow instructions correctly.

(Continued on next page)

3. Observe: The atmosphere in your office when a positive attitude dominates and when a negative one dominates.

   Write: A brief description of each.

   Positive: everyone getting along, happy, cooperative, people working hard + getting things accomplished, helpful, considerate

   Negative: Everyone edgy, every one stressed out, people don't get along, crabby, Snap @ each other, no cooperation, not really getting work done,

4. Observe: Two supervisors.

   Write: How their attitudes influence the attitudes of their staffs.

   Positive: want to do work + get it done; happy to be at work; want to get things done right; help each other

   Negative: Don't want to show up to work; Don't do quality work; employees don't ~~come~~ come to work or help each other out

Attitude Adjectives

Make two lists, positive and negative, and keep going until you run out of words.

Positive	Negative
happy, optimistic, out-going, helpful, cooperative, agreeable, don't complain, does work well, works hard, does quality work, people like to be around them, smile a lot, encouraging, dependable, on-time, fun, good to be around, accepts constructive criticism	unhappy, crabby, don't want to be around others, disagreeable, complain all the time, no one wants to be around this person, doesn't do work, takes frequent breaks, frequently has to redo work, always frown or have a scowl, puts others down, not dependable, never on time, takes criticism personally + gets very angry, takes anger out on others

Improve Your Writing Skills

Write an essay on what work means to you.

Work is important to me. I think that work provides me with an opportunity to be creative and to show what I can do. I think that having a good job that I like will make work fun. Work also gives me an opportunity for recognition; a lot of times if you complete a job well you will be recognized for your efforts. Work is also an opportunity to interact with others and to learn from others. Work also provides for an opportunity to constantly learn.

Your attitude is showing

Elwood Chapman

Career Opportunities in the Office

Objectives

After completing this chapter, you will be able to do the following:

1. List the clerical job classifications that have employment opportunities for the nineties.
2. List the types of companies that have clerical employment opportunities for the nineties.
3. List the job duties, working conditions, and qualifications of an office clerk.
4. List the job duties, working conditions, and qualifications of a secretary.
5. List the job duties and qualifications of an account clerk.
6. List the job duties and qualifications of a customer service representative.
7. List the job duties and qualifications of a hospital unit clerk.
8. List the job duties and qualifications of a medical records clerk.
9. List the job duties and qualifications of a receptionist.
10. List the job duties and qualifications of a peripheral equipment operator.
11. List the job duties and qualifications of a reprographics clerk.

New Office Terms

back-office jobs
civil service jobs
Employment Development
  Department
employment in services
full-time work schedule

job sharing
Occupational Outlook Handbook
replacement needs
service-producing industries
temporary office workers

Before You Begin . . .

Answer the following questions that preview material covered in this chapter:

1. *What is the employment outlook for clerical jobs in the 1990s?*
2. *What are the job duties and qualifications of a general office clerk?*
3. *What are the job duties and qualifications of a medical clerk?*

Garrett recently completed business classes that included training in word processing, spreadsheets, and data bases using a microcomputer. He was a good student and is excited to be able to look for full-time work in an office. The only problem is that he does not know what jobs are available to someone with his training.

Garrett remembers that his neighbor Rochelle works for the **Employment Development Department** (EDD), a state department that handles unemployment. He makes an appointment to meet with Rochelle at her office. Garrett wants information concerning the projected employment growth of clerical jobs. He also wants information on skills required for clerical jobs, since he is not certain which jobs he is qualified for.

At the meeting, Rochelle first explains to Garrett that much of the information he wants is contained in a publication entitled *Occupational Outlook Handbook.* This handbook is published once every two years by the U.S. Department of Labor, Bureau of Labor Statistics. Using it as a reference, Rochelle shares with Garrett some information on job prospects for the future.

You may find a job through newspaper want ads. However, these same ads can also teach you what skills employers are requiring for clerical jobs.

■ OCCUPATIONAL OUTLOOK

Employment in administrative support occupations, including clerical occupations, is expected to increase from 21.1 million to 29.1 million jobs between the years 1990 and 2005. At first glance, you might think the prospect for work in the clerical field is poor. However, the Department of Labor predicts that because of their high number of jobs and substantial replacement needs, clerical occupations will offer abundant opportunities for qualified job seekers in the years ahead.

Garrett asks Rochelle what the handbook means by **replacement needs.** Rochelle explains that these are needs to fill job openings because people leave occupations. Some people transfer to other occupations to change careers. Others stop working, return to school, assume household responsibilities, or retire.

Most job openings that arise are the result of replacement needs. Therefore, even occupations with little or no employment growth may still offer many job openings. *Employment growth* is an increase in the number of job openings that occur because new jobs are created in a certain occupation.

Garrett is told that advances in office technology affect the statistics and classifications for future clerical jobs. Technological advances in mail sorting equipment, for example, will slow demand for Postal Service clerks. Increased use of word processing equipment will lead to a decline in the number of typists and an increase in the need for workers with word processing skills.

Operations that involve interaction with others will generally grow faster than **back-office jobs,** which have little or no contact with the public. Jobs that involve interaction with the public, such as receptionist and information clerk jobs, are expected to grow at a much faster rate than the average for all occupations. Table 2–1 shows that employment as a receptionist is expected to increase by 34 percent into the year 2005. Note that 3 of the top 20 largest-growing occupations are from the clerical field. Which ones are they?

Rochelle also shares information with Garrett on the types of companies that have the best outlook for employment. She states that the service-producing industries will be hiring the most workers in the 1990s. **Service-producing industries** are businesses that exist to provide a service to the public. They do not produce a tangible product, as does a goods-producing industry. They include banking, insurance, health care, education, data processing, and management consulting.

■ TABLE 2–1
The Twenty Largest-growing Occupations (1992–2005)

OCCUPATION	NUMBER OF JOBS TO BE ADDED	PERCENTAGE INCREASE
1. Food preparation workers	1,190,000	38%
2. Food and beverage service workers	1,124,000	26
3. Kindergarten, elementary, and secondary school teachers	1,113,000	34
4. Retail salespersons	877,000	21
5. Registered nurses (RNs)	765,000	42
6. Computer systems analysts	737,000	10
7. Truck drivers (light and heavy)	708,000	26
8. Cashiers	669,000	24
9. General office clerks	654,000	24
10. Nursing aides and psychiatric aides	616,000	44
11. Preschool workers	611,000	65
12. Janitors and cleaners	600,000	20
13. Guards	408,000	51
14. Secretaries	386,000	12
15. Teacher aides	381,000	43
16. General managers and top executives	380,000	13
17. Adjusters, investigators, and collectors	367,000	66
18. Receptionists and information clerks	305,000	34
19. Accountants and auditors	304,000	32
20. Restaurant and food service managers	227,000	46

Source: *Occupational Outlook Quarterly* (Bureau of Labor Statistics), Spring 1994.

Employment in services—a subgroup within the service-producing sector—is expected to rise above 40 percent by the year 2005, making it the fastest-growing industry division. Jobs in this subgroup will be found in large corporations and government agencies, as well as in small businesses.

Job growth in legal services and business services (advertising, accounting, word processing, and computer support, for example) will be exceptionally rapid. Employment in health services also will make impressive gains as demand for health care continues to expand.

All this information concerning clerical occupational outlook seems to satisfy Garrett, but now he needs information on the types of jobs he is qualified for. Rochelle encourages him to attend a job classification workshop that is being sponsored by the Employment Development Department. She says this may answer his final questions concerning job classification.

R ecall Time

Answer the following questions:

1. Who publishes the *Occupational Outlook Handbook?*
2. Will the number of clerical jobs increase or decrease in the 1990s?
3. Are most new jobs in the clerical area due to more work or to the replacement of workers who leave?
4. Will receptionist job openings show a slow, average, or faster-than-average growth in the 1990s?
5. What is the projected growth rate of employment in services through the year 2005?

JOB CLASSIFICATION

The presenter at the job classification workshop that Garrett attends divides office clerical jobs into three categories. The different categories include individuals with the following:

1. minimum clerical skills
2. average clerical skills
3. advanced clerical skills or work experience

The presenter spends time discussing each category. The discussion includes job titles, typical duties, qualifications (including skill requirements), and working conditions. The presenter refers frequently to the *Occupational Outlook Handbook* during the workshop.

Real job descriptions that have been collected from private employers and from government agencies are passed out at the workshop. The job descriptions from the government agencies were collected from federal, state, county, and city organizations. These government agency jobs are often called **civil service jobs.**

Michelle has been working for six months as a general office clerk for a large company. Her supervisor has been nice and even let Michelle leave early one day because Michelle had some personal business to attend to.

A clerk-typist job opening has become available in the accounting department. Michelle is qualified and would like to apply for the transfer. It would mean more money and more interesting work.

Michelle feels guilty because her supervisor has been so nice. She is afraid to tell her supervisor she wants the transfer. Michelle is thinking of forgetting about the opportunity.

What advice would you give Michelle?

Minimum Clerical Skills

Here is the information for the first category—workers with minimum clerical skills.

Job Titles Job titles in the minimum clerical skills category include file clerk, mail clerk, clerk, and staff clerk.

Typical Duties Typical duties of workers in the minimum clerical skills category include processing correspondence and invoices, filing documents, entering data on records, typing labels and envelopes, operating copy machines, and processing mail. The filing duties may be performed entirely with paper or by computerized filing and retrieval systems.

Qualifications Skills required of workers in the minimum clerical skills category include touch typing (no minimum speed is usually required), basic spelling, and reading skills. Employers also look for people who like detailed work. Employers prefer high school graduates for these positions. However, since these are entry-level positions, some employers consider an applicant's willingness to work and learn more important than any special training or education.

Working Conditions Most workers in the minimum clerical skills category work in clean, well-lighted offices right alongside other clerical workers. If the company has a central filing room, however, these workers may be separated from other departments. Although they do not do a lot of heavy lifting, these clerks must frequently stoop, bend, and reach.

Job Descriptions Following are two actual job descriptions provided by real companies.

Job Description 1

Title: Office Services Assistant
Company: Construction Firm
Job Responsibilities: Organizes, stores, and retrieves records; sets up rooms for meetings and conferences; maintains paper supplies for copy machines;

OFFICE TIP

Take notes on everything. Don't trust anything to memory for the first few weeks of a job.

delivers incoming office supplies and materials; assists in mail room; provides a variety of other assistance as requested.

Required Skills and Experience: High school education or equivalent; familiarity with an office environment; industrious worker with self-motivation; good communication skills; willingness to assist with a wide variety of requests. If previously worked, must have an excellent attendance record.

Job Description 2

Title: Mail Clerk
Company: Advertising Firm
Description of Duties: Sorting and distribution of incoming and outgoing mail. Responsible for processing invoices and orders. Responsible for fax machine orders.
Minimum Qualifications: Prefer one year of experience in a related mail room environment.
Special Equipment to Be Used: Postage meter for decollating, folding, stuffing. Data printer.

Average Clerical Skills

Here is the information for the second category—workers with average clerical skills.

Job Titles Job titles in the average clerical skills category include general office clerk, staff clerk I, office helper, and account clerk.

Typical Duties Duties in the average clerical skills category include a variety of tasks without concentrating in any one particular area. Workers in this category perform many different tasks in support of general office, business, or administrative operations. Work assignments are set in accordance with the needs of the employer. Some days may be spent filing or typing, others may be spent entering data at a computer terminal. General office clerks also may operate photocopiers and calculators, answer telephones, and deliver messages.

Experienced workers in this category may handle more demanding tasks. These could include maintaining financial or other records, verifying statistical reports for accuracy and completeness, and handling and adjusting customer complaints. Other duties could include taking inventory of equipment and supplies, answering questions on departmental services and functions, and helping prepare budgetary requests.

Qualifications Skills required of workers in the average clerical skills category usually include the ability to type a minimum of forty words per minute (wpm); a basic knowledge of microcomputers; the ability to operate ten-key calculators by touch; and basic math, English, and spelling skills. Employers usually require a high school diploma, and some require knowledge of word processing. Workers in this category usually work with others. Therefore, they should be cooperative and should be able to work as part of a team.

LARGE OFFICE/SMALL OFFICE: What's Your Preference?

Work Performance

It is common for administrative assistants in large offices to work for more than one boss. In a large law office, for example, an administrative assistant may work for two attorneys. This is also true in many other businesses. Therefore, an administrative assistant must be able to schedule the work to meet the needs of all the bosses. An administrative assistant must be able to set priorities. He must also have the personality to be able to take directions from and interact on a regular basis with more than one boss.

In a small office, an administrative assistant usually does the work for and reports to only one boss. Therefore, the daily work is scheduled around only one person. Any priorities can be set with that one boss. Once a work routine is established, an administrative assistant will find it easier to do the work for only one boss.

Both the situations described above have advantages and disadvantages. Would you prefer to work as an administrative assistant in a large office or a small office? Why?

Working Conditions For the most part, working conditions for workers in the average clerical skills category are the same as those for other office employees in the same company. Employees in this category who are on a **full-time work schedule** usually work a standard forty-hour week. Nevertheless, one in four works part time.

In addition, a significant number of general office clerks work as temporaries. **Temporary office workers** are employees who work for a few days or a few weeks at one company until a job is completed. They also work at companies to replace employees on vacation or out ill. Temporary office workers usually work through private companies known as temporary employment placement services.

Job Descriptions Following are two actual job descriptions provided by real companies.

Job Description 1

Title: Clerk I
Company: Publishing Company
Job Responsibilities: Provides backup relief to the company receptionist. Coordinates supplies and equipment including moves and delivery. Handles vendor inquiries. Clerical duties include filing and invoice coding.
Required Skills: Typing 40 wpm, strong interpersonal skills, detail oriented.

Roberto has been working for five years as a general office clerk for the same family-owned company. The company has always been successful and has always hired enough office workers for the busy times.

For the past year, the company has not been doing well financially and has had to lay off employees, including office workers. At the same time, the office workers who remain must take on more and more work. Roberto occasionally has to do some of the work previously done by word processors.

A new executive has been hired who promises to turn the company around and make it financially successful again. In the meantime, all the employees must continue to take on extra work and maintain a positive attitude that things will improve.

Roberto does continue to take on extra work and even does a little overtime without any extra pay. He believes the company has been good to him for the past five years, so he now owes it extra effort during this difficult time.

Do you agree with Roberto's attitude? Why or why not?

Job Description 2

> Title: Principal Clerk
> Company: Medical Clinic
> Job Responsibilities: Scheduling, coordinating, and preparing for patient visits. Taking and delivering accurate telephone messages. Maintaining appointment schedules through computer input. Other duties as assigned.
> Required Skills: Accurate typing and computer skills preferred. Excellent communication skills. Excellent interpersonal and public-contact skills. Ability to work independently and under pressure.

Advanced Clerical Skills

Here is the information for the third category—workers with advanced clerical skills or work experience.

Job Titles Job titles in the advanced clerical skills category include secretary, administrative assistant, and stenographer.

Typical Duties Workers in the advanced clerical skills category are at the center of communications with a firm. They process and transmit information to the staff and to other organizations. They perform a variety of administrative and clerical duties that are necessary to run and maintain organizations efficiently. They schedule appointments, give information to callers, organize and maintain files, fill out forms, and process correspondence using word processing software on microcomputers.

In today's automated offices, more and more secretaries are assuming responsibilities previously handled by managers and professionals. For example, using personal computers, secretaries now run spreadsheet, data-base management, and graphics programs. Their role is to help ensure that information gets to the people who need it in a timely fashion. This role is becoming more critical with companies tending to view information as a valuable commodity for gaining a competitive edge on their rivals.

Qualifications Skills required of workers in the advanced clerical skills category include a typing speed of over 55 wpm; word processing abilities; and proficiency in spelling, punctuation, grammar, and oral communications. Employers also prefer workers in this category to have an aptitude for numbers. Good judgment, organizational ability, and initiative are important for the more responsible positions.

Employers stress that flexibility is especially important in this category. Continuing changes in the office environment, many made possible by the computer, have increased the demand for workers who are flexible. Workers must be prepared to be retrained whenever an employer introduces new equipment. The frequency with which such equipment is changed or updated makes retraining and continuing education an integral part of these jobs. Thus, employers seek workers who understand and accept the inevitability of change.

Working Conditions Workers in the advanced clerical skills category usually work in offices that are clean and free from high noise levels except during peak typing periods. Their jobs often involve sitting for long periods, and typing often requires working from materials that are difficult to read. This category of work lends itself to flexible working arrangements. A significant number of people work as temporaries. A few participate in **job sharing,** which is an arrangement in which two people divide responsibility for a single job.

Job Description Following are two actual job descriptions provided by real companies.

Job Description 1

> Title: Administrative Assistant
> Company: Public Television
> Job Responsibilities: Using word processing software, types, edits, and distributes proposals, correspondence, memorandums, reports, and contracts. Coordinates the preparation of materials between the Underwriting and the Design departments. Maintains effective system of information retrieval. Arranges meetings, conferences, and luncheons. Prepares purchase orders, expense vouchers, personnel requests, and time sheets. Other duties as assigned.
> Desired Qualifications: Two years secretarial experience. Typing 65 wpm. Strong detail-orientation and proofing skills. Good organizational and communication skills.

Job Description 2

> Title: Secretary II
> Company: Private University
> Description of Duties: Provides administrative support to the department. Miscellaneous duties include word processing, scheduling meetings, making

---

O F F I C E   T I P

Want to stop the printer without turning it off? Press the online button. Are you ready to resume printing? Press the online button again.

---

travel arrangements, copying, and maintaining files. Assists in preparation of graphs and reports. Backup for order entry.

Minimum Qualifications: two or more years secretarial experience. Ability to handle heavy workload in a fast-paced environment. Strong organizational skills. Team player.

R ecall Time

Answer the following questions:

1. Does a staff clerk have as much responsibility as a secretary?
2. What typing speed is required of a file clerk?
3. What is a job title of an employee who works on a variety of tasks without concentrating on one particular area?
4. What is the minimum typing rate usually required of a general office clerk?

OTHER AREAS OF EMPLOYMENT

Garrett decided to attend a final workshop sponsored by the Employment Development Department. This workshop covered a variety of clerical-related jobs. The presenter shared information on occupations that are expected to rise faster than average into the year 2000.

Account Clerks

Typical duties Account clerks compute, classify, and record numerical data to develop and maintain financial records. They record debits and credits, compare current and past balance sheets, and monitor loans and accounts payable and receivable to ensure that payments are up-to-date.

Account clerks prepare bank deposits, compile data for cashiers, verify and balance receipts, and send in deposits. They also may post transactions on computer files and update these files when needed.

Qualifications Account clerks need to possess basic accounting knowledge and have a good math aptitude. They must be able to operate a ten-key calculator, have accurate data-entry skills, and be able to process financial details quickly. Account clerks need to be proficient with computers, be detail oriented, and have a knowledge of basic business filing rules.

Customer Service Representatives

Typical Duties Customer service representatives handle customer inquiries, problems, or complaints following company guidelines. They receive and process orders by telephone from customers, field sales representatives, brokers, and dealers.

Customer service representatives also present new products and promotional offers to customers. They are encouraged to identify opportunities to improve customer service.

OFFICE TIP

Ask for extra work in slow times.

Qualifications The qualifications needed to work as a customer service representative normally include a high school education, general office experience, and excellent verbal and written communication skills. Customer service representatives need to be detail oriented and have good math skills; have a sound knowledge of the company's product or services which may require technical knowledge; and have the ability to make decisions.

Hospital Unit Clerks

Typical Duties Hospital unit clerks prepare and maintain patient charts with initial information and maintain/update charts with physicians' orders. They complete daily requisitions for diagnostic tests, and they initiate, verify, and distribute various hospital reports in a timely manner.

Hospital unit clerks distribute mail, maintain office supplies, and chart forms for all shifts. They also are required to perform other clerical duties as assigned.

Qualifications Hospital unit clerks must have knowledge of medical terminology. They must have the ability to work effectively with the public and the ability to follow oral and written instructions. Many medical facilities require that prospective hospital unit clerks have current work experience or that they have completed an equivalent unit clerk training program.

Medical Records Clerks

Typical Duties Medical records clerks review medical records for completeness and coordinate the follow-up on delinquent or deficient medical records. They may also process birth and death certificates, maintain birth and death logs, and compile statistics as needed. Medical records clerks process incoming and outgoing mail, answer telephones, photocopy material, maintain supplies, and may type a variety of correspondence such as letters, reports, forms, and memorandums.

Qualifications Medical records clerks must have a knowledge of medical terminology; one year's experience as a medical records clerk is preferred. They must possess good verbal and written communication skills, have legible handwriting, and be detail oriented. Word processing ability is usually required, as is knowledge of numeric filing.

Receptionists

Typical Duties Receptionists greet customers and other visitors, determine their needs, and refer callers to the person who can help them. Their day-to-day duties vary a great deal, depending on where they work. In large business firms, they provide identification cards and arrange escorts to take customers or clients to the proper office.

When they are not busy with callers, receptionists may perform clerical duties such as typing, filing, and mail processing. Increasingly, receptionists use automated office equipment such as word processors or personal computers in the course of their work. Most receptionists also handle incoming telephone calls using a multiline telephone system.

Qualifications Skills required of receptionists include typing (minimum 30 wpm) and other general office skills. Personal characteristics are very important in this occupation. Receptionists should like meeting people and have a desire to be helpful and informative. A neat appearance, a pleasant voice, and an even disposition are important. Because receptionists do not work under close supervision, common sense and a thorough understanding of how the business is organized help them handle various situations that arise.

Peripheral Equipment Operators

Typical Duties Peripheral equipment operators are responsible for the performance and upkeep of the peripheral equipment such as printers, disk drives, and tape readers. They also assist the computer operator by preparing printouts and other output for distribution to computer users.

Peripheral equipment operators may maintain logbooks listing events such as machine malfunctions. With the increasing trend toward networking—making connections between computers—a growing number of peripheral equipment operators are assisting with the upkeep of minicomputers and personal computers.

Qualifications Previous work experience is the key to landing a position as a peripheral equipment operator. Employers look for specific, hands-on experience on the type of equipment that they use. A high school diploma and some business school training are usually required for entry-level positions. Peripheral equipment operators must be able to communicate well to work effectively with computer operators and programmers.

Reprographics Clerks

Typical Duties Reprographics clerks accept copy-work orders at a counter, for either in-house personnel or outside customers. They complete order forms, operate photocopy and/or printing equipment, collate, staple, and bind.

Reprographics clerks use communication skills when they telephone clients and/or co-workers, or people within the company, when questions arise about the work and when the work is completed.

Qualifications The qualifications needed for a reprographics clerk normally include the ability to operate copy equipment, to be service oriented, and to possess good communication skills. Reprographics clerks

The paperless office has never arrived and probably never will. Copy work is an ongoing task in all businesses.

also need to be capable of working in a fast-paced environment and to be capable of standing for long periods of time.

R ecall Time

Answer the following questions:

1. What are two job duties normally required of a medical records clerk?
2. Besides greeting visitors, what other duties might a receptionist perform?
3. What is the minimum typing speed usually required of a receptionist?
4. What are two job duties normally required of a customer service representative?
5. What are two job duties normally required of a reprographics clerk?
6. List three qualifications needed to be an account clerk.

■ SUMMARY

Many job openings will continue to exist in clerical occupations well through the year 2005. Although some jobs will be available for individuals with minimum clerical skills, most opportunities will be for individuals with average or above-average clerical skills.

In addition to the technical knowledge and skills of microcomputer operation and typing, written and verbal communication skills are required for most clerical occupations. Employers prefer hiring individuals who are high school graduates. Jobs requiring the greatest responsibilities require the greatest skills.

Do you qualify for any of the clerical positions discussed in this chapter? Use the following checklist to determine which clerical level you are most qualified for.

Minimum Clerical Skills
____ Touch typing
____ Basic spelling skills
____ Basic reading skills

Average Clerical Skills
____ Typing—minimum 40 wpm
____ Knowledge of microcomputers
____ Knowledge of word processing
____ Basic math skills
____ Basic spelling skills
____ Basic English skills

5.   Advanced Clerical Skills
        —— Typing—minimum 55 wpm
6.   —— Proficiency in word processing
        —— Proficiency in oral communications
        —— Proficiency in grammar, punctuation, and spelling
        —— Aptitude for numbers
        —— Adaptability and versatility
        —— Organizational ability
        —— Initiative
        —— Office experience

In Conclusion . . .

When you have completed this chapter, answer the following questions:

1. What is the employment outlook for clerical jobs through the year 2005?
2. What are the job duties and qualifications of a general office clerk?
3. What are the job duties and qualifications of a medical records clerk?

QUIZ

*Write a **T** if the statement is true or an **F** if the statement is false.*

_____ 1. EDD stands for Employment Development Department.

_____ 2. The *Occupational Outlook Handbook* predicts that employment in clerical occupations will decrease through the year 2005.

_____ 3. Retirement of workers has no effect on the projected outlook for job openings in clerical occupations.

_____ 4. Receptionists usually work in back-office jobs.

_____ 5. Secretarial jobs are expected to increase to the year 2005.

_____ 6. Job growth in advertising and accounting will be very slow to the year 2005.

_____ 7. Government agency jobs are often called civil service jobs.

_____ 8. Employers prefer high school graduates for minimum clerical skills jobs.

_____ 9. Most minimum clerical skill jobs require only paper filing duties.

_____ 10. Most average clerical skills jobs require a minimum of forty words per minute in typing.

_____ 11. Hospital unit clerks do not work with the public.

_____ 12. Employment of receptionists is expected to grow at a much faster rate than the average for all occupations through the year 2005.

_____ 13. Account clerks need not know how to operate a ten-key calculator.

_____ 14. Customer service representatives have no contact with the public.

_____ 15. Communication skills are helpful for reprographics clerks to have.

Employment Test

You may be required to pass an employment test when applying for a job. The following is an example of a test given by one company. See if you can pass it.

Your Name _____   Time Begun _____

Date _____   Time Stopped _____

Part I. Math

1. $497.3 + 6.2 + 30.5 + 7 + 92.34 =$ 2. $6389.45 - 23.6 =$

3. $25 \times 15 =$ 4. $\$7.80 \times 5 =$ 5. 2400 divided by $25 =$

Part II. Checking

On the answer lines to the right, write "C" if the sums of the following problems are correct and "I" if they are incorrect.

1.	2.	3.	4.	5.	6.	
						1._____
						2._____
7	9	6	0	8	3	3._____
6	4	6	0	7	9	4._____
1	3	6	5	7	6	5._____
13	16	18	10	22	18	6._____

Part III. Spelling

If any of the following words are misspelled, write the correct spelling to the right of the word. If the words are spelled correctly, write the word *correct* to the right of the word.

a. personel _____   f. discused _____

b. advertising _____   g. ledger _____

c. engeneer _____   h. proceed _____

d. supercede _____   i. excede _____

e. bussines _____   j. invoice _____

(Continued on next page)

Part IV. Alphabetic Filing

1.	A—Cr	4.	Jes—Me	7.	Rx—Th			
2.	Cs—F	5.	Mf—Pi	8.	Ti—W			
3.	G—Jer	6.	Pj—Rw	9.	X—Z			

In the file drawers above, customer files are filed alphabetically. Each drawer has a number. In which drawers would you place the files listed below? Write the correct drawer number on the line to the left of the name.

a. _____ Solano Bakery

b. _____ Yarnell Cheese

c. _____ Barnes Culinary

d. _____ Place & Place Products

e. _____ 5-Hour Deliveries

f. _____ Rennett Corporation

g. _____ Jerrett Pies

h. _____ Tin Recycled

i. _____ Kraft Dairy

j. _____ McMillan Bros.

k. _____ Modems for Less

l. _____ Customer Satisfaction

Part V. Numeric Filing

1.	100—248	4.	487—519	7.	701—799			
2.	249—318	5.	520–623	8.	800—865			
3.	319–486	6.	624—700	9.	866—900			

In the file drawers above, customer files are filed numerically. Each drawer has a number. In which drawers would you file the numbers listed below? Write the correct drawer number on the line to the left of the customer file number.

a. _____ 251

b. _____ 273

c. _____ 625

d. _____ 432

e. _____ 157

f. _____ 503

g. _____ 824

h. _____ 612

i. _____ 675

j. _____ 888

k. _____ 380

l. _____ 732

Zip Codes

The following is an example of classifying and recording numeric data. Account clerks and data-entry clerks do this type of work. Ask your instructor whether you should handwrite, type, or use a micro-computer for this exercise.

List the zip codes and their locations in <u>numeric</u> order using the state and the first two zip numbers as the column heading. The state listings are **Massachusetts 02, New York 10, Florida 33, Illinois 61, Texas 76, California 94.**

For example:

MASSACHUSETTS 02

02159	Boston
02360	Plymouth
02542	Otis AFB
	etc.

NEW YORK 10

10004	Governors Island
10024	New York
10310	Staten Island
	etc.

Following are the locations to be grouped.

Arlington	76004	Berkeley	94710
Boca Raton	33434	Boston	02159
Boynton Beach	33436	Bradenton	33506
Bronx	10467	Brooksville	33512
Champaign	61820	Clearwater	33518
Concord	94518	Daly City	94015
Euless	76040	Fall River	02726
Fort Lauderdale	33313	Fremont	94536
Fort Worth	76117	Fort Pierce	33452
Fort Myers	33904	Governors Island	10004
Hayward	94541	Homestead	33032
Irvington	10533	Lakeland	33802
Larchmont	10538	Mountain View	94040
Napa	94559	New York City	10024
New Bedford	02747	Newton	02649
North Attleboro	02763	Oakland	94602
Otis AFB	02542	Peoria	61650
Plymouth	02358	Round Ridge	10576
Richmond	94806	Rockford	61102
San Mateo	94404	San Angelo	76903
San Francisco	94112	Staten Island	10310
Taunton	02780	Truro	02666
Waco	76703	Walnut Creek	94598
Wichita Falls	76305	Yonkers	10710

Commonly Misused Words

Good written communication skills are important for all office workers. Listed below are some commonly misused words. Use your dictionary to find the meaning of the word; then use the word in a sentence.

Word: Affect
Meaning: _____
Sentence: _____

Word: Effect
Meaning: _____
Sentence: _____

Word: Ascent
Meaning: _____
Sentence: _____

Word: Assent
Meaning: _____
Sentence: _____

Word: Capital
Meaning: _____
Sentence: _____

Word: Capitol
Meaning: _____
Sentence: _____

Word: Compliment
Meaning: _____
Sentence: _____

Word: Complement
Meaning: _____
Sentence: _____

Word: Disinterested
Meaning: _____
Sentence: _____

Word: Uninterested
Meaning: _____
Sentence: _____

Word: Farther
Meaning: _____
Sentence: _____

(Continued on next page)

Word: Further
Meaning: _____
Sentence: _____

Word: Flare
Meaning: _____
Sentence: _____

Word: Flair
Meaning: _____
Sentence: _____

Word: It's
Meaning: _____
Sentence: _____

Word: Its
Meaning: _____
Sentence: _____

Word: Lay
Meaning: _____
Sentence: _____

Word: Lie
Meaning: _____
Sentence: _____

Word: Peek
Meaning: _____
Sentence: _____

Word: Peak
Meaning: _____
Sentence: _____

Word: Principal
Meaning: _____
Sentence: _____

Word: Principle
Meaning: _____
Sentence: _____

Word: Stationery
Meaning: _____
Sentence: _____

Word: Stationary
Meaning: _____
Sentence: _____

Use of Reference Materials

Some employees are required to complete reports by gathering information from registers, charts, lists, or other reference materials. The following exercises will give you experience in this area.

Exercise A

An employer is planning a meeting for all company supervisors that will be held at a local hotel. Refer to the Conference Price List from the hotel as you answer the following:

a) How much should the breakfast budget be if you order:

2 gallons of coffee	40 muffins
1 gallon of tea	3 trays of fruit

b) How much should the evening budget be if you order:

25 petits fours	10 mud pies
3 dozen Danish cookies	30 soft drinks

c) You can get 12 slices from the zucchini bread. How much is saved by ordering 4 zucchini loaves instead of 48 muffins?

d) A gallon of coffee serves 16 cups. How many gallons would you order to plan for 70 cups?

e) A pitcher of orange juice serves 12 glasses. How many pitchers would you order to plan for 90 glasses?

CONFERENCE PRICE LIST

MORNING COMBINATIONS	Quantity	Price
Coffee	Gallon	$20.00
Tea	Gallon	20.00
Orange juice	Per pitcher	16.00
Fresh fruit	Per tray	19.50
Date nut bread	Per loaf	17.50
Zucchini bread	Per loaf	17.50
Whole wheat muffins	Each	2.25

EVENING COMBINATIONS	Quantity	Price
Fresh fruit	Per bowl	$15.00
Petits fours	Each	1.50
Soft drinks	Each	1.75
Danish cookies	Per dozen	8.00
Fruit punch	Per gallon	18.00
Mud pies	Each	1.75

(Continued on next page)

Exercise B

At Lucas Advertising, the employees must record mail charges for each client. Referring to the Mail Expense Register below, what was the total April charge for:

a.) Chevron _____
b.) Levis _____
c.) Admin _____

MAIL EXPENSE REGISTER FOR APRIL			
Charge to	**Amount**	**Charge to**	**Amount**
Levis	14.89	Chevron	8.90
HewPac	7.13	Levis	2.90
Levis	43.90	Cal Milk	.75
Levis	.56	Chevron	3.78
PacTel	8.90	Levis	.55
Levis	.45	Chevron	8.90
Admin	6.60	Levis	2.67

Choosing Your Office Career

Objectives

After completing this chapter, you will be able to do the following:

1. Describe in detail the life you dream of five, ten, and twenty years in the future.
2. List the eight steps in career decision making.
3. List the work values that are important to you.
4. List four topics on which you will need to gather career information.
5. List three sources of career information that are published by the U.S. Department of Labor.
6. Describe your own personal attributes.
7. Describe the responsibilities and requirements of careers in which you may be interested.
8. Develop a plan of action to reach your life-style and career goals.

New Office Terms

Aptitude
Dictionary of Occupational Titles (DOT)
extrovert
flextime
fringe benefits

Guide for Occupational Exploration (GOE)
introvert
life-style goal
personality
work values

Before You Begin . . .

Answer the following questions that preview material covered in this chapter:

1. *What personal attributes should you consider when choosing a career?*
2. *What types of career information should you consider when choosing a career?*
3. *What types of information should you include in a plan of action to reach your life-style and career goals?*

Are you dreaming about the future when you should be planning it? Not that dreaming should be discouraged—the dream comes first—but a dream is just a dream without a plan.

The 1990s has introduced employment opportunities of greater variety and degrees of complexity than ever before. Your education and skills have prepared you for a career in the modern office. But maybe you're confused or uncertain as to exactly where you fit in and what kind of company needs what you have to contribute. And where are the jobs, anyway?

The U.S. Department of Labor predicts that one of every six new jobs through the year 2005 will be in health services. The demand for office support staff will be huge. Telecommunications, information services, and the cable television industry are other areas exploding with career opportunities.

Once you've identified your career goals and the life-style to which you aspire, you're pointed in the right direction. It then becomes a matter of following a series of logical steps to reach your destination.

■ CAREER CHOICE AND LIFE-STYLE

Planning for and making a career choice is one of the most important undertakings of your life. It gives you a sense of direction and a sense of purpose. But many career choices are tentative, and that's OK. You should feel free to change your mind as you learn more about what the world of work has to offer.

Office careers provide a wide variety of work both for the new business school graduate and for the experienced professional. And work environments are equally varied. For example, an administrative assistant could be employed by the racing office at Hollywood Park Race Course, at the headquarters of IBM, at the Metropolitan Museum, or at the studios of MTV. Doctors' and lawyers' offices employ administrative assistants. So do schools and hospitals. Although your clerical and computer skills may be similar to those of your friends, different work environments and types of businesses provide an exciting realm of possibilities.

Whatever your career choice, your earnings must support your life-style. This includes your rent and utilities, car payments and insurance, clothing and personal products, and leisure activities. The responsibilities of marriage and children and perhaps owning a house or other property require a substantial salary. In choosing your career, consider the potential for advancement.

You will get more from work than just money. Your work will satisfy, to a greater or lesser extent, your social, psychological, and self-esteem needs. Your work probably will become the central activity around which you plan your daily life.

■ MAKING CAREER DECISIONS

Does it sound as though your work will control your life? In many ways it will, but you may choose the type of work you do. So, if there's a secret to a fulfilling life, perhaps it's choosing the type of work that will provide the life-style you want to live in the future. You have a right to do exactly that—and with proper planning, you can take control of your life.

Of course, many people *don't* take control of their lives. They don't plan for a career. They make a choice all right, but it's a choice to give up control—to just let things happen to them. You can make a better choice than that. You will most likely make an intelligent career choice if you follow a decision-making procedure.

Whether you know it or not, you follow certain procedural steps in making any important decision. Some choices are so simple that we don't even recognize the procedure. Choices about which TV show to watch are easy. Choosing which car to buy requires more thought, but you may not follow a step-by-step procedure for doing so.

The following eight steps work especially well for making decisions about your career.

1. *Define your need or want.* What do you want out of life? Think about your daydreams and picture your hoped-for future life-style. Consider your values and interests.
2. *Analyze your resources.* Your skills and aptitudes (natural abilities) are the resources you contribute to a career.
3. *Identify your alternatives.* Your alternatives are the careers that you want to learn more about. You have probably already thought about the careers or jobs that you believe would be interesting. Select at least three career fields for in-depth research, and you will have some alternatives to compare.
4. *Gather information on your alternatives.* Information on careers includes responsibilities and requirements, working conditions, benefits, and opportunities.
5. *Evaluate your alternatives.* Review all the information you have gathered on alternatives. Compare each alternative with your personal attributes. Would the work activities be interesting? Do the activities, responsibilities, and working relationships match your values? Do you have the skills required? If not, do you have the aptitudes to learn the required skills? If further training and education are re-

quired for advancement, how will you complete them? Does this work mesh well with your personality? Can you realistically expect to earn enough to support your long-range life-style plans? Is it likely that this field will have ample opportunities when you begin working?

6. *Make your decision.* Which alternative is best for you? Which is second best? If one alternative is clearly best, then you will probably stick with this decision. Most people, though, need to keep reviewing their career decision for months or even years (see step 8). Things can and often do happen that make another career alternative more appealing or appropriate, so think of your initial career decision as a flexible one. No matter how certain you feel about your decision, you may want to change it later.

7. *Plan your action.* Your plan of action is an outline of what you must do to reach your career goal—and thus have your desired life-style. This will require setting some planning goals, which are the stepping-stones toward bigger goals.

8. *Evaluate your decision.* After making your decision, continue reviewing it to determine whether it is, indeed, the best choice for you. Either you will become even more convinced that it is a wise decision or you will begin to have lingering doubts about whether it is appropriate. If the latter occurs, then review your other alternatives again. If you decide that another choice would have been better, then change your career goal. Before you change your career goal, though, make certain that the new choice matches more closely with your long-range plans for your life-style.

EXPLORING PERSONAL ATTRIBUTES

Your personal attributes are your own needs, values, interests, data-people-things preferences, skills and aptitudes, and personality. Once you assess your personal attributes, you can determine which careers will match them.

An easy way to organize the information you discover about your personal attributes (and later, what you learn about career alternatives) is to record all of it in a notebook. Divide your notebook into four sections: Personal Attributes, Career Alternatives, Career Choices, and Plan of Action. As you explore your personal attributes, record this information in the first section. As you gather information about career alternatives, record it in the second section. Use the third section to record information on how your personal attributes match with each of several career alternatives. Finally, use the fourth section to develop a plan of action that will guide you toward your chosen career.

Needs

When you were younger, you probably began to plan your future by thinking about—daydreaming about—how you would like to live some-day. Our plans are based on daydreams, and we should never stop dreaming and planning. Do you continue to picture how you want to live in five, ten, or even twenty years? How does that picture compare with the life-style you have today? As you picture your hoped-for life-style, think about the following:

- where you live
- your relationships with family and friends
- community, social, and religious activities
- the work you do to earn a living
- how you spend your leisure time
- the type of car you drive

Would you like to continue with your present life-style? If not, what changes would you like to make?

Your life-style is an expression of ideas and feelings that you believe are desirable, important, and worthwhile. These ideas and feelings are called values. As you daydream about and plan your future life-style, you will picture ways you hope to express your values. The way you want to live in the future is your **life-style goal.** You must have a clear understanding of your values to picture clearly your future life-style goal. If you are unsure of your own values, this picture of the future will remain blurry.

Values

A clear set of values makes it relatively easy to focus on the future. You can set goals and plan how to reach them because you know where you're going.

Your values have been formed throughout your life, and they will continue to change as you grow older. When you were a child, your values probably mirrored those of your family. Since then, teachers, friends, and co-workers have affected your values, too.

Throughout life, it is easy to get confused about what is important. We are constantly testing reality because we're unsure about a lot of things. Perhaps you are in the process of questioning some of your values now.

Consider what your family, friends, and others think is important, but decide for yourself what is important to you. As you change and refine the values you believe in, they will guide your decision making throughout your life.

We all have general values that define how we live our daily life. Certain values define needs we expect to fulfill through work, and they are sometimes known as **work values.** Work values may include such things as

- fame
- economic well-being
- creativity
- religious activity
- prestige
- security

Consider whether you would want a job in which your working relationships are mostly with other people, data, or things.

- independence
- friendships
- close family life
- humanitarianism

You will be a happier person if your work is compatible with your values than if your work demands opposing values. For example, if fame is an important value, you will likely be happier as a performer than as an accountant. If security is an important value, you will probably be happier as an accountant than as an aspiring-but-often-unemployed actor. Think about the work you have done and the work you are preparing to do. Are your values and your career choices compatible?

Interests

As you have discovered, an important criterion for choosing a career is to find work that is interesting. No work is all fun, but you know that you are happier doing work that you find interesting. Think about the career you have chosen. How do the activities you expect to be doing on the job match with your interests?

As you continue to meet new people and explore new ideas and activities, you will probably discover that you will develop new interests. These new interests may open up new possibilities for you in the world of work. Maintaining an interest in your work is an important part of developing a satisfying life-style.

Data-People-Things Preferences

All jobs require working with data, other people, and things. On some jobs, though, such as that of a bookkeeper, you would work primarily with data (information). On other jobs, such as that of receptionist, you would work primarily with people. On yet other jobs, such as that of a copy machine operator, you would work primarily with things (machines).

Have you considered your data-people-things preferences? Do you prefer activities involving other people? Are you fascinated by working with things, such as building models? Think about the jobs you have had. What were your working relationships with data, people, and things? How has this consideration influenced your choice of careers?

Skills and Aptitudes

An awareness of your interests and data-people-things preferences has helped you choose work that you want to do. However, simply finding work that sounds interesting is no assurance of success—and you won't enjoy your work long unless you are successful. You have already developed some general skills that will help you succeed, such as getting along with others.

You may have taken some tests to help you discover your particular aptitudes. An **aptitude** is the potential for learning a skill. Becoming aware of your aptitudes has given you another tool to help you make

After graduation from high school, Recado accepted a job in his uncle's secondhand furniture store. He was not very interested in the business, but he made enough money to "get by." A couple of years later he enrolled as a part-time student in the local community college because some of his friends were attending. Again, he was not very interested in the classes he chose and did not do very well in school.

1. How will Recado's attitude of letting things happen to him affect his chances of creating a satisfying life-style?
2. Describe your attitudes and actions that have helped you make your career choice.

career choices. But discovering your aptitudes is only a beginning. You must continue to develop your skills to make them valuable tools in the workplace. As you continue to work, you may discover that you have other aptitudes. Just as discovering new interests may lead you to new job possibilities, discovering new aptitudes and choosing to develop them will also broaden your choices.

Personality

Your **personality** is the outward reflection of your inner self. It is apparent in how you look, speak, and act. All employers look for cheerfulness, enthusiasm, honesty, neatness, self-control, tact, and a good sense of humor.

Success in certain careers depends a great deal on certain other personality traits. Perhaps the simplest way of categorizing personality types is to divide everyone into two groups, extroverts and introverts. An **extrovert** is a person who has an outgoing personality. If you make friends easily and enjoy the company of a lot of people, then you are probably an extrovert. You will probably want to work where you can interact with a variety of other people. You might enjoy being a receptionist in a busy office where you can greet and talk with lots of people.

An **introvert** is a person with a quiet personality. If you are uncomfortable in a room full of strangers and have difficulty making new friends, then you are probably an introvert. You might enjoy a job as a bookkeeper, where you can work primarily with information and will not be interrupted frequently by other workers.

Neither personality type is better than the other, but each type is more appropriate for certain careers. As you may have guessed, most people fall somewhere between the extrovert and introvert extremes, but you are probably closer to one personality type than to the other.

Just as we have measurement instruments for values, interests, and aptitudes, we have tests for personalities, too. They are not tests in the usual sense—there are no right or wrong answers. But if you would like more information to help you define your own personality, then a personality test may help. Certain personality tests show how similar your personality is to that of most workers in particular careers.

$\mathbb{R}$ecall Time

Answer the following questions:

1. Think about your present life-style. What parts of your life-style do you like? What parts would you want to change? How will the career you have chosen help you do that?
2. What interests and aptitudes do you have that you think correspond with the career you have chosen?
3. Raymond is particularly interested in a clerical job in the field of travel. Besides interest, what else is important in evaluating whether a person is "right" for a job?
4. A clerk's job at the library involves categorizing and labeling books, working alone in a back room. As the employer, what personality traits would you look for when hiring someone for this position?

■ EXPLORING CAREERS

Although your future life is sure to take some unexpected turns, the dreaming and planning for the future that you do now will leave less to happenstance and allow you to take control of your life. If you have not settled on a career goal, the following information on exploring careers can help you make that decision. Even if you have already decided on a career goal, look again at some other careers—or at some specific jobs within your chosen career field. As explained in the discussion of the decision-making process, career goals should be kept flexible, and they should be continually evaluated.

Although you can explore careers in many ways, plan to gather information on the following four topics. (A variety of sources of this information are available.)

- responsibilities and requirements
- working conditions
- opportunities and benefits
- emerging career options

Responsibilities and Requirements

The most important information you will need about jobs and careers is a description of the daily work activities. These are the work activities you will do if you select a particular job or career. As you explore each career and later consider individual jobs, ask yourself, "What are the duties and responsibilities?" Consider whether you would enjoy performing these duties and carrying out these responsibilities.

If the duties and responsibilities appeal to you, determine the requirements for success in this career or on this particular job. If you want to earn promotions and pay raises, you will need more than the simple entry-level skills required for a beginning position. How many of these skills have you already developed? Do you have the aptitude to learn high-level skills in this career? What additional training and education are needed for advancement? Where can you get the required training and education?

Some careers are more compatible with your values and your personality type than others. As you investigate each job or career, consider whether the responsibilities and requirements are compatible with your own values and personality type.

Working Conditions

You will probably spend about forty hours each week (that's two thousand hours each year) on a job, so investigate the working conditions of any job or career you may consider. Most office-type work is done in a pleasant environment, usually indoors and often in air-conditioned, well-lighted offices. Even so, the working conditions can vary considerably. Some offices lack air-conditioning and thus are often too hot. Others are noisy or are located in cramped quarters.

The level of stress on a job, whether physical, mental, or emotional, also falls into the category of working conditions. Most office jobs are not too physically demanding, but many require more work than you can comfortably complete in eight hours a day—which leads to mental and emotional stress.

Other working conditions worth checking include data-people-things relationships and the hours of work.

Opportunities and Benefits

When you discover several careers in which the work activities and working conditions appeal to you, research the opportunities and benefits to workers.

Check on the usual salary for beginning workers, and find out how much you can earn after working two, three, five, and ten years. Are the fringe benefits appealing? **Fringe benefits** are the extra payments or services, in addition to salary, that you get from your employer. They usually include medical and dental insurance, paid sick days, and paid vacations. Larger companies generally have more extensive benefit packages than small employers, often including contributions to a retirement plan, profit sharing plans, or the right to buy stock in the company for less than the market price. The banking industry has the reputation for reliably good fringe benefit programs. The "fringe" package is in addition to your salary, and it is often to your advantage to accept a smaller salary when the benefit package is especially good because benefits are not taxable the way your paycheck is.

Standard packages in large corporations usually include between six and twelve paid holidays each year, in addition to one (sometimes two) week's vacation after one year's service. Vacation days increase with the number of years worked, up to four or even five weeks after twenty years. You may also be paid for as many as thirteen sick days each year. In large corporations, often you will be paid for these days even if you are not out sick, so it is to your advantage to stay healthy.

If you do become ill, having a good health insurance plan can take a great weight off your mind. Health insurance is the biggest employee benefit expense most companies have, and large corporations have much more bargaining power with insurance companies because of the large numbers of subscribers they represent. This means that if you work for a large corporation, you are likely to receive much more extensive health coverage than if you work in a small business. Because the cost of health care is so high, the first benefit many job seekers assess when researching a company is its health insurance program.

In unionized industries such as airlines, unions will manage most benefits of union employees. In return, members pay dues and abide by union rules.

Fringe benefits for some positions may include the use of a company car, as well as travel, meal, or uniform allowances. A special private lunchroom or restaurant at a large company's offices may be available to some employees. Airline workers are often envied because of their right to travel free on flights wherever their airline flies—a real "perk." More and more companies are providing child care. Some companies provide recreational facilities for employees to use during the lunch hour or other free time.

When you find one or several careers in which you feel you can succeed and that are interesting and rewarding, investigate the expected availability of jobs. You may not want to prepare for work that has limited opportunities or that would require you to move to another city or section of the country.

Emerging Career Options

Several career options have become more available to office workers in recent years. The most prevalent (widespread) are temporary work assignments, flextime, and working at home. These primarily affect where and when you work rather than the type of work activity.

Temporary Work Assignments Several nationwide companies (such as Manpower and Kelly Services) and many smaller companies have for many years provided businesses with temporary office workers. These companies have also provided opportunities for many office workers to experience a variety of working environments.

Office workers have more opportunities than ever to work for temporary agencies, and doing so has some obvious advantages. If you are a beginning worker with good office skills, your limited experience may disqualify you from some desirable permanent jobs. Your good skills will probably qualify you as a temporary worker, however. Many

LARGE OFFICE/SMALL OFFICE: What's Your Preference?

Careers

You will usually find many more career advancement opportunities in a large office than you will find in a small office. The main reason is that more positions are available in a large office. The more employee positions, the more chances for advancement. In a large office, it is common to find advancement positions such as office assistant I, office assistant II, and office assistant III. These steps up the career ladder often result in higher salaries and more work responsibility. Also, large offices are often parts of big companies that have more offices in other locations. This means even more advancement possibilities and more options should you decide you'd like to move to a different part of the country.

Career advancement opportunities in a small offices are usually limited. This is because fewer positions are available in a small office. Once an employee reaches a certain level in a small office, he finds little chance for career advancement. In many cases, the only possibility for promotion is to accept a position in a new job category. For example, if you work as a typist-clerk in an insurance office, your only advancement option might be to become a claims adjuster.

Are you the kind of person who will want to move up the career ladder, or will you be content with a steady job that you know you can do well? To advance, would you prefer to try new and different kinds of jobs, or would you rather continue using your office skills and training at higher levels?

beginning workers are gaining experience and sharpening their skills as temporary workers.

Another reason to consider working for a temporary agency is to try working on a variety of jobs and in a variety of environments.

Some people—especially mothers with small children—may want to work less than full time. If you want to work a schedule other than eight-to-five, most temporary agencies will give you work assignments to match your schedule.

Flextime Some companies allow workers certain latitude in setting their own hours for coming to work. **Flextime** means a system for allowing workers to set their own times for beginning and finishing work within a range of available hours. The concept of flextime has been around for years, and it is now being accepted by more and more companies.

Working at Home During the mid-1980s, many people purchased their own desktop computers for home use. These machines made it possible to write letters, reports, and other documents at home just as

Many companies now allow some employees to work at home.

easily as in an office. In fact, some workers have fewer interruptions at home and are thus more productive at home.

More and more companies are hiring part-time or temporary office workers and allowing them to complete all or most of their tasks at home using desktop or laptop computers. Sometimes, the computers are provided by the company.

By working at home, you save the time you would spend going to and from an office every day. You also save on gasoline and other car costs, and you eliminate the frustration you would have to endure if you passed through congested traffic. Some companies allow parents of small children to work at home. This allows parents to remain in the home with their children and may save some of the money otherwise spent on child care costs.

Many types of work that do not require the use of a computer are done at home, too. However, the computer has made it feasible for more office workers to stay at home and complete their work. An increasing number of people have begun their own office services businesses in their homes, too. You may want to consider this as an alternative as you consider your career options.

Sources of Career Information

Numerous sources of career information are available. You can find many of them in a local public library or elsewhere within your community.

The Library Begin your career research in your local public library. Most libraries have career books, magazines, pamphlets, films, and videotapes.

Most libraries have copes of the following three books published by the U.S. Department of Labor. They provide a wealth of career information.

- *Occupational Outlook Handbook*
- *Guide for Occupational Exploration*
- *Dictionary of Occupational Titles*

The *Occupational Outlook Handbook (OOH)* includes detailed information on more than two hundred occupations, and it is updated every two years. The *OOH* is easy to use and provides the following types of information:

- nature of the work
- working conditions
- employment
- training, other qualifications, and advancement
- job outlook
- earnings
- related occupations
- sources of additional information

Begin your career research in your local library.

The **Guide for Occupational Exploration (GOE)** organizes jobs into twelve interest areas. Each interest area is further divided into work groups and subgroups. The *GOE* provides the following types of information:

- the kind of work done
- skills and abilities needed
- interests and aptitudes
- how to prepare for this kind of work

The **Dictionary of Occupational Titles (DOT)** includes descriptions of more than twenty thousand jobs. In the main section, "Occupational Group Arrangement," it lists an identification number for and describes in some detail the duties of each job. Copy down the identification number, then turn to the appendix and learn the data-people-things relationships for a job. The *DOT* is somewhat more complicated to use than the *OOH* or *GOE*, so read the instructions in the front before you start using it.

The Community The business community near your home can also serve as an excellent source of career information. You can benefit from this source in two ways. First, you can gather career information by interviewing several people who earn their living doing the type of work you are considering. Second, you can get some real on-the-job work experience.

Your library research will likely provide an introduction to several careers that interest you and prompt some specific questions. You can probably find answers to these questions by interviewing someone in your business community who has years of experience in the career that interests you. You may know people who work in the careers you are considering. Call them up, explain your interest in their career, and ask

Patty had been sure about her future ever since she could remember. "I definitely want to be a flight attendant," she always told people. But Patty began to look around and to think about her long-term goals. She explored her own interests and aptitudes through a variety of tests at her local business college. She also explored careers and found others that would satisfy her interest in traveling. She was pleased to have discovered new options and began considering which choices would best meet all her goals.

Renee also had always been convinced that she wanted to be a flight attendant. She worked at a number of part-time jobs that she hated and struggled to save enough money to pursue the training she needed.

1. Describe Patty's and Renee's attitudes toward choosing their careers.
2. How might Patty's attitude be helpful on the job?
3. Based on their attitudes, which person is more likely to succeed in establishing a satisfying career?

if you may interview them. Most people are flattered by an interest in their work, and they enjoy talking about what they do. If you can, arrange for an interview at the job site so you can see the equipment and materials used. Before your appointment, prepare a list of questions to guide you during your interview.

Perhaps there are opportunities to learn about careers that interest you at your current place of employment. If there are people at your workplace doing work that interest you, express your interest to them. They may be able to provide you with some on-the-job experience that will be valuable in helping you learn about your future career.

Volunteer opportunities can also be a way to learn more about a career that interests you and can give you some on-the-job experience. Check with nonprofit organizations in your community to see what opportunities are available.

CHOOSING A CAREER

The work you do to earn a living will probably become the central activity in your life. It will influence every aspect of your life-style. Perhaps no decision in your life will be more important than your choice of career.

Unfortunately, many people never get around to making a conscious career decision. Some spend more time planning a wardrobe or deciding which car to buy than they do planning a career. They don't seem to understand that the work they do will control much of their future life. Unable to make a conscious choice, these people fall into some type of work through happenstance and simply drift through life. They do make a decision, but it is an unconscious decision to give away control of their life.

Having explored your personal attributes and careers, it is time to make your career choice. You may feel reluctant to make such an important decision today, this month, or even this year. However, the sooner you choose a career, the sooner you will have a direction for your life. Remember, no career choice is final, so you can always change your mind. Indeed, you *should* change your career choice whenever you determine another one is better for you.

■ DEVELOPING YOUR PLAN OF ACTION

Some people with good intentions get as far as choosing a career but never get around to developing a plan to reach their goal. If you have not done so already, plan now how you will reach your career and life-style goals. Include the following types of information in your plan:

- training and education
- money for training and education
- jobs leading to your career and life-style goals
- major changes in your personal life

Begin by setting some planning goals. These are the relatively minor goals you must achieve before you can achieve your bigger goals.

Goals must be specific. Saying you want to be a success or you want a simple life-style is much too general. Describe your life-style goal in detail.

Goals must be realistic. Setting goals that are impossible to reach is worse than having no goals at all because such goals will constantly frustrate you.

Actually putting your goals into writing helps you to think more clearly and to organize your thoughts. Begin by evaluating your life-style. Think about the life-style you are hoping to achieve in the next five, ten, and twenty years. Then think about the career you have chosen and what your career goals are for the next five, ten, and twenty years. Are your career goals and life-style goals compatible?

Obviously you have already established some planning goals to help you reach your career goals. The courses you are taking are part of those planning goals. Successfully completing this course work might be considered a short-range goal. Defining the kind of job you hope to find once you have completed your training is an example of a medium-range goal. Advancements in your career are examples of long-range goals.

With better planning, most people could have a more satisfying life-style than the one they live. You can have a satisfying life-style because you know how to take control of your life. You know how to explore your personal attributes, explore careers, and make important decisions. You also know how to develop a plan of action that will guide you toward your ultimate career and life-style goals. Your plan of action can do these four things for you:

- Organize your activities
- Keep you on schedule

- Help you set priorities
- Give you a feeling of accomplishment when you reach your goals

As you achieve your short-range goals, you will become more confident. You will know that you can achieve your longer-range goals, too.

R ecall Time

Answer the following questions:

1. Suzy is considering a front-office job for a busy trucking company. What should she find out about her potential working conditions before she makes her final decision?
2. What are some advantages to temporary office work through an agency?
3. Jorge is interested in department store customer service. What sources can he find in the library to research this career?

■ SUMMARY

Your career choice will be one of the most important decisions of your life. Your work will affect every aspect of your daily life. Such an important decision requires a step-by-step decision-making procedure in which you define your desired future life-style; analyze your skills and aptitudes; identify your career alternatives; get information about those alternatives; evaluate the alternatives; make your decision; develop a plan of action to reach your career goal; and continue to evaluate your decision until you are convinced it is the best for you or decide to change your career goal to one that suits you better.

Exploring your personal attributes can be helpful in selecting a career that makes you happy. In assessing your own personal characteristics, include a description of the life-style you hope to lead; your personal and work values; your interests; your preferences for working with data, people, or things; your skills and aptitudes; and your personality type.

Exploring career characteristics is equally as important as assessing yourself. The most vital information about jobs and careers concerns the duties and responsibilities of a job. Try to find a match between your own needs, values, interests, and skills and the requirements of a job. Examine the working conditions of a job or career. Are they compatible with your personal preferences? Are the job opportunities and benefits agreeable to you? Investigate the expected availability of jobs in a field. Include temporary work and working at home in your list of options.

Your public library contains valuable information about careers. Many libraries contain extensive resources for your career research. Three books published by the U.S. Department of Labor provide particularly detailed information about jobs and careers: the *Occupational*

Outlook Handbook, the *Guide for Occupational Exploration,* and the *Dictionary of Occupational Titles.*

Contact with your local business community also can provide excellent career information. One approach is to interview people who are working in jobs that interest you. Perhaps the best way to find out about a particular job or career is firsthand experience. Work experience programs or part-time jobs allow you to try out a type of work with on-the-job experience.

Choosing a career goal is truly taking control of your life. It is like sitting in the driver's seat and choosing a destination. To make sure you arrive at the destination, you take along a road map—a plan to reach your destination. This plan of action includes setting goals for the training, education, and jobs that will lead you to your ultimate career and life-style goals.

When preparing for and choosing your office career, do you

- think about how you would like to live in the future?
- ask yourself how different types of work would affect your overall life-style?
- believe that career choices should sometimes be changed?
- want to take control of your own life?
- use a decision-making procedure for important decisions?
- record all your career information in a notebook?
- consider what your family and friends think is important, but decide for yourself what is important to you?
- know the types of work that would interest you?

In Conclusion . . .

When you have completed this chapter, answer the following questions:

1. *What personal attributes should be considered when choosing a career?*
2. *What types of career information should be considered when choosing a career?*
3. *What types of information should be included in a plan of action to reach your life-style and career goals?*

Review and Application

REVIEW YOUR VOCABULARY

Match the following by writing the letter of each vocabulary word in the space to the left of its description.

_____ 1. system for allowing workers to set their own work hours

_____ 2. outward reflection of your inner self, apparent in how you look, speak, and act

_____ 3. person who has an outgoing personality

_____ 4. extra payments or services, in addition to salary, that you get from your employer

_____ 5. resource that organizes jobs into twelve interest areas

_____ 6. person with a quiet personality

_____ 7. way you want to live in the future

_____ 8. needs we expect to fulfill through work

_____ 9. resource that includes descriptions of more than twenty thousand jobs

_____ 10. potential for learning a skill

a. aptitude
b. _Dictionary of Occupational Titles (DOT)_
c. extrovert
d. flextime
e. fringe benefits
f. _Guide for Occupational Exploration (GOE)_
g. introvert
h. life-style goal
i. personality
j. work values

DISCUSS AND ANALYZE AN OFFICE SITUATION

1. James has accepted an office job with an accounting firm. The job promises to be a perfect match with James's interests and skills. During the first few weeks of work, however, his employer asks James to change his work hours—to come in later and stay later. This conflicts with the schedule James has arranged to spend time with his family. James's family is very important to him, but he does not want to lose his new job.

   What should James do?

2. Robert enjoys and is skilled at working on cars. He thinks it would be great to have his own garage someday. But when a job at a local repair shop came up, Robert took it for the extra money. After two years, Robert is still at the shop—and the idea of having his own garage has become just a dream.

   What was missing in Robert's approach to his career? What could he have done differently?

PRACTICE BASIC SKILLS

Math

1. When considering your life-style goals, part of what you must consider is how much money you wish to earn. If you earn $25,000 in one year when the inflation rate is 5 percent, you must earn an extra 5 percent the following year just to stay even.

   Suppose you will earn $25,000 in one year, and the inflation rate remains at 5 percent over the following twenty years. How much will you need to earn in 5 years to have the same buying power? In 10 years? In 20 years? (Note: You will need to calculate each year separately.)

English

1. Regardless of what career you choose, you will be required to use Standard English on the job. It is a good idea to begin now using Standard English so that it becomes a habit for you. In the paragraph below, circle the words that are not Standard English.

   I need a job bad. I'm into music, computers, and cars. Any ideas would be majorly appreciated. I gotta go now, but call if you hear something. If my roommate or myself isn't there, leave a message on the machine.

Proofreading

1. Whatever your new career entails, you will probably be required to write with correct spelling, punctuation, and grammar. Read the passage below and circle the items that are not correct.

Employment Skills for Office Careers

Report on the Monday Morning Meeting

The mondya morning meeting was ttenned by jane smith, Mary Ann Worsley, George atwood, and mee. The problms with the new action plan was discussed in detale with everyon finally agreein that it filled the needs it was deesigned to fill.

Next there was a descussion about the recycling of our newspapers. We worked out a methud of picking up the pappers each tuesday to take to the down town center.

The meetin was over by ten oclock.

1. Write out a description of your desired future life-style.
2. What is your long-range career goal? If you haven't made your decision yet, write down one of the career goals you are most interested in. List some short-range and medium-range goals that will help you achieve your long-range goal.

QUIZ

*Write a **T** if the statement is true or an **F** if the statement is false.*

_____ 1. Daydreaming is a waste of brainpower and cannot help you to be a success.

_____ 2. Once you have made a career decision, you will only be wasting precious time if you change it.

_____ 3. Evaluating a decision involves asking teachers and counselors to decide if it is the correct choice.

_____ 4. An important factor in choosing a career is what your life-style needs are going to be.

_____ 5. The hobbies and fun things you do can be a good indicator of what kind of career you would do well in.

_____ 6. A job need not be interesting to be fully satisfying.

_____ 7. People who prefer data to things would be happier working in bookkeeping than in sales.

_____ 8. Your personality is an important factor in the kind of work that you will choose.

_____ 9. Learning the responsibilities and requirements of a job is not as important as whether the boss is a friendly, outgoing person.

_____ 10. Fringe benefits should not be a factor in making a job decision.

_____ 11. Working for a temporary agency should be used only as a last resort, if you cannot find permanent work.

_____ 12. Doing volunteer work at a local hospital can be good experience for a first office job.

(Continued on next page)

_____ 13. The *OOH, DOT,* and *GOE* are publications that can help you to find a job that is suited to you.

_____ 14. Even if you do not make a conscious career choice, the chances are you will end up in the job that is right for you.

_____ 15. Deciding on long-range goals is the first step in making a career plan.

Your Self-Profile

As you read and studied chapter 3 you probably learned more about what you want out of life and how your career can make it all happen. Complete this self-profile and save it for later comparison with the demands and opportunities of various careers.

Your Values

Based on what is important to you in life, list your top four values:

1. _____   3. _____

2. _____   4. _____ .

Your Interests

Based on activities you find most interesting, list your top four career interests:

1. _____   3. _____

2. _____   4. _____

Your Life-style Goals

Based on your view of the life-style you are trying to achieve, what do you see as the four most important elements of your life-style ten years in the future?

1. _____   3. _____

2. _____   4. _____

Abilities, Aptitudes, and Personality

Based on your past work experience and other outside activities describe how your abilities, aptitudes, and personality can help you in your future career.

_____

_____

_____

_____

Using Library References

As you learned from the text, one of the best sources of career information is the library. Select two careers that are suited to your personality, interests, and abilities. Then use the *Occupational Outlook Handbook (OOH)*, the *Dictionary of Occupational Titles (DOT)*, and the *Guide for Occupational Exploration (GOE)* to gather information on these careers. Ask your instructor or librarian for help when using these or other references they may recommend. Photocopy and use the following checklist to research each of your career choices.

Career Research Checklist

Name of Career _____

Library References Used _____

_____

Values

■ What values are important in this career?

_____

Salaries and Fringe Benefits

■ What is the beginning salary for this career? _____

■ What is the average salary for this career? _____

■ What fringe benefits do workers in this career usually receive?

_____

Education or Training Required

■ What education is required for this career? _____

_____

■ Once a person has entered this career field, will more education or training be necessary or helpful?

_____

_____

(Continued on next page)

Duties and Responsibilities

What are the normal duties and responsibilities of this career?

_____

_____

_____

Skills and Aptitudes Required

What skills and aptitudes are necessary in this career? _____

_____

Helpful Personality Traits

What personality characteristics would be helpful in this career?

_____

_____

_____

Work Environment and Relationships

Is the work done indoors or outdoors? Describe the environment.

_____

_____

Is the work performed while sitting, standing, or moving?

_____

Is there anything dangerous about the work? If so, describe it.

_____

_____

_____

Will this career involve working with mostly data, people, or things?

_____

Career Information Interviews

You have learned that a good way to get information about a particular career is to speak with someone who works in that career. An interview with such a person is called a *career information interview*. Use the following questionnaires to guide you in conducting two career information interviews.

Select a company or a person you would like to interview and call for an appointment. Introduce yourself on the telephone and explain the purpose of your call. It may be helpful to say that the interview is a school assignment.

INTERVIEW #1

_____

Date and Time of Appointment

_____   _____

Consultant's Name   Career/Type of Work

Questions to Ask

Duties and Responsibilities

■ What are the normal duties in your job? _____

_____

Skills and Aptitudes Required

■ What skills and abilities are necessary in this career?

_____

_____

Helpful Personality Traits

■ What personality characteristics would be helpful in this career?

_____

_____

Work Environment and Relationships

■ What are the typical working conditions in this profession?

_____

_____

(Continued on next page)

Do you work with mostly data, people, or things? Explain. _____

_____

Education or Training Required

What education or training is required for your career? _____

_____

Once a person has entered this career field, will more education or training be necessary or helpful? Explain.

_____

Values

What values are important in this career? Why? _____

_____

Salaries and Fringe Benefits

What is the average beginning salary in this field? _____

How quickly do salaries go up with experience? _____

What do the most successful people earn? _____

What fringe benefits could someone expect? _____

Career Outlook

Is it likely that there will be many new job opportunities for people to enter this type of work?

Why or why not? _____

_____

Additional Comments

Is there any additional information that might be helpful to someone who is interested in pursuing this career? What is it?

_____

_____

INTERVIEW #2

_____
Date and Time of Appointment

_____
Consultant's Name

_____
Career/Type of Work

Questions to Ask

Duties and Responsibilities

What are the normal duties in your job? _____

_____

Skills and Aptitudes Required

What skills and abilities are necessary in this career?

_____

_____

Helpful Personality Traits

■ What personality characteristics would be helpful in this career?

_____

_____

Work Environment and Relationships

What are the typical working conditions in this profession?

_____

_____

Do you work with mostly data, people, or things? Explain.

_____

_____

(Continued on next page)

Education or Training Required

What education or training is required for your career?

_____

Once a person has entered this career field, will more education or training be necessary or helpful? Explain.

_____

_____

Values

What values are important in this career? Why?

_____

_____

Salaries and Fringe Benefits

What is the average beginning salary in this field? _____

How quickly do salaries go up with experience? _____

What do the most successful people earn? _____

What fringe benefits could someone expect? _____

Career Outlook

Is it likely that there will be many new job opportunities for people to enter this type of work?

Why or why not? _____

_____

Additional Comments

Is there any additional information that might be helpful to someone who is interested in pursuing this career?

_____

_____

Making a Flexible Career Decision

As you read in chapter 3, making a career decision, even if it is one you will change later, is better than making no decision at all. You will achieve your goals only by taking control of your life and setting a course for yourself.

Review the self-profile that you completed in Activity 3–1. Then select the two careers that interest you most. Fill in the following blanks for each of these career choices. When you have finished, select one of them as your career choice. Remember that if you discover later that this choice is inappropriate, you can correct it. But today, even a choice you may change later is better than no choice at all.

NAME OF CAREER _____

Values

Does this career match my values? _____

Salaries and Fringe Benefits

What is the salary range, from the beginning salary to the salaries of the highest-paid workers in

this career? _____

Would my salary be adequate to support the life-style I want to live in five, ten, or twenty years?

_____

Will this career provide all the fringe benefits I will need? _____

Education/Training Required

What requirements for pursuing this career have I already completed?

_____

What requirements must I complete before I can enter this career?

_____

What additional requirements must I complete to advance in this career?

_____

Considering my grades and attendance record at school, are these educational and training require-

ments realistic for me? _____

(Continued on next page)

How will I pay for the cost of this education and training?

_____

_____

Career Duties and Responsibilities

Do the duties and responsibilities of this career sound interesting? _____

Skills and Aptitudes Required

Do I have the skills needed to succeed in this career or the aptitudes to develop them?

_____

Type of Personality Needed

Do I have the type of personality needed in this career? _____

Work Environment Relationships

Is the working environment satisfactory? _____

Are the number of hours and the time of day worked compatible with my future life-style?

_____

Do the requirements for working with data, people, and things in this career match my own

preferences? _____

Career Outlook

Will there be a demand for more workers in this career when I am ready to begin work?

_____

Am I willing to move to another location to find a job in this career? _____

Narrowing Career Choices

Is this career a wise choice for me? _____

Explanation of this decision:

_____

_____

NAME OF CAREER _____

Values

☐ Does this career match my values? _____

Salaries and Fringe Benefits

☐ What is the salary range, from the beginning salary to the salaries of the highest-paid workers in this career? _____

☐ Would my salary be adequate to support the life-style I want to life in five, ten, or twenty years?

_____

☐ Will this career provide all the fringe benefits I will need? _____

Education/Training Required

☐ What requirements for pursuing this career have I already completed?

_____

☐ What requirements must I complete before I can enter this career?

_____

☐ What additional requirements must I complete to advance in this career?

_____

☐ Considering my grades and attendance record at school, are these educational and training requirements realistic for me? _____

☐ How will I pay for the cost of this education and training?

_____

_____

Career Duties and Responsibilities

☐ Do the duties and responsibilities of this career sound interesting? _____

(Continued on next page)

Skills and Aptitudes Required

■ Do I have the skills needed to succeed in this career or the aptitudes to develop them?

_____

Type of Personality Needed

Do I have the type of personality needed in this career? _____

Work Environment and Relationships

Is the working environment satisfactory? _____

Are the number of hours and the time of day worked compatible with my future life-style?

_____

Do the requirements for working with data, people, and things in this career match my own

preferences? _____

Career Outlook

Will there be a demand for more workers in this career when I am ready to begin work?

_____

Am I willing to move to another location to find a job in this career? _____

Narrowing Career Choices

Is this career a wise choice for me? _____

Explanation of this decision:

_____

_____

A Plan of Action

As you learned from chapter 3, planning goals are important stepping-stones that guide you toward your ultimate career goal. In this activity you will write specific and realistic planning goals. These goals will become your *plan of action* and will include short-range, medium-range, and long-range planning goals.

Review the section "Developing Your Plan of Action." On a separate sheet of paper, write your short-range, medium-range, and long-range planning goals. Be as specific and as realistic as possible. Write down the dates when you want to complete these goals. Arrange your goals in order according to what you need to accomplish first, second, and so on. Finally, rewrite all your planning goals and dates under the appropriate headings on this page.

Your Plan of Action

Short-Range Goals   Complete by

_____   _____

_____   _____

_____   _____

_____   _____

Medium-Range Goals   Complete by

_____   _____

_____   _____

_____   _____

_____   _____

Long-Range Goals   Complete by

_____   _____

_____   _____

_____   _____

_____   _____

Ultimate Career Goal   Complete by

_____   _____

In the Real World

Interview three persons who you feel are successfully managing their careers and ask them these questions. You may photocopy this page to use during each interview.

1. Is this how you planned your career, and, if not, how did you end up where you are now?

_____

_____

_____

_____

2. What other jobs have you had and how did those experiences contribute to your present success?

_____

_____

_____

_____

3. Do you have any advice for someone unsure of what she wants to do? What advice do you have for someone who knows what she wants to do?

_____

_____

_____

_____

Sounds Like a Plan

Evaluate what you expect from the work experience and how your expectations can be met using the following guidelines:

1. Define your needs.

_____

_____

_____

2. Identify your talents and abilities.

_____

_____

_____

3. Research the opportunities in your area of interest.

_____

_____

_____

4. Organize your resources.

_____

_____

_____

5. Know your alternatives.

_____

_____

_____

Finding and Applying for a Job

Objectives

After completing this chapter, you will be able to do the following:

1. Name a legal form that you must have before you can begin working.
2. List six sources of job leads.
3. Organize your job hunt, including the use of job lead cards.
4. Secure job leads from a variety of sources.
5. Correctly fill out an application form.
6. Write a letter of application.
7. Write a resume and a cover letter.
8. Prepare for and dress appropriately for an interview.
9. Conduct yourself properly and answer questions appropriately in a job interview.
10. Use Standard English in a job interview.
11. Follow up a job interview properly.

New Office Terms

cover letter
direct calling
employment tests
job lead card
letter of application
letter of inquiry

private employment agencies
public employment agencies
resume
reverse chronological order
Standard English

Before You Begin . . .

Answer the following questions that preview material covered in this chapter:

1. *How will you go about looking for a job?*
2. *When you hear about a job that you would like, what action will you take?*
3. *What will you do to prepare for a job interview?*

You may have chosen an office job as your ultimate career goal—or, at least, you may have some ideas about the job you would like for now. If not, first ask yourself this important question: What jobs can you do well and would you enjoy? You will probably think of several related office jobs. It is important to know the type of work you would like and the names of one, two, or several jobs for which you wish to apply *before* you start looking.

You may want an office job to gain experience as a stepping-stone into the career you have chosen. Even if you have not made your career choice, you still may want a part-time job. You may want to earn some money for recreational activities, new clothes, a car, or educational expenses.

■ LOOKING FOR A JOB

Whatever your reason for wanting to work, getting the job you want will be a job in itself. You may be well qualified, but so are many others. You will be up against some good competition, and you must convince the employer that *you* are the best candidate. You can do this better than most others if you are motivated, energetic, and prepared.

If you really want to find a job, and you're willing to spend the time required, some proven ways of going about it will make your job hunt more efficient and effective. Begin with two important steps that will put you ahead of your competition. Then learn where to look for job leads, how to follow them up with an application, and how to prepare for and conduct yourself in a job interview.

First, most people spend less than five hours a week looking for a job. That's not enough. Plan to invest as much time per week looking for a job as you will spend working on the job after you're hired!

Second, most people are not well organized for a successful job hunt. Follow the suggestions in this chapter and you will spend your job-hunting time efficiently. You will learn in detail how to go about organizing your job hunt. Then you will learn how and where to find job leads and how to expand your collection of job leads. You will even learn how to find a job without any job leads!

Organizing Your Job Hunt

Remember, job hunting is quite a job itself, and you must be willing to work hard at finding the right job. You will be using a variety of sources

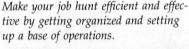

Make your job hunt efficient and effective by getting organized and setting up a base of operations.

Employment Skills for Office Careers

"Ross! Guess what?" hollers Yolanda. "I found a good job lead this morning! When I was waiting for the bus, I spotted an ad in the newspaper for part-time clerical help at Mesa Realty."

"Really? What are the qualifications?" asks Ross.

"Oh, they're all listed in the ad. . . . You know, 'no experience necessary, bilingual desired' and . . . oh, I've got the ad here in my purse."

Yolanda unsuccessfully digs around in her purse for the little ad. In frustration, she dumps her purse contents onto her desk. "I can't find it! I'll just have to find another copy of the newspaper."

1. Will Yolanda conduct a well-organized job search?
2. Is it likely that Yolanda will be able to keep paperwork organized as an office clerk?
3. Is it likely that the job at Mesa Realty will still be available by the time Yolanda applies for it?

to secure job leads. Write down all your job leads so you will be able to follow up on them.

Before you begin your hunt, set up a base of operations and collect the supplies you will need. Then be sure you have the legal documents you will need.

Base of Operations   A good way to organize your job hunt is to set up a base of operations. This can be a section of your bedroom or another room in your house or apartment. If you have a study desk, designate one drawer for job-hunting materials. You will need a chair and a telephone nearby—preferably at your desk. These are the basics. A section of a filing cabinet will help you organize your job hunt, too. You will need a typewriter or computer with a word processing program when you begin to prepare application documents.

Supplies   You will also need some supplies. The following should be enough to get you started:

- *a logbook.* Any loose-leaf notebook will serve the purpose. If you have a computer at home, use the word processing program to keep a log of your progress.
- *one hundred index cards for recording job leads.* Use a 4×6-inch or 5×8-inch size.
- *an appointment calendar.* Get one that has room for hour-by-hour notations.
- *lined notebook paper.* If you do not have a computer readily available, you will need some lined notebook paper for rough drafts of application documents. You probably already have this on hand.
- *one hundred sheets of good-quality bond paper.* Use twenty-pound or twenty-four-pound weight and 8½×11-inch size. This will be used for resumes and cover letters. White, cream, or light gray are the most preferred colors. About fifty matching envelopes should be enough.

- *stamps.* Use these for mailing application documents.
- *other helpful office supplies.* These include colored pencils or high-lighters, scissors, paper clips, a stapler, transparent tape, and a wastebasket.

Finding the right job is difficult enough when you are well organized. Good organization allows you to concentrate your time and your effort on getting and following up leads, completing application documents, and going to interviews. If you are not well organized, you will waste time waiting in line at the post office for stamps or making repeated trips to the stationery store.

Use your computer or logbook to record everything connected with your job hunt. Record the calls you've made, the calls you plan to make, and names, numbers, and ideas. Do this every day. Then, each evening, go through your logbook and cross out things you have completed and things that are no longer important.

Use your index cards to make job lead cards like the one shown in figure 4–1. A **job lead card** is an index card on which you record all relevant information about an available job. This is an efficient system because you can easily rearrange your leads however you want, perhaps placing the most promising ones on the top. You may want to keep a separate set of cards ordered according to the time and date of scheduled interviews.

Write the name of the person you should contact and the company name, address, and phone number on the front of the card. Write the source of the lead in the lower left corner. If your source is a newspaper want ad, tape the ad to the card as shown in figure 4–1. Use the back of the card to record whatever you do to follow up the lead. Record the date when you call to request an interview, and the time and date of the interview. Also write down the name of the person you are to see and, if necessary, directions to the company. Later, write down your impression of the interview and whether you are offered the job.

Use a second card to write down whatever information you can learn about the company, such as the product it makes, the service it provides, or other pertinent information. (The "Know the Company" section later in this chapter explains how to find information about companies.) Then staple this second card, with information about the company, to your job lead card. Just before your interview, review your notes about the company.

If you have a computer that you can use daily in your job search, set up your job lead information using a data-base program. Record the same information you would if you were using job lead cards. Then print out the information you will need before each application or interview.

You may use your appointment calendar to keep track of any appointment related to your job hunt. In fact, it's a good idea to put all your appointments in this calendar. Then you won't schedule an interview at the same time you have a dental appointment.

Many calendar programs are available for personal computers (PCs). If you are using a computer for other job search functions, you may want to use a calendar program, too.

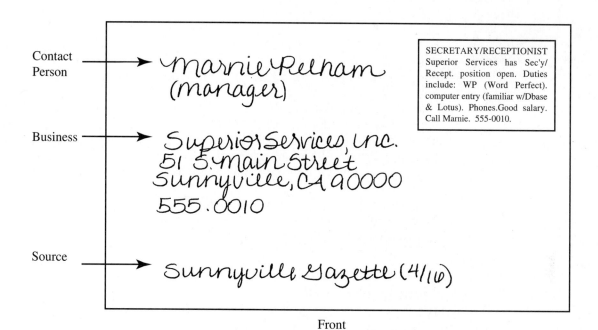

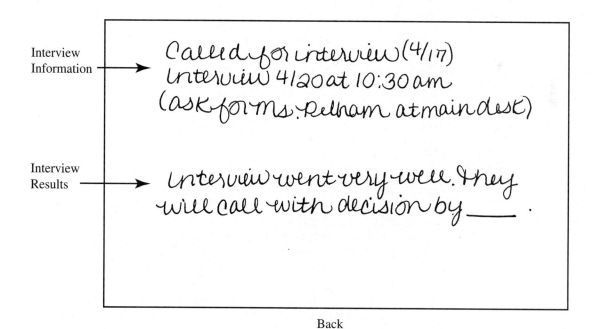

Friends may know of job openings from their own job hunt.

Your lined notebook paper, bond paper, stamps, and other office supplies will all come in handy when you start writing letters, filling out application forms, and preparing resumes.

Social Security Card The final part of being organized for your job hunt is to be sure you have a Social Security card. You probably won't be hired if you don't have a Social Security card. It is illegal for an employer to pay you until you have provided your Social Security number. Even if you can get someone to hire you, the employer cannot pay you until you have your card.

In 1988, Congress passed a law requiring every person who is five years of age or older and is claimed as a dependent on federal income tax form 1040 to have a Social Security card. Chances are you already have one. If not, fill out an application and mail it today or tomorrow. If you do not have one, you may miss out on a job that you would really like.

You can get an application form for a Social Security card at your local Social Security office. Look up the address in your telephone directory. These applications may also be available at your local post office.

Finding Job Leads

How do you go about finding job leads? The first step is to contact all the sources available that might produce a job lead. Sometimes job lead information is incomplete. For example, you may learn that a local insurance company is looking for an office worker. You don't know the job title or the qualifications for the job. You may not even know who you will need to see to apply. Follow up even skimpy leads and fill in the missing information yourself. Finding a job you can do well and enjoy requires finding as many job leads as possible and then following up promptly on each one.

Where do you begin looking for sources of job leads? Among the most productive are members of your own family, friends, former employers, newspaper advertisements, and employment agencies.

Networking A system of networking to track down job leads can be most productive. Start with your own family members. Do they know of any openings where they work? They might have contacts at other companies or have friends who know who is hiring. You probably know of one or two people who have recently started jobs and are willing to share information from their own search.

Make a list of family friends, personal friends, neighbors, and acquaintances through clubs, teams, or organizations of which you are a part. This is your primary network. Add to that the people who know the people you know and your network expands many times over.

Use your network to make contacts at companies where you would like to work. Make calls. But don't ask them if any jobs are available. Instead, ask them for advice on finding a job, making clear the type of job you are seeking. This approach avoids the usual "Sorry, we don't have anything

now, but we'll keep you in mind." This is not a promise nor is it something that will be remembered when something does come up.

Most people are flattered when asked for advice and will sincerely try to be helpful. Advice from someone on the "inside" can be invaluable.

Inexperienced job seekers will wonder if it is appropriate to contact influential family friends. It is as long as you are qualified to do the work. Many of the best jobs are never advertised because they are filled by friends of employees. Also, don't be hesitant about asking influential family friends for references. This is not only appropriate, but necessary.

Former Employers Have you previously held a job? Former employers are often good sources of job leads whether you worked in an office or just held a temporary baby-sitting job. Former employers who were satisfied with your work will most likely want to help you find a job.

Newspaper Advertisements Many employers place classified ads in the local newspaper when they need to fill office jobs. Make it a habit to read the help-wanted ads. Some papers separate jobs according to type, such as accounting, clerical, secretarial, and so on. Newspaper ads are a good source of job leads, and you may also learn a lot about the local job market. You may learn how much money is offered for each type of work and the qualifications needed for the type of job that interests you.

Follow up promptly on every ad that might lead to the job you want. If you wait even a day or two, you may be too late.

Avoid ads that require you to make a deposit of money or to enroll in a course and pay a fee. Such ads are not offering jobs at all but are attempts to sell you something.

Public and Private Employment Agencies Employment agencies match workers with jobs. When employers call an agency about a job opening, the agency writes out the qualifications, salary offered, and other details on a job order form. An agency employee reviews the

Finding and Applying for a Job

Many people find jobs by looking in the employment section of a newspaper and calling or writing to a company. Generally, large businesses often place detailed ads describing a position and starting salary. Some companies use an employment agency to advertise, interview, and find a suitable employee for them. Many large businesses have a personnel department, sometimes called the *human resource department.* The people who work in this department place newspaper advertisements for job openings, review applications, and do initial interviewing and screening. If you pass this screening process, then you interview with the manager or supervisor of the department you will be working for. You can go through several interviewing steps before you get a job.

Small companies usually don't have a personnel department. The manager or supervisors themselves may place an advertisement, receive applications, and conduct interviews. This often means that you have fewer interview stages than when applying for jobs in large offices. Another difference is that in small offices, the employees are more aware of job openings, and they have more direct access to the person doing the hiring. As a result, they often suggest friends or relatives for job openings before ads are even placed in a newspaper. This type of "word-of-mouth" communication often plays a much bigger part in finding a job in a small office than it does in a large office.

Would you stand a better chance of getting a job in a large office or a small office? Why?

records of those who have completed application forms and refers several applicants for interviews.

Most cities have both public and private employment agencies. **Public employment agencies** provide free job referral service because they are supported by taxes and operated by the federal or state government. Fill out an application form at the public employment agency near you. You will be interviewed to determine your interests and qualifications. Then, when a job is listed that matches your interests and qualifications, the agency will call you. You will be told about the company and the job duties, then referred for an interview if you are still interested.

Private employment agencies are not supported by taxes, so they must charge a fee for finding you a job. The fee is either a flat rate or a percentage of the first few months' salary. Employers are often willing to pay the placement fee for higher-level professional jobs. However, if you are a beginning worker, you will probably have to pay the fee charged by a private employment agency. Private employment agencies sometimes have job leads that aren't listed with public agencies. If you are not getting all the leads you want, you may want to consider applying at a private agency.

Expanding Your Collection of Job Leads

Get all the leads from firsthand sources that you can. Then expand your collection based on the leads you already have. Here is how to do it. Every time you follow up on a lead that does not result in a job, ask for suggestions about whom you might contact. From each lead you follow up on that doesn't result in the job you want, try to get at least one or two new leads.

A lot of other people are looking for work, too. You may not get just exactly the job you want, and you may turn down some jobs offered to you. If you have a lot of leads, you can simply follow up on the next one. Having a lot of leads will keep you from getting discouraged when you are turned down or if one particular job is not what you want.

Finding a Job without Leads

The ideal is to have a lot of job leads. The more leads you have, the better your chances of getting a job you can do well and will enjoy. However, if you don't have a lot of leads, you may need to do some direct calling. **Direct calling** is contacting employers by telephone or in person when you don't know whether they have any job openings. This is a much less effective way to go about job hunting than knowing where the jobs are at the start.

If you decide to try some direct calling, you may have luck by contacting the personnel offices of companies where you would like to work. Some companies list jobs available on a bulletin board, and you can check regularly for any new openings that have been listed.

For ideas, company names, and addresses of places you might call directly, refer to the yellow pages of the telephone directory. You will

Check job vacancies listed on bulletin boards of companies where you would like to work.

probably have better luck going in person than inquiring about a job on the telephone. Either way, direct calling will take a lot of time. However, if you contact enough employers, you may find a job this way.

A variation of direct calling is writing a letter of inquiry. A **letter of inquiry** is simply a letter asking whether a specified type of job is available. Suppose you would like to work in an office of a certain company, but you don't know whether the company has a vacancy. Look up the company's number in the telephone directory and call. Ask the person who answers for the name of the person who hires new employees. If you learn that department heads hire new employees, ask for the name of the head of the department in which you would like to work. Confirm the spelling of any names you get, and thank the person who gave them to you. Then write down the address of the company, and write a letter of inquiry. Address your letter to the person who does the hiring. An example of a letter of inquiry is shown in figure 4–2.

R ecall Time

Answer the following questions:

1. Fred says he has been looking for a job for three weeks, but he is always downtown relaxing with his friends after accounting class and on weekends. What suggestions can you give him to help make his search more fruitful?
2. What legal form should a person have obtained before beginning to look for work?
3. What are six common sources of job leads?
4. How can you use index cards to record job leads and your response to them?

▪ APPLYING FOR A JOB

Follow up promptly on job leads. Seek out new leads. Keep the process going. Remember: looking for a job is a job in itself.

Follow up after an interview. If a week has passed and you have not heard anything, call and inquire about the position for which you have applied. If the job is still open, restate your interest in it. This is not being a pest. This is showing a potential employer that you have perseverance and enthusiasm—two attractive qualities in an employee at any level.

You will be applying to employers who are looking for the person best qualified to fill a job. Employers will decide whom to hire based generally on their overall impression of each applicant and more specifically on their appraisal of an applicant's ability to do the work.

How do employers get the information they need to choose the best applicant for a job? From you. Before your first interview, prepare a

Employment Skills for Office Careers

120 San Marcos Rd.
Orlando, FL 32802
March 1, 19___

Ms. Carole White
Personnel Director
Jensen Computers
710 Chapala Street
Orlando, FL 32802

Dear Ms. White:

My computer science instructor, Mr. Reynolds, recently advised me to write to learn whether you expect to hire additional word processors for the summer.

I have completed courses in WordPerfect and Microsoft Word, and I type 75 words per minute on five-minute speed tests.

If you expect to hire additional word processors for the summer, may I have an application form? If you wish to call me, my home telephone is 832-1246.

Sincerely,

Caitlin Justice

Caitlin Justice

---

personal data sheet listing all the information about you that an employer may need.

Most employers will ask you to fill out an application form. This is a form used to summarize your job qualifications. Most forms are short—from one to four pages—and most ask the same or similar questions. However, most companies design their own application forms, so each one is a little different from the next.

For many office jobs, employers expect an applicant to present a resume (pronounced rez-oo-may). A **resume** organizes, usually on one or two pages, all the facts about you related to the job you want. A resume should always be accompanied by a cover letter, which is an abbreviated **letter of application.**

A complete letter of application—a sales letter in which you, as the applicant, try to convince an employer that you are the best person for a particular job—includes a description of all your qualifications. However, if you prepare a resume, your cover letter will not duplicate anything in your resume. Instead, the cover letter will simply introduce you to the employer and perhaps explain how you learned about the job. The cover letter also provides an opportunity to highlight one particular qualification that makes you appear especially well qualified for the job.

For some jobs, you may be asked to take one or even several **employment tests.** These may include skills and aptitude tests, psycholog-

Fran finds out through her computer club that a member's company is about to expand its local offices. The member, Nick Petersen, suggests that Fran call Ms. Wiley to find out if Coleman Accounting is hiring yet.

The next morning, Fran calls Ms. Wiley and introduces herself. She tells Mrs. Wiley that she had heard Coleman Accounting might need some clerical help and that Nick Petersen suggested she call to find out. Ms. Wiley says the company has already started interviewing for two positions but is still accepting applications.

"Why don't you come to our office today and fill out an application?" she suggests. "I will be here this afternoon and I could meet with you."

"That would be great, Ms. Wiley," says Fran.

"All right then, can you come by around four thirty with your resume?" asks Ms. Wiley.

"Yes," says Fran. "I'll see you then. Good-bye."

"I'll have to bring my personal data with me to fill out the application efficiently," thinks Fran.

Kofi also finds a good job lead. He locates an ad on the bulletin board at his business college for an assistant to the manager of a local insurance company. The ad reads "Must type 40 WPM. No experience necessary. Will train."

"A management assistant," says Kofi. "Imagine the skills I can sharpen and the new things I can learn in the insurance industry! I need to compose a cover letter and send it with my resume right away!"

1. Are Fran and Kofi prepared to put their best efforts into following up job leads?
2. What attitudes will guide the way you follow up job leads?

ical tests, and general abilities tests. The test most often given to applicants for office jobs is a typing test.

Performing well on employment tests doesn't guarantee you will be hired. Almost all employers will require an interview before deciding whether to hire you.

If you are not qualified for a job, you probably will not get it. Of course, you don't want a job for which you aren't qualified, either. Taking such a job would be setting yourself up for failure. If you are qualified for a job, the way you present your qualifications may determine whether you are hired.

What do employers look for in forming an overall impression of each applicant? The most important thing is that an applicant use Standard English. Make a habit of always using Standard English in a business setting.

Standard English

Usually, an employer will first learn about your qualifications by reading your application form, resume, or letter of application. Later, in the interview, you will have a chance to explain why you think you can do the work. Use Standard English in everything you write and everything you say to an employer. **Standard English** is the correct style of speaking and writing that you learned in school. It is the standard way of communicating in business because it means the same thing to everyone.

This is emphasized because most people do not use Standard English for all their communication. Standard English is not always necessary or even appropriate. When you write a note to a friend, you probably don't worry much about form. When you're chatting with a friend, you may use slang or other popular words. That is informal communication, and it makes for interesting conversation. However, in business, most communication is formal—and that means using Standard English.

Standard English means standard grammar, spelling, usage, and pronunciation. Some people use standard grammar but nonstandard pronunciation. This will not make a favorable impression at a job interview. Do not use a word unless you know for certain how to say it and what it means.

Employers will have several chances to judge your English. From the application form, they will look at whether you use and spell words correctly. If you submit a resume or letter of application, they will notice your ability, or inability, to use Standard English. If they see poor grammar or misspelled words, your application will probably be filed in the wastebasket. Employers get a lot of applications, and they don't usually waste their time interviewing those who don't use Standard English. Finally, during the interview, they will listen as you speak, and they will note your grammar and pronunciation.

Your Personal Data Sheet

A good way to prepare for the job application process is to complete a *personal data sheet*. This is simply an outline of all the information you may need later when you fill out application forms or prepare resumes.

When you are in an employer's office filling out an application form, you may have difficulty remembering the correct spelling of former employers' names, their addresses, and their telephone numbers. Maybe you will forget the exact dates that you attended a former school. These problems are solved if you prepare a personal data sheet in advance. An example is shown in figure 4–3.

Application Forms

For an employer, an application form summarizes information about an applicant's qualifications so the employer can decide which applicants to interview. For you, the application form is an opportunity to show that you are qualified to do the job. Follow these suggestions to improve your chances of being chosen for an interview.

- Complete the application form as neatly as possible. Many application forms ask you to print. Make sure all words are spelled correctly by taking a pocket dictionary with you when you expect to fill out an application form.
- If you complete the application form at an employer's office, use a pen. Usually, though, you can take the application form home and fill it out. If so, use a typewriter—unless the form specifically requests that you print. If you type your form, carefully align the

Personal Data Sheet

Name _____ Social Security Number _____
Address _____
Date of Birth _____ Place of Birth _____
Telephone _____
Hobbies/Interests _____
Awards/Honors/Offices _____
Activities/Sports _____
Other _____

Educational Background

	Name	Address	Dates Attended From	To
High School				
College or				
Further Education				
Course of Study			GPA	
Favorite Subject(s)				

Employment History (Begin with current or most recent.)

Company _____ Telephone _____
Address _____
Dates of Employment: From _____ To _____
Job Title and Duties _____
_____
Supervisor _____
Last Wage _____ Reason for Leaving _____

Company _____ Telephone _____
Address _____
Dates of Employment: From _____ To _____
Job Title and Duties _____
_____
Supervisor _____
Last Wage _____ Reason for Leaving _____

Company _____ Telephone _____
Address _____
Dates of Employment: From _____ To _____
Job Title and Duties _____
_____
Supervisor _____
Last Wage _____ Reason for Leaving _____

References (Names of persons who can provide information about your personal, school, or work background.)

	Name	Address	Telephone Home	Work	Relationship
1.					
2.					
3.					

typing on the printed lines. Practice on an extra form so that your application will have a neat appearance.

- Don't skip over any questions. If a question doesn't apply to you, put "NA," meaning "Not Applicable," or draw a short line in the space.
- Use your correct name on the form. Include your first name, middle initial, and last name. State your complete address, including your zip code.
- Some applications ask for your marital status. Employers cannot legally require you to answer this. If you do, just state whether you are single or married.
- Many applications ask for your job preference. List a specific job title. Never use the word *anything*. Employers want a specific answer here.
- Most application forms ask for a listing of schools you have attended. Include the name of all the schools you have attended along with the dates of attendance. You may refer to your personal data sheet for this.
- The application will ask about your previous work experience. Most request this listing in **reverse chronological order,** beginning with your most recent job. If you haven't had much experience, include even short-term jobs or volunteer work.
- Most forms ask for references. These are the names of people who know you well and will recommend you for the job. Plan ahead and ask permission to list people's names as references. Good references include teachers or friends established in business. Do not list classmates.
- Most forms request your signature at the end. Write—don't print— your name using your first name, middle initial, and last name.

Carefully review the application form shown in figure 4–4.

Resumes

Employers accepting applications for office jobs often expect applicants to submit a resume. Your resume may be typed on a typewriter or word processor or prepared on a computer using a word processing program. If you use a typewriter, clean the typewriter keys and put in a new ribbon before you start.

Some typewriters, word processors, and computer programs offer different type styles, sometimes called fonts. If you have a choice, choose an easy-to-read style such as Times Roman or Helvetica. Avoid italicized and unusual fonts. Word processors and computer programs allow the use of boldface (heavy-faced) type for main headings, which is a nice touch.

Most people use twenty–pound paper for their resumes. But twenty-four–pound paper with some cotton content, though slightly more expensive, is more impressive. White, cream, and light gray are probably the best colors. Avoid pink, green, or any dark colors, as they don't photocopy cleanly. Purchase matching envelopes and extra paper for cover letters when you choose your resume paper.

Application for Employment

All qualified applicants will receive consideration for employment and promotion without regard to race, creed, religion, color, age, sex, national origin, handicap, marital status, or sexual orientation. This application is effective for 90 days. If you wish to be considered for employment thereafter, you must complete a new application.

Date _____

Name _____ Telephone (_____) _____

      Last   First   Middle Initial   Area Code

Address _____

      Number & Street   Apt. #   City   State   Zip

Length of time at that address _____ Previous Address _____

Position you are applying for _____ Rate of pay expected $ _____ per month

Were you previously employed by us? _____ If yes, when? _____

Typewriting words per minute _____ Shorthand or speedwriting words per minute _____

Other business machines _____

State any other experiences, skills, or qualifications that you feel would especially fit you for work with the company

_____

Applying for: Full-time ____ Part-time ____ Days ____ Evenings ____ Midnight ____ Alternating ____ Any _____

Are you at least 18 years of age? _____ Will you take a physical examination? _____

List any friends or relatives working for us _____

	Name	Relationship
	Name	Relationship

Referred to our company by _____

School	Name and Location	Course of Major	Graduated
Elementary			☐ Yes ☐ No
High School			☐ Yes ☐ No
College			☐ Yes ☐ No
Business or Trade			☐ Yes ☐ No
Other (Specify)			☐ Yes ☐ No

Do you plan any additional education? _____ If yes, describe _____

List in order all employers, beginning with your most recent employment:

Name & Location of Company	From Mo Yr	To Mo Yr	Salary	Supervisor	Reason for Leaving
1)					
2)					
3)					

Describe the work you did with:

Company #1. _____

Company #2. _____

Company #3. _____

May we contact the employers listed above? _____ If not, indicate by number which one(s) you do not wish us to contact _____

CERTIFICATION OF APPLICANT

I hereby certify that the facts set forth in the above employment application are true and complete to the best of my knowledge. I understand that if I am employed, falsified statements on this application shall be considered sufficient cause for dismissal, and that no contractual rights or obligations are created by said employment application.

Signature of Applicant _____

If you have completed a personal data sheet, then you already have most of the information you will need to prepare your resume. Many styles of resumes are used. If you want to see a variety of ways to present this information, you can buy an inexpensive book on resumes at your local bookstore. However, if you are a student or a recent graduate, use a reverse chronological resume format such as the one shown in figure 4–5.

■ FIGURE 4–5
Sample Reverse Chronological Resume

Carmen Fisher
1715 Bliss Street
Winfield, KS 67156
(316) 221-4565

Objective
An entry-level position as an accounting clerk with opportunities for advancement.

Education
1990–1992 Winfield Business College. Certificate in Accounting

1987–1990 Winfield High School. Graduated in upper 10%. Courses included:
      Office Procedures, 2 semesters
      Bookkeeping, 4 semesters
      Word Processing, 2 semesters
      Keyboarding, 2 semesters
      Business Math, 2 semesters

Special Skills
Keyboarding speed test score: 81 WPM

Experience
7/92–8/94 TELLER
      First State Bank
      Winfield, KS

      Accepted cash and checks, issued receipts. Computed principal, interest, and discounts using a calculator and computer. Typed loan forms and documents.

6/90–9/91 BOOKKEEPER (part time)
      Merchandise Mart
      Winfield, KS

      Used DAC Easy computer account program to record cash receipts and payments and to maintain accounts receivable and accounts payable ledgers. Assisted in preparing payroll records and printing payroll checks.

Personal
Hobbies include solving difficult math problems and conundrums.

References
Available upon request

As a young job seeker, you can probably provide all pertinent information on a one-page resume. Employers are busy people, and they prefer resumes that present the facts in as few words as possible. Even applicants with twenty years of experience usually try to limit their resumes to two pages. So be brief. Provide the following types of information on your resume.

1. *personal identification*—your name, address, and telephone number.
2. *career goal*—a brief statement about the career you are working toward. Make sure that this fits with the specific job you are seeking. For example, if you are applying for an accounting job, then you might state controller as your career goal.
3. *educational background*—all the schools you have attended from high school on. Don't list elementary schools, middle schools, or junior high schools. List any colleges or technical schools and your high school. Begin with the school you most recently attended or still attend. List any degrees, diplomas, certificates, or licenses earned. Then add any awards or honors you have received.
4. *work experience*—jobs you have held, beginning with your present or most recent job. If you've had a lot of short-term jobs, list only four or five that are most related to the one you are seeking. List dates of employment, company name, and your work activities. For brevity and impact, use active verbs to describe your duties. Complete sentences aren't necessary here. For example, you might say "Planned travel arrangements, compiled reports, and prepared weekly statements." If your experience is limited, list any part-time or temporary work.
5. *references*—names of three people who will vouch for your dependability, skills, and good work habits. If this section won't fit on the page, just state "References available on request."

Write, rewrite, and polish your resume until it is exactly right. Then type it or print it from your computer. Use a good photocopier to make clear copies on your special resume paper. As you get new job leads, customize your resume to fit each job. By doing this, you can state your qualifications in ways that fit the job for which you are applying.

Type or print (from your computer) a cover letter. A **cover letter** simply states how you learned about the job and why you are especially interested in it. You can say why you can do a good job for the company, and you may want to emphasize one or two facts that make you especially qualified for the job. Figure 4–6 shows a sample cover letter.

Employment Tests

If an employer requires one or more employment tests, you may be asked to complete the testing before your job interview. This is likely if the testing session will require more than a half hour—or if the employer wants to see the test results before interviewing you. Many employers who require testing will schedule tests just before your interview.

1715 Bliss Street
Winfield KS 67156
April 6, 19___

Ms. Julie Atkins
Kennedy Accounting Services
1700 South Main Street
Arkansas City, KS 67005

Dear Ms. Atkins:

Your job for an accounting clerk, advertised in Sunday's Courier, caught my
attention immediately. I think you will agree that my qualifications, listed on the
enclosed resume, match your requirements for this job very closely.

Two months ago I participated—along with several hundred top students enrolled in
accounting—in the state scholarship examination sponsored by Emporia State
University. Today, I learned that I placed third in this statewide examination.

After you have reviewed my resume, I would like very much to make an
appointment for an interview. I will call in a few days to schedule a time convenient
to you.

Sincerely,

Carmen Fisher

Carmen Fisher

Probably the most commonly used employment test is the typing (or
keyboarding) skills test. Many employers screen applicants for office
jobs this way because the test is quick and easy to administer. Usually
it is just a five-minute test during which you type from a printed copy
as fast as you can, trying not to make mistakes. If an employer needs a
person who can type sixty words a minute but most applicants type
only forty or fifty, then it is worth the five minutes to give the test.

You may apply for a job that allows you to learn while you work.
This is on-the-job training. In this case, an employer may ask you to
take a test to measure your aptitude for learning a particular skill or
group of skills. Aptitude tests require more time than the quick five-
minute typing test. Employers who use them feel that they are worthwhile, though, because they identify who will be able to learn required
job skills.

Some office jobs require good math skills. If you apply for one of
these jobs, you will likely be asked to take some type of math test.

Some employers use other general academic tests that measure your
ability in English usage, vocabulary, and spelling. The purpose of these
tests is to help an employer decide whether you are qualified for a job.
If you do not have the qualifications for a job, you will not want it.

You may be asked to take a skills test. Consider this an opportunity to show what you can do.

Some employers give personality and psychological tests to screen job applicants. These tests are designed to indicate how well suited you are to the job and how well you will get along with co-workers and/or customers.

It is normal to be a little nervous when you take a test but try not to worry too much about employment tests. Nevertheless, if you know that you will be taking an employment test, don't go to a party the night before. You will perform better on almost any test if you are well rested.

R ecall Time

Answer the following questions:

1. You are filling out an application for a receptionist's position at a local insurance office. You are having trouble completing the section asking you to list your prior experience because you cannot remember the addresses or phone numbers of your former employers. What could you have prepared that would help you in this situation? What should you do now?
2. Why is it important to fill out a job application neatly? What does it tell an employer if you misspell words and write illegibly?
3. What are the main areas of information listed on a resume? How long should your resume be?
4. Violet is applying for a job in the accounting department of an auto parts store. What basic skills should she brush up on before going for her interview and possible employment tests?

INTERVIEWING FOR A JOB

If your application form or resume is impressive enough, an employer will want to interview you for a job. An interview is a formal meeting between you and an employer. It is your best chance to convince the employer that you are qualified to do the job. It is also the employer's best chance to evaluate your overall qualifications.

Some interviews are as short as five minutes and others go on for several hours. However, a group of psychologists analyzed job interviews and found that the first minute is the most critical. If you make a good first impression, you will be blessed with a *halo effect* that will cause the interviewer to feel positive about you throughout the interview. If you don't impress the interviewer in the first minute, your chances aren't very good regardless of how well the rest of the interview goes.

The interview, then, is the most important part of the entire job seeking process. What can you do to increase your chances of a successful interview? Plan ahead by following these steps:

1. Prepare for the interview
2. Communicate effectively
3. Sense when the interview is over
4. Follow up the interview

Prepare for the Interview

Preparing has several advantages. If you know ahead of time what you want to say, you can communicate it more effectively. If you know something about the company, you will have a better idea how to phrase your questions and answers. Finally, being prepared will boost your confidence and help you to make that critical good first impression.

Your preparation should include learning about the company, selecting the clothing you will wear to the interview, and gathering the materials you will need to take with you. By thinking about these things ahead of time, you will allow enough time to get ready for your interview. You may want to practice interviewing with a family member or a friend, but once you leave your house for the interview, you will be on your own.

Know the Company   During the interview, you will want to show that you are interested in the company, not just the money you can earn from working there. So your first step in preparing for the interview is to do some research on the company. Begin by asking people you know who might have information about the company. Do you know any of the company's current employees or someone who previously worked there?

Many companies print pamphlets that provide details about their products or services. Others have catalogs that will give you an idea of

As in this photo, the interviewer may make some notes during the interview. Show your interest in the company by asking some appropriate questions about the company as well as the job.

what the company produces. You may be able to pick these up from the company well before your interview. Advertisements and press releases may provide additional information. Pay special attention to information that fits with your education, interests, or experiences—and remember to use this information during the interview.

As you research a company, keep in mind the types of questions you may be asked that relate to the company itself. For example, many interviewers ask such questions as, "Why do you want to work for this company?" or "What interests you about working here?"

As you learn about the company, write down the questions you will want to ask the interviewer. For example, you may want to ask how the job became available, what your working relationship with other employees will be, and what opportunities exist for advancement within the company.

You will probably be a little nervous at the beginning of every interview. However, if you know what to do and say, you may be more self-confident—and you likely will become less nervous as the interview progresses. Knowing some things about the company helps. The best confidence builder is to prepare for the interview by practicing your interviewing skills. Perhaps your instructor will allow you and others in your class to do some role-playing in which you practice interviewing skills.

Dress Appropriately Avoid extremes of any type—clothing, jewelry, hairstyle, makeup, and scent. A conservative, dark suit and tie is best for men. A stylish, yet dignified dress is best for women. Appropriate dress shoes in good repair are essential. They will be noticed.

To most employers, personal cleanliness and neatness are equally important. Hair should be clean, well-cut, and not worn in a fussy or distracting style. Nails should be clean and not too long.

Make sure your oral hygiene is excellent, and if you smoke, refrain the day of your interview. A breath mint will not eliminate the smoke odor that clings to hair and clothing. Many companies now prohibit smoking in their offices and some even have unwritten policies about not hiring smokers.

Take the Things You Need Assemble the items that you want to take with you to the interview. Include your job lead card and notes on the company, your personal data sheet, your resume, and your list of questions to ask. You will probably take some notes, and you may need to fill out some forms, so take a good pen and a notebook.

Allow Enough Time If it has been a week or more since you made your appointment, call to confirm that the interviewer is still expecting you. Then start getting ready early. After you are dressed, read your resume through carefully several times. This will help you answer questions about your qualifications. Check your job lead card for the address and leave in time to arrive about ten minutes early. Allow some extra time if you have to travel across town—you might be delayed in traffic. On your way to the interview, mentally review what you have prepared.

Go Alone Never take anyone with you for a job interview. Some people have taken along a friend for support, but employers are not favorably impressed by this. When you arrive, introduce yourself to the receptionist and give the name of the person with whom you have an interview appointment.

Communicate Effectively

When you meet the person who will interview you, smile. Smiling will help more than anything to create a favorable first impression.

The second thing you can do to create a good impression is to shake hands properly. Wait for the interviewer to offer her hand. When the interviewer offers to shake hands, grasp her hand firmly. Some employers think a wimpy, "limp fish" handshake reveals a weak personality. But don't squeeze too hard, either. You don't want to begin your interview by hurting the interviewer! Some interviewers don't offer to shake hands. In that case, you won't shake hands.

Don't sit down until you are asked to sit down. If you aren't asked to sit, then remain standing—the interview will be a short one. The interviewer will probably suggest that you sit beside or in front of the desk. If you have a choice of where to sit, take a seat beside the desk. With no barrier between the two of you, you have a psychological advantage. As you sit, lean slightly toward the interviewer. This tells the interviewer that you are interested.

If the interviewer offers to shake hands clasp her hand firmly. But don't squeeze too hard, and don't pump when you shake hands.

Jeanne Lumbert
Vice President, Operations
Manpower, Inc./California Peninsula

Q: Mrs. Lumbert, what do you look for when interviewing applicants for clerical positions?

A: Packaging is the first thing that consumers see when deciding to purchase an item. Companies spend billions of dollars creating the right packaging for their product in order to attract consumers. People are no different. Your appearance gives a first impression of *you*. If that impression is positive, you've made it past the first step. Like a typical consumer, once the "packaging" is acceptable or impressive, an employer is more open to discovering if the product inside the packaging is as "good as it looks." In other words, when you walk into an interview, that first impression elicits a positive or negative reaction from the employer in a matter of seconds. If it's negative, the rest of the interview will be an uphill battle to overcome that first impression. If it's positive, you've at least gotten their attention—and that's the edge that can lead to success!

Once you pass that interview, there are three other traits that help you become successful in the business world—a good attitude, flexibility, and the ability to accept and learn from positive criticism.

Q: What recommendations do you have for an applicant to prepare for an interview?

A: Have a resume regardless of the amount of, or lack of, prior work experience. More and more companies are requiring resumes from our company before they will even consider someone for a *temporary* assignment.

Come prepared to the interview with all the necessary statistics on yourself (your mailing address, prior dates of employment, immigration requirements, etc.).

Have some idea of a specific job or type of work you're interested in and qualified to perform. Telling an interviewer "What do you have? I can do anything" doesn't impress a prospective employer. It would be better to say something like "I've done reception work, filing and light word processing but I'm open to doing any other work you think I'm qualified to handle." Now you have indicated skills you have *and* you are letting the employer know you're flexible.

You will have a folder containing your resume and other papers, and you may have a briefcase or purse. Keep your folder in your lap and place your briefcase or purse on the floor by your chair. Even if there is room to do so, never put anything on the interviewer's desk.

Don't let your eyes roam across papers on the interviewer's desk—what is there is none of your business! Look the interviewer in the eye most of the time, shifting your eyes only now and then so you don't appear to be staring. Those who fail to maintain good eye contact are often considered insecure or are perhaps suspected of trying to conceal something.

The interviewer will determine the interview tone, pace, and style. Some interviewers will be serious and businesslike, others will appear more outgoing and cheerful. Try to respond in the same tone and pace that the interviewer projects. In the usual style of interviewing, you will be asked a series of questions, and eventually you will get a turn at asking your own questions.

During the interview, speak clearly, listen closely, and show by gestures or facial expressions that you understand and are receptive to the interviewer's thoughts.

Table 4–1 gives a list of questions commonly asked during interviews. When answering questions, pause to give yourself time to compose an

1. What type of work are you looking for?
2. Have you done this type of work before?
3. Why are you leaving your present job?
4. How often were you absent form your last (or present) job?
5. What did you dislike about your last (or present) job?
6. How did you get along with your boss and co-workers?
7. What are you greatest strengths?
8. What are your greatest weaknesses?
9. What do you hope to be doing in five years?
10. How do you feel about this position?
11. Can we check your references?
12. How does your experience qualify you for this job?
13. How do you take direction?
14. Can you take criticism without feeling hurt or upset?
15. Can you work under pressure?
16. Do you like detail work?
17. Do you prefer working alone or with others?
18. Have you ever been fired or asked to resign?
19. What type of people do you find it difficult to work with?
20. How well do you work with difficult people?
21. What salary do you expect?
22. What did you like most about your last job?
23. What do you know about this company?
24. Do you have any questions?

■ TABLE 4–1
Questions Often Asked during an Interview

answer that is concise but thoughtful. This requires listening very carefully to complete questions before you formulate your answer. It is all right to write down a word or two to help you remember something you want to say in answer to a question—but never interrupt. Good listening skills will help you pick out patterns in the interviewer's questions. You may be able to detect the direction of a line of questioning—organization skills, leadership qualities, or other qualifications. If so, focus your answers on these areas of interest.

When asked about your skills and experience, elaborate somewhat. Answer questions concisely, but avoid one-word or one-line answers. Refer to your resume or other notes to help you with answers. If you think that the interviewer hasn't understood your answer or that you haven't expressed yourself clearly, try again. Stay on the topic until you are sure that your message has been received.

When preparing for an interview, many people overlook certain approaches to interview communication. These include how the interviewer may open the interview and certain questions that are either illegal to ask or difficult to answer. Others include nonverbal communication (body language) and being prepared to ask appropriate questions of the interviewer.

Some Problem Areas Some interviewers may open the interview with "Tell me about yourself" or "What can I do for you?" This type of opening is difficult because the question is so broad. Your job is to narrow the focus and direct your answer to support your candidacy for the job.

By preparing for such questions, you can respond appropriately without rambling on. State that you are interested in a particular job and explain why you are qualified to do the work. Don't describe your career goals—the interviewer will mainly be interested in what you can do now.

Some personal questions are illegal, but your interviewer may ask them anyway. Questions about marital status, family planning, child care arrangements, and age are illegal—unless they are real job qualifications. But if they are asked, it may be to your advantage to deal with them as honestly and tactfully as possible.

Other difficult questions that you should prepare for are probing-type questions, such as "What are your greatest weaknesses?" These questions are variations of "Tell me about yourself." Again, disregard the general question and focus your answer on your strengths—your personal skills and abilities that pertain directly to the job. Try to match the company's needs with your abilities. Give examples to support your answers. You can even use a question on your greatest weakness to your advantage. You might mention a weakness that will enhance your qualifications on this particular job. For example, on a job that requires great organization, you might mention that your greatest weakness is that you simply cannot stand disorder and seem to overorganize things. Do not reveal a weakness that will disqualify you for the job.

You may be asked whether you quit or were fired from your last job. Avoid saying anything negative about former employers. Most inter-

It was four-thirty on Friday afternoon. Jack Tuttle entered the personnel office of Harcourt Accounting Associates five minutes prior to his scheduled interview with the personnel director. When he introduced himself to the receptionist, Ms. Woodruff, she told Jack that she was very sorry, but the director, Ms. Johnson, would be unable to meet with him today. Ms. Woodruff said that she would be happy to reschedule the interview for the following week.

Jack was visibly disappointed. He had given up a date with his girlfriend to attend an out-of-town football game for this interview.

"Why can't Ms. Johnson interview me today?" Jack asked.

"Something unexpected came up. I'm sorry," replied Ms. Woodruff. "Can you come in on Monday afternoon?"

"Then why didn't you call me or leave a message? I cancelled an important meeting myself to be here," Jack felt angry toward Ms. Woodruff.

"I would have called you, but she just told me twenty minutes ago that she would be unable to interview any more applicants today. Would you like to come in next week?"

"I guess so," Jack was still unhappy, but he was resigned to returning another day. "I'll check my calendar and call you on Monday."

Based on Jack's conversation with Ms. Woodruff, respond to these questions:

1. What was Ms. Woodruff's first impression of Jack? If the personnel director asks Ms. Woodruff about the applicants she could not interview on Friday, how will this affect Jack's chances of getting the job?
2. When Jack does get a job, how well will he get along with the other employees?
3. What could Jack do to improve his relationships with others on the job?

viewers will identify with other employers and will interpret your criticism as incompetence or uncooperativeness on your part. Simply explain, briefly and unemotionally, why you left your last job. Don't make any excuses. If you expect to receive a bad recommendation from an employer, suggest other references who will attest to your qualifications.

Nonverbal Communication Two of the first exchanges you will communicate with the interviewer are shaking hands and making eye contact. These are nonverbal ways of communicating, usually called body language. If this topic interests you, you can find a number of books on body language in your local library.

You will communicate in other nonverbal ways during an interview, and how you do this will significantly affect your chances of being offered the job. In answering questions, the *manner* in which you speak conveys messages to the interviewer. The tone and volume of voice, rising and falling inflections, and facial expressions are all meaningful. They will impart enthusiasm for the job and the company—or lack of it. Be aware of the mood of the conversation and be ready with either a smile or a serious expression, depending on what is appropriate.

Be aware, too, of your interviewer's body language. You will usually notice some nonverbal clues that will help you understand whether you

Watch your interviewer's body language. If the interviewer does not seem interested in what you are saying, move on to something else.

are coming across effectively. If the interviewer appears disinterested or impatient, you might want to move on to another topic that may elicit more interest and express more enthusiasm yourself to change the mood.

Appropriate Questions to Ask The interviewer will expect you to ask some questions. If you aren't invited to ask questions and a pause occurs in the conversation after the interview is well under way, ask whether you may ask some questions. Your first questions should show a sincere interest in the company, in the job, and in the employer's needs related to the job. If the interviewer hasn't discussed salary and fringe benefits, it is all right to ask about them—but ask these questions last.

Make a list of questions you may want to ask before you go for your interview. Then you will be more likely to remember them and to ask them in an appropriate order. The interviewer will probably cover some of the topics on your list during the interview, so you won't have to ask all your questions. If you think of others as the interview progresses, make a brief note to remind yourself to ask them later.

Use good judgment about how much time to take up asking questions. If you sense that the interviewer is on a tight schedule, ask only your most important questions.

Sense When the Interview Is Over

Try to get a feeling for when the interview has run its course. Many interviewers will stand and say something like "Well, I think I have all the information I need" or "Do you have any other questions?" Unless the interviewer looks rushed, it's all right to ask one or two brief questions at this point—but don't delay your exit more than a minute or two. If the interviewer hasn't mentioned when a decision will be made on the selection of a candidate for the job, ask about that.

1715 Bliss Street
Winfield, KS 67156
April 26, 19___

Ms. Julie Atkins
Kennedy Accounting Services
1700 South Main Street
Arkansas City, KS 67005

Dear Ms. Atkins:

Thank you for the interview yesterday afternoon regarding the position as an
accounting clerk. I enjoyed talking with you and learning more about your
accounting needs.

Having discussed this position in greater detail, I am more interested in the job than
ever. I also feel even more certain that I can fulfill your needs.

If I may provide any further information for your consideration, please call me at
home any afternoon after three. My number is 221-4565.

Sincerely,

Carmen Fisher

Carmen Fisher

In some cases, you may have to take responsibility for closing the
interview. If the conversation seems to be drifting, reemphasize your
strong points, say that you want the job (if you do), thank the interviewer for his time, and leave. On your way out, thank the receptionist
or secretary.

Follow Up the Interview

You can profit from every interview, no matter what the outcome, if you
take time to evaluate the experience. Ask yourself if a little more planning
and preparation would have helped. Did you mention everything about
your qualifications that would have helped you get the job?

In the evening after the interview, write a thank-you note to your
interviewer. It should go in the mail the very next morning. While the
interview is still fresh in your mind, you can refer to a particular point
discussed. Mention some fact that sets you apart from other applicants.
The thank-you letter is an opportunity to add any important information in support of your application that you may have neglected to
mention or emphasize during the interview. Figure 4–7 shows a sample
thank-you letter.

If you haven't heard from the company within a week to ten days,
give the interviewer a call. State your name and that you were inter-

viewed for a particular job. Then ask, "Have you made a decision on who will be hired for this job?" If you are told that a decision has not been made, say something like "I would very much like to work for this company, and I know that I can do a really fine job for you." Showing this extra interest may tip the scales in your favor.

R ecall Time

Answer the following questions:

1. Why is the first minute of an interview important? What do you need to do in the first minute to improve your chance of being chosen for the job?
2. Joe and Laura are both interviewed for the same typing job at Hayward Lumber. Joe answers all the questions Ms. Hayward asks and is very polite and quiet. Laura asks Ms. Hayward several questions about the company and tells her she has heard the company is thinking of opening another branch. Even though her typing skills are not as good as Joe's, Laura gets the job. Why does Ms. Hayward choose Laura?
3. What will you wear to an interview with Ms. Bailey at the National Bank's main office downtown?
4. You are applying for a job as a switchboard operator in a physician's office. The doctor opens the interview with, "Tell me about yourself." How do you best respond?
5. What items will you bring with you to an interview to be sure you are well prepared?

■ SUMMARY

Finding openings and applying for jobs is the last step before entering the working world. How well you perform this step will determine whether you get the job you would most like or have to settle for something much less interesting. Following certain guidelines will help make your search for a good job successful.

First, when beginning your job search, give it plenty of time. You will need to be well organized, having a logical system for keeping track of leads and follow-ups. Before you begin to call prospective employers, be sure that you have a Social Security number. Also, have a general idea of the job leads for which you qualify.

Make use of as many different sources of leads as possible, from newspaper ads to employment offices to school and family. Follow up all leads promptly, either calling an employer directly or writing a letter of inquiry if that is required. When you are asked to fill out an application, be prepared. Have all the information you may need with you on a personal data sheet and type or print the application clearly. Take the time to write a concise resume and have copies of it available. Brush up on the math or English skills you may be tested on and be sure to use Standard English when speaking or writing to prospective employers.

Before you go to be interviewed for a job, be sure you are well groomed and properly dressed. Make sure you have discovered enough about the company that the employer will see that you are interested in more than just the salary. Take your resume and notes on any questions you may have about the job and company. Be prepared by anticipating the types of questions you are likely to be asked and thinking ahead of time about how you will answer them. Practice describing your qualifications out loud, perhaps in front of a mirror.

Remember that the first minute of an interview is extremely important. Try to make a good impression through a firm handshake, a smile, and a pleasant, enthusiastic demeanor and by responding to the interviewer's tone and body language appropriately. Look the interviewer in the eye and try to overcome any nervousness. Ask pertinent questions but don't be pushy or aggressive. Use common sense and good manners.

Be aware of when the interviewer is trying to wind up. Bring the interview to a close yourself if it begins to move to general conversation and you sense the interviewer has all the information needed. Follow up the interview with a call or a letter, emphasizing your special qualifications and thanking the interviewer for her consideration.

When looking for and applying for a job, do the following:

- Keep records of all your leads and how you followed up on them.
- Use all available sources for job leads.
- Follow up leads promptly.
- Keep a personal data sheet handy for filling out applications.
- Have copies of a resume ready when needed.
- Recognize the need to use Standard English in both speaking and writing.
- Be clean and neat and well dressed for interviews.
- Find out all you can about the company before an interview.
- Be prepared to explain your qualifications for and interest in a job.
- Appear relaxed and competent in an interview.
- Ask questions to show your interest in a company.
- Sense when an interview is over, and leave on a high note.
- Evaluate your performance at an interview.
- Write a follow-up letter.

In Conclusion . . .

When you have completed this chapter, answer the following questions:

1. How will you go about looking for a job?
2. When you hear about a job that you would like, what action will you take?
3. What will you do to prepare for a job interview?

Review and Application

Match the following by writing the letter of each vocabulary word in the space to the left of its description.

_____ 1. form that organizes all the facts about you related to the job you want

_____ 2. organizations that charge a fee for finding you a job

_____ 3. letter inquiring whether a specific type of job is available

_____ 4. letter that always accompanies a resume

_____ 5. method in which your most recent job is listed first

_____ 6. correct style of speaking and writing

_____ 7. item on which you record all relevant information about an available job

_____ 8. items that may include skills and aptitude tests, psychological tests, and general abilities tests

_____ 9. contacting employers by telephone or in person when you don't know whether they have any job openings

_____ 10. organizations that provide free job referral service

_____ 11. written request for work

a. cover letter
b. employment tests
c. job lead card
d. letter of application
e. letter of inquiry
f. private employment agencies
g. public employment agencies
h. resume
i. reverse chronological order
j. Standard English
k. direct calling

DISCUSS AND ANALYZE AN OFFICE SITUATION

1. Bradley hears about a general office work job that has just opened up at a local real estate office. He thinks the job would be perfect for him, especially since he hopes to make his career in real estate. However, he has made a date with his girlfriend for this afternoon and is reluctant to change the date. He decides to call the real estate office tomorrow instead.

   What might Bradley have done differently to better his chances of getting the job?

2. Alice is going to an interview with Mr. Beasely of Beasely Electronics. Her friend Judy used to work there. Judy tells Alice that Mr. Beasely is a nice guy, always joking around with the employees and buying them coffee on their breaks. When Judy sees that Alice is dressing quite conservatively for her interview, she tells her it is not necessary—everyone just wear jeans at work; even Mr. Beasely. She laughs when she sees Alice's resume, saying her previous experience at a pizza restaurant will not help her get this job—and she should leave the resume at home. Alice is confused.

   Should Alice take Judy's advice? Why or why not? How can Alice have the best chance of getting the job?

PRACTICE BASIC SKILLS

Math

1. You think you will like both the jobs you have been offered, but you are trying to decide which will be the best for you financially.

   The job at Jones Lumber pays $5.18 per hour for the first 40 hours each week and double time ($10.36 per hour) for any hours after the first 40 each week. It pays $50 per month toward health insurance and allows full-time workers one paid sick day per month.

   The job at Smith's Electrical pays $6.08 per hour with $1.00 per hour extra on Saturdays. No health insurance is paid for part-time employees.

   You plan to work about 20 hours per week while attending business college—8 hours on Saturdays and a few afternoons after class. Which job gives you the most income per month, including fringe benefits? Assume a four-week month.

English

1. Remember that it is important to use Standard English in the business world. In the following passage, underline examples of non-Standard English.

After I'm graduating, I start a new job. The boss and me go way back. I'll get the choice assignments and the big bucks no doubt. It'll be great to see how far I go. Irregardless, I know this job will be way cool.

Proofreading

1. Retype or rewrite the following paragraphs of a letter of application, correcting all errors.

Im a student at Fairview Community College, and will graduate in june this year. I have been in the business education, porgram, and worked as a aide in various offices on campus. I also-worked for a semester at lawrence radio and TV, where I ansered the phone on Saturday and wrote some checks as well.

I hope to get a degree in accounting, and I have a good undertanding of math and bookkeeping. I really think this this job would be good for me, and I no I could do it well. May I call for aninterview? My phone number is 9632145.

APPLY YOUR KNOWLEDGE

1. Write a letter of inquiry to a local business to learn whether any office positions are open.
2. Prepare a resume listing all the parts in the sample resume shown in figure 4–5.

QUIZ

*Write a **T** if the statement is true or an **F** if the statement is false.*

___ 1. A job lead card is sent to you by a prospective employer to invite you for an interview.

___ 2. You should plan to spend about four hours a week on your job search.

___ 3. Most employers won't hire you without a Social Security card.

___ 4. It's not a good idea to ask friends or family members for job leads.

___ 5. Public employment agencies don't charge a fee to help you find work.

___ 6. Direct calling is a way of finding job openings when you don't have any leads.

___ 7. Most people are hired based on what they write on their application forms.

___ 8. A resume is a letter that tells prior employers that you are ready to come back to work.

___ 9. You should not bring your personal data sheet with you when going to apply for a job.

___ 10. If the employer asks you what job you are applying for, you should say you will do anything.

___ 11. You shouldn't ask other students to be references for you on job applications.

___ 12. Asking questions of the person interviewing you for a job is a bad idea.

___ 13. Preparing for an interview includes taking a shower and brushing your teeth.

___ 14. The most important part of the interview is the last two minutes.

___ 15. If you are asked to tell about yourself during a job interview, it is a good idea to try to stick to your qualifications for one specific job.

Making Job Lead Cards

You will have a better chance of finding the job you want if your job leads are well organized. One efficient way of organizing your job leads is to record each lead on a separate index card.

Look at the sample job lead card below. On the front of the card, in the center, is the name, title, address, and phone number of the person to be contacted. The source of the lead is written in the lower left-hand corner. This might be a friend, teacher, or a newspaper ad. The time and date of a scheduled appointment is written in the upper right-hand corner. On the back of the card is a brief description of the company and any pertinent information about the job. Try to learn as much as you can about a company before you apply to work there. The local chamber of commerce can be a good source of information.

Front

Appointment 4:00 Fri.

Mr. Gerald King
Personnel Manager
St. Mark's Rehab. Ctr.
1842 Thompson Avenue
966-3254

News Press (Sun. 9/12)

Back

Private rehabilitation center for
patients recovering from head injuries.
Modern state-of-the-art facility.
Acquiring new computer system for
business office. Expanding services.
Opportunity for advancement.

(Continued on next page)

Fill out a job lead card for each of the jobs listed below.

■ You are interested in working at the Channel City Medical Clinic. You have done some research and found that this clinic has grown steadily over the past ten years. It now employs more than three hundred people. You have learned through a friend who works there that the company is expanding its outpatient services and will be hiring new office workers. You called and found that Angela Baker, office supervisor, does the hiring. You made an appointment to see her on October 3 at 3:00 p.m. The clinic is located at 1175 Canton Street, and the phone number is 678–1906.

■ A local desktop publishing firm called Wordstyles placed a classified ad in your local newspaper. Wordstyles wants to interview applicants for word processing. You learn that the company is only two years old and employs nine full-time employees. When you call, you find that George Kramer, the owner and manager, will be interviewing you. Your appointment is set for Thursday, October 5 at 10:00 a.m. The firm is located at 915 Sycamore, and the phone number is 964–5925.

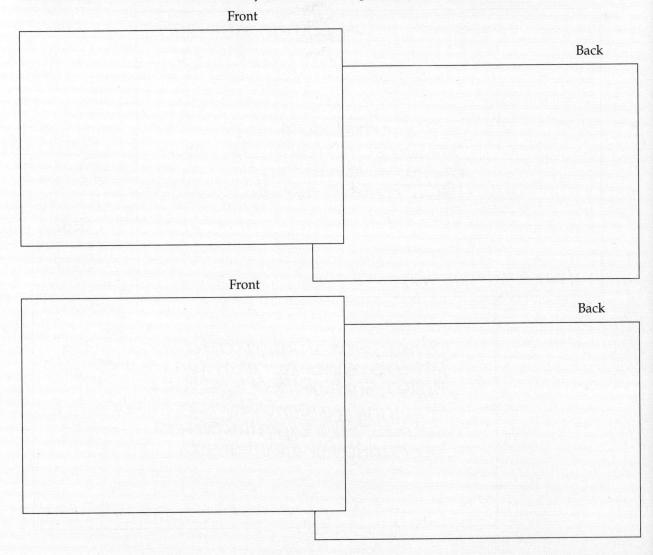

Front

Back

Front

Back

Using Help-Wanted Ads

Newspaper advertisements are an important source of job leads. Reading the want ads in your local newspaper can also give you information about the local job market.

Read the samples of help-wanted ads (numbered 1 through 9) on the next page. Study the job information in these ads, then write in the correct ad numbers for the following questions.

1. Which ads mention interpersonal skills?

_____

2. Which ads require a resume?

_____

3. Which jobs offer fringe benefits?

_____

4. Which ads mention educational requirements?

_____

5. Which jobs require experience?

_____

(Continued on next page)

1. ADMISSIONS COORDINATOR

In this position, you'll be responsible for admitting new residents to our hospital. Some community relation is also involved.. This full-time position requires excellent communication skills. A knowledge of MCal/MCare and marketing is helpful. For consideration, contact the Personnel Dept. at:

Beverly La Cumbre Convalescent Hospital
3880 Vid Lucero
Santa Barbara, CA 93110
(805) 687-6651
Equal Opprtunity Employer

2. SECRETARY

Downtown Los Angeles based health care organization is seeking an experienced secretary to join our team.

Ideal candidate will be proficient in word processing/Lotus 1,2,3, and possess first class communication and organizational skills. Excellent benefits. Please send resume and salary history to our personnel department:

UniMed America
20500 Nordhoff Street
Chatsworth, CA 91311
Attn: Deborah Hecksel
E.O.E.

3.
LEGAL SECRETARY. Our growing firm has an immediate opening for an experienced litigation secretary in our Santa Barbara office. Excellent opportunity for someone who possesses strong spelling, grammar & typing skills.
We offer medical, dental, life, profit sharing & pd parking. Please send resume & salary history to our L.A. office: Bonne Jones, Bridges, Mueller & O'keefe, Attn: Rose Bazan, 3699 Wilshire Blvd. 10th fl. L. A. CA 90010 800-234-5602

Secretarial

4. EXECUTIVE SECRETARY

As an industry leader, the Visiting Nurse Association of Los Angeles (VNA-LA), has attained unparalleled performance in the home health care arena. We are currently looking for an experienced Executive Secretary.

In this exciting, fast-paced environment, you will directly support the President of the VNA-LA in a variety of challenging secretarial/administrative duties. This high-profile position requires a detail-oriented team player with 5 years secretarial experience, shorthand skills, 60 wpm typing/word processing ability (WordPerfect desired), excellent interpersonal skills and the ability to work with minimal supervision.

VNA offers competitive salaries and comprehensive benefits. To join us, please contact Carolyn Fields, Executive Assistant at (213) 386-7200, or send your resume with salary history to:

The Visiting Nurse Association of Los Angeles, Inc.
A Working Commitment to Home Care

520 S. LaFayette Park Place
Suite 500
Los Angeles, CA 90057

Equal Opportunity Employer

5. SECRETARY
LEGAL ADMINISTRATIVE SECRETARY

Legal Department has opening for a detailed oriented secretary to assist traveling legal staff with scheduling, reports and correspondence. 3 years min. exper, xlnt phone skills, proficient WordPerf 5.0, transcribing and writing skills req'd. Flexibility and good sense of humor pref'd preferred.

Send detailed resume and salary history to:
HUMAN RESOURCES-LEGAL
PO BOX 76917, Los Angeles
CA 90076, EOE

6.
Medical   No Fee
FRONT OFFICE

Need bilingual indiv. w/ general office skills to manage front desk in local chiropractic office. PC knowledge, math skills & pleasant demeanor req'd. Salary $7.50 to $9.00 hr. Flexible benefits.

LANDMARK
PERSONNEL SERVICES
965-7300

7.

The Rehabilitation Institute
AT SANTA BARBARA

COME WORK AND GROW WITH US!

We offer a variety of career opportunities in the busy physical rehabilitation field.

OUTPATIENT SCHEDULE SPECIALIST

Seeking an energetic, detail-oriented individual with excellent organizational, communication and public relations skills to join our Outpatient Center team. Responsibilities include coordination of therapy scheduling and transportation requests, data entry, and other clerical duties. Must have working knowledge of computers, wordprocessing skills, ability to respond well to pressure and deadlines, and High School diploma or equivalent. Related experience working with physically challenged individuals and knowledge of medical terminology is preferred.

CLINICAL SECRETARY, PER DIEM

We are seeking a detail-oriented, organized individual with excellent public relations skills to perform reception and secretarial duties for the Nursing Department, Responsibilities, include transcription, processing of physicians' orders, and ordering supplies. The applicant must have a high school diploma or equivalent; knowledge of medical terminology; typing speed of 20 wpm; and excellent written and verbal communication skills. One year recent experience as a ward clerk preferred.

8. EDP OPERATOR ASSISTANT

Full-time position to support our Data Processing Department on the NCR 9300 system. Minimum of two years experience on mainframe or mini system required. Previous Mac experience preferred. Duties include: Operator tasks (B/U, EOD, etc.); data entry; data management; ordering & inventory of computer related supplies and some general support. Strong organizational and time management skills a must.

Please contact Personnel at 964-9640 ext. 189 or send your resume to:

The Rehabilitation Institute
at Santa Barbara
427 Camino Del Remedio
Santa Barbara, CA 93110
Attn: Personnel Dept.
EOE

9. Legal Secretary
FOR
Price, Postel, Parma

Tired of working for mediocre people? Want to work with and for the elite in an environment where excellence is not only expected but rewarded? We are looking for an exper. secretary who enjoys the stimulation and pressure of litigation. The successful applicant will be working with two associate attorneys who enjoy what they do and see their secretary as part of the team. Wordprocessing exper. a must, WordPerfect an advantage. Julie Scott will be delighted to hear from qualified applicants. Call 962-0011

Filling Out an Application Form

The application forms that you fill out when you are ready to apply for a job will be much more impressive if you practice filling out similar forms beforehand. In this activity, you will fill out the application form found on page 151. Complete the form as neatly as possible. You may refer to the suggestions for filling out application forms on pages 121–124 of your text.

(Continued on page 151)

Santa Barbara
Medical
Foundation
Clinic
AN EQUAL OPPORTUNITY EMPLOYER

4213 STATE STREET
POST OFFICE BOX 62106
SANTA BARBARA, CA 93160
(805) 964-8916

ALL QUESTIONS ON THIS FORM
CONFORM TO EQUAL OPPORTUNITY
REGULATIONS

APPLICATION FOR EMPLOYMENT

NAME	LAST	FIRST	MIDDLE	PHONE		SOCIAL SECURITY NO.	TODAY'S DATE

PRESENT ADDRESS — CITY — STATE — ZIP — HOW LONG A RESIDENT OF THE SANTA BARBARA AREA?

POSITION DESIRED — AVAILABLE TO START — DO YOU HAVE ANY PHYSICAL CONDITION WHICH MAY LIMIT YOUR ABILITY TO PERFORM THIS JOB?　YES　NO

TYPE OF EMPLOYMENT
REGULAR　　　FULL TIME
TEMPORARY　　PART TIME
SUMMER　　　HOURS PREFERRED:

ARE YOU 18 YRS. OR OLDER?
YES
NO

ARE YOU PREVENTED FROM LAWFULLY BECOMMING EMPLOYED IN THIS COUNTRY BECAUSE OF VISA OR IMMIGRATION STATUS? (PROOF OF CITIZENSHIP OR IMMIGRATION STATUS WILL BE REQUIRED UPON EMPLOYMENT.)　YES　NO

NAME AND ADDRESS OF PARENT OR GUARDIAN IF A MINOR

IF EMPLOYED IN THE POSITION FOR WHICH YOU HAVE APPLIED, WOULD YOU BE IN A SUPERVISORY, SUBORDINATE OR CO-WORKER (i.e. WITHIN THE SAME DEPARTMENT) RELATIONSHIP TO ANY RELATIVE OR MEMBER OF YOUR HOUSEHOLD?　YES　NO　IF YES, PLEASE SPECIFY
(CLINIC POLICY MAY AFFECT WORK ASSIGNMENT OF RELATED EMPLOYEES.)

NAMES OF CLINIC PHYSICIANS OR EMPLOYEES WITH WHOM YOU ARE PERSONALLY ACQUAINTED

NAME, ADDRESS AND PHONE OF PERSON TO NOTIFY IN CASE OF EMERGENCY　PHONE

HAVE YOU EVER BEEN CONVICTED OF A CRIME, OTHER THAN TRAFFIC INFRACTIONS?
YES　　NO　　IF YES, WHEN, WHERE AND DISPOSITION OF CRIME:

HAVE YOU EVER BEEN ARRESTED FOR A CONTROLLED SUBSTANCE, NARCOTIC OR DRUG OFENSE AS SPECIFIED IN SEC. 11590 CA HEALTH & SAFETY CODE?
YES　　NO　　IF YES, PLEASE EXPLAIN:

(NOTE: ARREST OR CONVICTION ARE NOT AN AUTOMATIC BAR FROM EMPLOYMENT. EACH CASE WILL BE CONSIDERED ON ITS OWN MERITS.)

REFERRED BY WHOM

ARE YOU A FORMER EMPLOYEE OF THE CLINIC? IF SO, UNDER WHAT NAME　　MINIMUM ACCEPTABLE SALARY (OPTIONAL)
YES　　NO

EDUCATION AND TRAINING

HIGH SCHOOL	NAME AND LOCATION		MAJOR SUBJECT		GRADUATE? YES　NO

JR. COLLEGE / BUSINESS COLLEGE	FROM	TO	COMPLETED YES　NO	DEGREE & MAJOR

COLLEGE			YES　NO	

POST GRADUATE WORK / SPECIALIZED TRAINING

TYPING (WPM)	SHORTHAND (WPM)	DICTATING MACHINE YES　NO	COMPUTER YES　NO	OTHER BUSINESS MACHINES (SPECIFY)

OTHER SPECIAL SKILLS OR INTERESTS PERTINENT TO POSITION DESIRED

SECOND LANGUAGES YOU READ, WRITE, OR SPEAK FLUENTLY

PREVIOUS EMPLOYMENT
INCLUDE MILITARY SERVICE AND VOLUNTEER WORK OF MORE THAN 3 MONTHS DURATION.　LIST MOST RECENT EMPLOYER FIRST.

FROM		EMPLOYER	ADDRESS	
	MO / YR			
TO		IMMEDIATE SUPERVISOR	PHONE	MAY WE CONTACT? YES　NO
	MO / YR			
HRS / WK		JOB TITLE & DUTIES		
SALARY START	$			
LAST	$	REASON FOR LEAVING		

FORM SBMFC 55-1600 REV. 1-90

(Continued on next page)

PREVIOUS EMPLOYMENT (CONTINUED)

FROM		EMPLOYER	ADDRESS	
	MO / YR	IMMEDIATE SUPERVISOR	PHONE	MAY WE CONTACT? YES NO
TO	MO / YR	JOB TITLE & DUTIES		
HRS / WK				
SALARY START $				
LAST $		REASON FOR LEAVING		

FROM		EMPLOYER	ADDRESS	
	MO / YR	IMMEDIATE SUPERVISOR	PHONE	MAY WE CONTACT? YES NO
TO	MO / YR	JOB TITLE & DUTIES		
HRS / WK				
SALARY START $				
LAST $		REASON FOR LEAVING		

FROM		EMPLOYER	ADDRESS	
	MO / YR	IMMEDIATE SUPERVISOR	PHONE	MAY WE CONTACT? YES NO
TO	MO / YR	JOB TITLE & DUTIES		
HRS / WK				
SALARY START $				
LAST $		REASON FOR LEAVING		

OTHER NAMES USED WHILE EMPLOYED (NOT REQUIRED IF CHANGED BY COURT ORDER) _____

DATES USED _____

PROFESSIONAL LICENSE OR REGISTRATION DATA

	TYPE	STATE	NUMBER	EXPIRATION DATE
1.				
2.				

PERSONAL REFERENCES

EXCLUDE FORMER EMPLOYEES, REFER TO PEOPLE WHO KNOW YOU WELL.   MAY WE CONTACT YOUR REFERENCES?   YES   NO

	NAME AND OCCUPATION	ADDRESS	PHONE
1.			
2.			

I certify that to the best of my knowledge, all information on this application is true and complete. If employed, I understand that any misstatements or omissions of any material facts may lead to disciplinary action up to and including termination. I authorize you to make such investigations and inquiries of my personal, employment, financial or medical history and other related matters as may be necessary in arriving at an employment decision. I hereby release employers, schools or persons from liability in responding to inquiries in connection with my application. I also understand that an employment offer will be contingent upon my passing a health screening exam which includes a **urine drug test** and possible blood alcohol test if deemed necessary. The basic exam and tests will be performed at no cost to me, however, if further tests are required to determine my health status these will be at my expense. I further understand that in the event I am employed, such employment is at will, and that termination may result at any time, with or without cause. Neither I nor the employer have agreed on any specific period of employment unless otherwise set forth in a separate contract.

SIGNATURE _____   DATE _____

Employment Skills for Office Careers

Frequent Interview Questions

One interviewing technique is for the interviewer to ask you to talk about yourself. In that case, you must do most of the talking. But the more common interviewing method is for the interviewer to ask you specific questions. The following are some of the questions most frequently asked during an interview. It will help you make a good impression during your job interviews if you have prepared your answers. Think about your responses, and write out your answers to each question.

1. What kind of work would you like to do?

_____

2. Do you want permanent or temporary work?

_____

3. What are your strengths and weaknesses?

_____

_____

4. Do you prefer working alone or with others?

_____

5. Why do you want to work for this company? (Pick any company)

_____

6. Which courses did you like best in school? Least?

_____

_____

7. What grades have you earned in your classes?

_____

8. What extracurricular activities did you participate in at school?

_____

_____

(Continued on next page)

9. Have you had any serious illnesses?

_____

10. Do you smoke?

_____

11. How do you spend your spare time?

_____

_____

12. What jobs have you had? Why did you leave?

_____

_____

_____

13. How do you feel about working overtime?

_____

14. What do you want to be doing in five years? In ten years?

_____

_____

_____

15. What salary do you expect?

_____

16. What questions would you like to ask?

_____

_____

_____

17. When can you begin work?

_____

Preparing a Resume

Many employers request resumes of applicants. You will have an advantage over other applicants if you prepare one really excellent resume and then use it as a basis for preparing resumes for other jobs. Use the worksheet below to fill in the information for your resume. Refer to the sample resume on page 125 of your text for help. After you have filled in all the information the way you want it, neatly type your resume on a sheet of white typing paper.

Name: _____

Address: _____

Phone: _____

Social Security Number: _____

CAREER
OBJECTIVE: _____

EDUCATION: _____

_____

_____

_____

_____

_____

_____

_____

SKILLS: _____

_____

_____

(Continued on next page)

WORK
EXPERIENCE: _____

_____

_____

_____

_____

_____

_____

_____

ACTIVITIES
AND AWARDS: _____

_____

_____

REFERENCES: _____

_____

_____

_____

_____

_____

_____

Writing a Cover Letter

From your reading, you know that sending a good letter of application to a prospective employer can get you an interview. However, sending a resume accompanied by a cover letter can be even more impressive. The cover letter should be brief and is essentially the same as a letter of application without the information about your education and experience.

Recept./Bkkpr.
Medical clinic seeks front/back office assistant.
Duties include scheduling appts., patient interaction, accounts payable and accounts receivable. Will train individual with appropriate background. Excellent starting salary and benefits. Send resume to: Valley Medical Clinic, Human Resources Dept., P.O. Box 2009, Wilmington, CA 90009.

314 Ocean Avenue
Goleta, CA 93017
October 1, 19___

Valley Medical Clinic
Human Resources Dept.
P.O. Box 2009
Wilmington, CA 90009

Dear Sir or Madam:

In today's Daily News, your company advertised an opening for a receptionist/bookkeeper. I would like to apply for this position. My resume is enclosed.

As you can see from my resume, I have worked in several jobs requiring interaction with the public. I also worked part time in the local high school accounting department while I attended Channel City Junior College. During the time I attended Channel City Junior College, I took several courses in medical assisting.

I would appreciate an interview at your convenience. I can be reached by telephone at 455–6782 in the evenings. Thank you.

Yours truly,

(Your name)

(Continued on next page)

Look at the sample want ad and cover letter on the preceding page. You may also want to refer to the sample cover letter and writing suggestions on pages 126 and 127 of your text.

Write a cover letter to one of the companies on your job lead cards. Write the first copy of your letter in the space provided below.

_____

_____

_____

_____

_____

_____

_____

_____

_____

_____

_____

_____

_____

_____

_____

_____

_____

_____

_____

(Continued on next page)

Revising Your Letter

Correct and revise your letter until it is perfect. Use the checklist below to help you make sure the form of your letter is correct. Place a check mark beside the suggestions you have followed in your letter.

- ☐ 1. The first paragraph tells where I learned about the job and that I want to apply for it.

- ☐ 2. The second paragraph emphasizes one or two facts that make me especially qualified for the job.

- ☐ 3. The last paragraph asks for an interview and includes my telephone number.

- ☐ 4. The heading of my letter includes my address and the date.

- ☐ 5. The inside address is correct.

- ☐ 6. I have used the proper salutation.

- ☐ 7. I have used the correct form for my closing.

- ☐ 8. I have included my signature in the proper place.

Before you rewrite your letter, read it to someone else to see if it sounds clear and businesslike.

Rewriting Your Letter

Type the revised version of your letter on a typewriter or computer in a form that is ready to mail.

Using Standard English

An employer's first impression of you can be the deciding factor in whether you are offered the job. It is therefore especially important to use correct grammar and pronunciation during your job interview. Below are sample job interview questions. Check the applicant's response that demonstrates Standard English that would be best to use in a job interview.

Mr. Price: Hello, Frank. Nice to meet you.
Frank:
1. You, too.
2. Hey, how's it going?
3. How do you do, Mr. Price?
4. Hi.
5. Great to meet you. Really great.

Mr. Price: Frank, I'd like to hear about your qualifications and experience. What were your grades like in school?
Frank:
1. OK.
2. Bs, Cs. Like that.
3. Never flunked a single class!
4. I maintained a B average, sir.
5. I'm way smarter than my grades.

Mr. Price: What was your area of special interest?
Frank:
1. Ummm . . .
2. Statistics class was my favorite.
3. All classes was interesting to me.
4. Anything about customer relations stuff.
5. I guess filing.

Mr. Price: Why do you think you'd like to work at this clinic?
Frank:
1. I feel my skills could be put to best use in the clinic business office.
2. I live not too far away so I could get here easy.
3. I'm broke. I need a job.
4. My friend works here. She says it's an okay place.
5. Gotta work someplace!

Mr. Price: Tell me about your previous work experience, Frank.
Frank:
1. Flippin' burgers, mostly.
2. I put myself through business college filing and assembling medical records at the hospital.
3. I work two years for my uncle in his store.
4. Well, uh, is baby-sitting work?
5. Previous to now, I'm a teller at Western Bank.

(Continued on next page)

Mr. Price: How do you feel about working overtime?
Frank: 1. Not real thrilled.
                 2. You get more money?
                 3. Overtime I could do maybe once a month.
                 4. Fine. It's an opportunity I would welcome.
                 5. My wife she would be mad about that.

Mr. Price: What salary do you expect for this position?
Frank: 1. I could get along good on nine bucks an hour.
                 2. Whatever . . .
                 3. I'd like to earn ten dollars an hour, Mr. Price.
                 4. When I'm askin' around, they said ten.
                 5. Man, with all these bills I got, I need major bucks.

Mr. Price: Thank you, Frank. I have more people to interview, so I'll be unable to make an offer today. But whatever my decision, I will call you by the end of the week.
Frank: 1. Thank you sir. That would be fine.
                 2. I don't have no phone.
                 3. No problem, man.
                 4. Well, OK.
                 5. Thanks. I'll be seein' ya!

Timed Employment Tests

The following are two examples of common types of timed employment tests given to entry-level applicants. Limiting yourself to five minutes for each, take these two tests.

ALPHABETIC FILING

Shown below are groups of names that represent correspondence to be filed. Preceding each group is a series of letters that represent a file drawer label. Select the one name in each group that *should not be* filed in the drawer under which it is listed. Circle the alphabetical letter in the answer column that indicates your choice.

1. FAR-GIZ
   (a) Farmer, Walter
   (b) Fay, Edward
   (c) Gleeson, Marjorie
   (d) Gagnon, Marcel
   (e) Ginsberg, Benjamin
	6. SCH-SHE
	   (a) Sebastina, Augustus
	   (b) Santos, Manuel
	   (c) Schenkel, Samuel
	   (d) Scot Ties Limited
	   (e) Sheehan, Martin

2. COR-DEX
   (a) Carnell, Prentise
   (b) Coughlin, Mary
   (c) Daniels, Kirk
   (d) De Martino, Vivienne
   (e) Dextraze, Edward
	7. MAN-MIN
	   (a) Manfred, Michael E.
	   (b) Menninger, V. B.
	   (c) Mimosa Nursery Company
	   (d) Mallory, Michele
	   (e) Memphis Tool Company

3. DRI-EIS
   (a) Driessen, D. M.
   (b) Drumm Veterinary Hospital
   (c) Eisner, David
   (d) Esposito, Salvatore
   (e) Eisenberg, Jacob
	8. STR-STU
	   (a) Stokely, Jennifer
	   (b) Stubben, Oscar
	   (c) Striker, Susan L.
	   (d) Streamer's Decoration, Inc.
	   (e) Stubbins, Barbara

4. MUR-ORM
   (a) O'Connell Realty
   (b) Murphy, Edward
   (c) Neumann, Geraldine
   (d) Moriarty, Daniel
   (e) Olgivie, Harris
	9. DUT-EAR
	   (a) Dutten Auto Supplies
	   (b) Eastman, Gail G.
	   (c) Earnest, Joseph T.
	   (d) Dutweiler, Peter
	   (e) Dworkin, Marlene

5. BUT-CEN
   (a) Byington, Kim
   (b) Buwalda, Mary
   (c) Cameron, William
   (d) Cermak, Marvin
   (e) Cellucci, Carmen
	10. LAB-MAB
	   (a) Mable, Irene M.
	   (b) Ludwig, Roberta
	   (c) Lincoln, Clark V.
	   (d) Levinson, Matthew
	   (e) Maple, R. T.

ANSWERS

1. A	B	C	D	E		5. A	B	C	D	E		9. A	B	C	D	E		
2. A	B	C	D	E		6. A	B	C	D	E		10. A	B	C	D	E		
3. A	B	C	D	E		7. A	B	C	D	E									
4. A	B	C	D	E		8. A	B	C	D	E									

(Continued on next page)

NUMERICAL MATCHING

Which number is the same as the first column? Write your answer at the right.

	(a)	(b)	(c)	(d)	(e)	
1. 897969	879696	899796	897969	989696	897868	_____
2. 423772	277324	423727	432772	423772	423227	_____
3. 378537	378357	387535	735378	378537	357837	_____
4. 195484	195484	915484	159848	195848	484591	_____
5. 463177	463717	463177	771364	436177	436771	_____
6. 944132	941423	941324	494231	944123	944132	_____
7. 777677	776777	777767	777677	767677	777676	_____
8. 246264	246246	264264	246264	224264	266246	_____
9. 511551	515115	511511	511555	511551	515151	_____
10. 189691	198691	189961	199891	188691	189691	_____
11. 593669	593696	593669	539669	593996	559669	_____
12. 424242	442424	424242	422424	242424	422242	_____
13. 666696	669669	666696	696966	696966	696696	_____
14. 303004	300304	303404	303004	303003	303404	_____
15. 111121	111221	121112	111112	121212	111121	_____
16. 348982	348892	348992	338982	349982	348982	_____
17. 471147	477147	471147	417174	411717	471117	_____
18. 322232	322322	322232	323222	233223	223332	_____
19. 600096	600069	606006	600696	600096	690096	_____
20. 843086	843068	863086	843086	834086	840386	_____
21. 744447	744747	744444	774747	744477	744447	_____
22. 369693	369693	366993	396693	399693	399693	_____
23. 242224	242242	242224	242724	244224	242244	_____
24. 000110	001010	111001	000110	001110	010010	_____
25. 329475	324975	329475	399475	329457	324475	_____

Getting Real—The Practical Part

A. Highlight or check off four ads in your Sunday newspaper for positions of interest to you and for which you feel qualified.

B. Locate listings for employment agencies in the yellow pages of your telephone book. Call and ask:

1. Is a fee charged when a client accepts employment, and, if so, who pays it?

2. What employment skills tests are offered?

C. Collect job leads from those already in the work force to get the idea of "networking."

D. Write sample letters of inquiry to businesses. Make sure spelling and punctuation are perfect.

On the Job: What to Expect

Objectives

After completing this chapter, you will be able to do the following:

1. List the purposes for which an employer usually withholds money from earnings.
2. List the topics usually covered by a company's written policies and procedures.
3. List and describe what most employers expect of their employees.
4. List and describe what you may reasonably expect from your employer.
5. Explain how you will behave if you are fired or laid off.

New Office Terms

grievance process
performance evaluation
probation
productivity

severance pay
termination
unemployment compensation
W-4 form

Before You Begin . . .

Answer the following questions that preview material covered in this chapter:

1. *What policies and procedures do you expect to learn about during your first days on the job?*
2. *What characteristics do most employers expect of their employees?*
3. *As a new employee, what can you reasonably expect of your employer?*

Think about your work experience. You may have had several jobs. Now you are preparing for work that you hope will lead to a rewarding career. How will your attitude toward work and your expectations of your work be different from your previous experience?

As you make a transition to a new job, look upon it as an adventure—a serious one, but an adventure nonetheless. You will have the opportunity to use the skills you have acquired and to learn new skills. You will probably have opportunities for new and greater responsibilities. You will also meet new people who share your interests in your chosen career.

Millions of people have successfully made this transition before you. It may help if you understand what kinds of things to expect when you are new on the job. You will likely want to know what the first days will be like, what your employer will expect of you, and what you can expect of your employer. You may even want to know what to expect if your employment is terminated.

YOUR FIRST DAYS ON THE JOB

Before you do any work, you will be required to fill out certain paperwork. You have probably already filled out an application for employment, which includes your address and telephone number, education, and prior work experience. You will need to fill out forms for tax withholding and other payroll forms. During your first days on the job, you will likely be introduced to other workers, read certain written policies and procedures, and even learn some unwritten rules.

Tax Forms, Withholding, and Payroll

The state and federal governments require all workers to pay taxes on the money they earn. The money collected in taxes supports the respective governments in the work they do and pays the salaries of government workers.

You are required by law to fill out a **W-4 form,** which provides certain information about the amount of taxes you will be paying (see figure 5–1, and Activity 5–1 at the end of this chapter). The amount you pay depends on how much money you earn (your gross salary), whether you are married, and how many allowances you claim. Each allowance represents one person for whom you provide financial support. An additional allowance is permitted for those who are blind or over age sixty-five. The more allowances you have, the less income tax you will have to pay. A single person usually has one allowance. A family has an allowance for the employee plus as many allowances as there are children claimed by this employee.

The information requested on the W-4 form include the following:

- your name with middle initial and your complete address (number and street name, city, state, and zip code)
- your Social Security number
- your marital status
- your total number of allowances
- a notation if you wish to have money withheld from your paycheck for other purposes
- other information concerning a possible exemption (Information on the W-4 form lists reasons why you may not be required to have money withheld—and are thus exempt from withholding.)
- a notation if you are a student
- your signature and the date you signed this document

■ FIGURE 5–1
A sample W-4 form

-------------------- **Cut here and give the certificate to your employer. Keep the top portion for your records.** --------------------

Form **W-4** Department of the Treasury Internal Revenue Service	**Employee's Withholding Allowance Certificate** ▶ **For Privacy Act and Paperwork Reduction Act Notice, see reverse.**	OMB No. 1545-0010 **19**___

1 Type or print your first name and middle initial	Last name	2 Your social security number

Home address (number and street or rural route)

3 ☐ Single ☐ Married ☐ Married, but withhold at higher Single rate.
Note: *If married, but legally separated, or spouse is a nonresident alien, check the Single box.*

City or town, state, and ZIP code

4 If your last name differs from that on your social security card, check here and call 1-800-772-1213 for more information . . . . ▶ ☐

5 Total number of allowances you are claiming (from line G above or from the worksheets on page 2 if they apply) . | **5**

6 Additional amount, if any, you want withheld from each paycheck . . . . | **6** $

7 I claim exemption from withholding for 19___ and I certify that I meet **BOTH** of the following conditions for exemption:
- Last year I had a right to a refund of **ALL** Federal income tax withheld because I had **NO** tax liability; **AND**
- This year I expect a refund of **ALL** Federal income tax withheld because I expect to have **NO** tax liability.

If you meet both conditions, enter "EXEMPT" here . . . . ▶ | **7**

Under penalties of perjury, I certify that I am entitled to the number of withholding allowances claimed on this certificate or entitled to claim exempt status.

Employee's signature ▶   Date ▶   , 19

8 Employer's name and address (Employer: Complete 8 and 10 only if sending to the IRS)	9 Office code (optional)	10 Employer identification number

---

Your employer will keep track of how much money you earn. In addition, on the basis of the information you have supplied on your W-4 form, your employer will determine how much money to withhold from each of your paychecks. Charts provide this information and computer programs do all the payroll calculations after the basic information is input.

Besides state and federal taxes, Social Security tax is withheld according to the percentage currently designated by the federal government. Your employer also pays part of your Social Security contribution. Other contributions may be made for such things as disability insurance, health insurance, and a retirement fund. Your employer also pays into one or two other funds for your benefit. It may seem complicated, but you should receive a complete statement of money withheld with every paycheck (see figure 5–2).

You may also be required to keep a time card or you may be instructed to keep track of the time you spend on the job by some other method. You may be asked to write down the time you arrive in the

■ FIGURE 5–2
A sample paycheck

Restaurants, Inc. Fort Worth, Texas			Morisot, Ramona R. Pay Rate: 4.50/hr.			Taxes Deductions	Year to Date
Description	Current		Year to Date		Federal Tax	$16.06	$401.50
	Hours	Earnings	Hours	Earnings	FICA	12.49	312.25
					Health	0.00	0.00
Regular	37	166.50	925	4,162.50	Dental	3.00	72.00
Overtime	0	0	20	135.00	Company Stock	0.00	0.00

	Earnings	Taxes	Deductions	Net Pay	Pay Period
Current Year to Date	166.50 4,297.50	28.55 713.75	3.00 72.00	134.95 3511.75	12-02-95 12-13-95

Restaurants, Inc.
Fort Worth, Texas 76179

No. 311264

Date ___Dec. 11___ 19 _95_

Pay to the Order of _____ Ramona R. Morisot _____

Amount ___One hundred thirty-four & 95/100___ Dollars

Dollars	Cents
134.95	

Texas Federal S&L

Ramona Morisot
2418 Hadley Street
Fort Worth, Texas 76179

Ann Winchell

morning, the time you go out for lunch, the time you return from lunch, and the time you leave in the evening. This record enables your employer to determine how much money you have earned. You should have agreed upon your rate of pay when you accepted the job. Figure 5–3 shows a sample time card.

Introductions

After you have finished your paperwork, your employer or your supervisor will likely take you around to the other employees for introductions. If no one conducts these introductions, your co-workers will probably come to you and introduce themselves.

Make it your policy to learn your co-workers' names and titles as quickly as possible. Make a mental note of the new names. If you have too many to remember, write the names and titles in a notebook as soon as you leave the work area. Go over these names several times so you can commit them to memory. Your new co-workers will be pleased if you are interested enough to call them by name.

It is good manners to determine how people in the office are addressed. Different levels of formality are used in different offices. In

Week Ending: September 12, 19—

Employee No.: 541-18-4324

Name: Paul Thorton

DAY	IN	OUT	IN	OUT	TOTAL
Mon	8:02	12:02	1:01	5:03	8
Tue	7:59	11:58	1:01	5:08	8
Wed	8:01	12:02	1:03	5:06	8
Thu	8:01	12:06	1:00	5:08	8¼
Fri	7:59	12:02	1:02	5:01	8
Sat					
Sun					

Total Time: 40¼ hours

Rate Per Hour: $10

Total Wages: $403.75 (incl. ¼ hr. OT)

■ FIGURE 5–3
A sample time card

some offices, people are addressed by their last names, such as Ms. Adams, Miss Brown, Mrs. Jones, or Mr. Green. In other offices, everyone is called by his or her first name. Make note of who gets called what and how visitors and customers are addressed, then follow these practices. It will help you fit into the work environment more quickly.

Written Policies and Procedures

Most companies have written policies and procedures. If your new job is with a large company, you may attend a formal orientation meeting for all new employees. At this time, you may be given a policies and procedures manual, sometimes called a policies and rules manual. The policies, procedures, and rules will likely be explained to you in detail in the orientation meeting.

If you do not attend an orientation meeting and no one explains the contents of a policies and rules manual, read through the manual very carefully. This can be important to your future employment with the company—so ask questions about any items you don't understand.

Policies and rules manuals contain different things in different companies. Some are large documents having many pages, others may be just a few pages. In companies with a union, you will also receive documents about policies and rules related to the union. The complexities of these documents depend, to some degree, on the complexities of the structure of your new company. Some companies feel that extensive definition is not necessary, and they have only a few rules and policies.

The topics addressed in a policies manual often include hiring procedures; work schedules and records; salaries, wages, and benefits;

Dorothy and Hooshang are hired at the same time at a large company that holds an orientation meeting for all new employees. The meeting is conducted on a Saturday morning and takes several hours. The company policies and rules manual is a main topic of discussion.

Dorothy is careful to take notes on the proceedings. She notices what people who work for the company wear. She also notices how they act to one another, discovering that they are rather formal and businesslike. She is glad to have the opportunity to discover all the new things about the company so she can quickly fit in and do a good job.

Hooshang sits next to Dorothy. He complains bitterly about having to spend his Saturday morning in a meeting of this sort. He had expected to be working Monday through Friday and resents having to cancel his Saturday plans. He spends time in the meeting grumbling and being distractive, not bothering to take notes or really pay much attention to the proceedings. Nor does he bother to notice how people who work for the company act. He feels he can read the documents later and find out all he needs to know.

At one point, Dorothy is forced to ask Hooshang to shush because he is becoming a real bother. The company representatives also notice Hooshang's behavior. Though they do not speak to him about it at the meeting, they make notes to put in his personnel file about his unpleasant and uncooperative attitude.

1. How would you describe Dorothy's attitude in the orientation meeting? Do you think she will carry this same attitude over into the office?
2. How would you describe Hooshang's attitude in the orientation meeting? Do you think he will carry this same attitude over into the office?

other benefits; probation periods; performance evaluations; termination of employment; grievance process; expenses and reimbursement procedures; and other categories. Every company's manual is unique, created especially for an individual company to meet its own needs.

Hiring Procedures One section of a policies and rules manual is usually devoted to explaining the procedures followed by the company when hiring new employees. It may be that only one interview is necessary, or a company may use a screening process that requires more than one visit. If a company is hiring a large number of people, it may interview several prospects at one time.

Many companies have personnel departments that do all the hiring. If this is the case, you may not meet your direct supervisor until your first day of work. People are hired in many ways, and the hiring procedures section of the policies manual will describe how your company does it.

Work Schedule and Records One section of the manual usually describes the work schedule, lunch breaks, coffee breaks, overtime, and so on. It also discusses the necessary records to document the work schedule kept by the employee and employer.

Salaries, Wages, and Benefits The salaries, wages, and benefits section of the manual describes how salaries are decided and how and when overtime is paid. Overtime refers to any hours worked over forty hours per week unless other arrangements have been agreed upon. Labor laws govern how many hours each day people may work. This section of the manual also details the availability of special programs that relate to the pay schedule, such as medical insurance and retirement plans.

Other Benefits Other benefits include such things as vacation time, sick leave, outside training opportunities, and bonus days for good performance. This section of the manual indicates how many vacation days you accrue (earn). It is common to earn one week's vacation for every six months worked. It is also common to earn one week's vacation after the first year, then two weeks' vacation after each subsequent year.

The number of paid sick days that an employee may accrue varies greatly from company to company. Some companies give one day of sick leave each month to be used only if you are ill. Other companies allow a paid sick day when you must stay home to care for a member of your family who is ill.

Probation Periods **Probation** is a period of time lasting, usually, three to six months after you are hired. During this time, you will accrue no benefits. At the end of the probation period, a formal evaluation should be conducted in a meeting between you and your immediate supervisor. If your job performance is unsatisfactory, you may be terminated. If your job performance is satisfactory, you will be considered a regular employee and will be eligible for all the benefits to which a regular employee is entitled.

Performance Evaluation A **performance evaluation** is a written statement outlining the strengths and weaknesses of your job performance. You will probably be evaluated at least once each year. Probation may be reinstated with poor job performance, and again termination is a possibility. You may learn to use the evaluation process to your advantage, discovering which things about your work you need to improve and taking steps to improve them.

Termination of Employment **Termination** means a notice for you to leave a job. In other words, you are fired. One reason for termination is a poor review. Other reasons are your being absent or tardy too often, stealing from the company, coming to work under the influence of alcohol or drugs, and disregarding company rules.

Grievance Process Your supervisor may do something you think is unfair. For example, she may give you a negative evaluation that you don't think is accurate or justified. The **grievance process** refers to the method a company uses to allow you to state your side in disputes with supervisors or other employees.

Expenses and Reimbursement You could be reimbursed for certain expenses, such as travel if it is required. These expenses will usually be spelled out in a policies manual along with the methods used to document them and methods of reimbursement.

Other Categories You may find some other categories in your new company's policies document. The ones listed here are only some of the possibilities. Whatever topics are covered in your company policies manual, it is your responsibility to read them completely, making sure that you have a thorough understanding of their content.

Unwritten Rules Throughout this book, discussions have focused on things you might expect and things that are expected of you in your office job. Many of these things are not written but are nonetheless rules of the job. They are part of the way the business office has been run—probably for a long while. You might refer to these as the *culture* of the office—its system of knowledge, beliefs, and behavior. Usually, the tone and style of an office culture is set by the company's owner or chief executive officer (CEO)—in other words, the main boss.

Some offices are very formal and frown on informal behavior. Some offices are so casual that they have no dress code or expectations of any kind except that you get the tasks that are assigned to you done on time and efficiently.

The unwritten rules in your new office must be learned through observing and asking questions. For example, recall the importance of understanding how people in the office are addressed. What are the special ways of getting work done, of passing information, of maintaining a specific attitude that might be part of the office behavior? Is casual dress the order of the day? Is informal English acceptable? You can acquaint yourself with the unwritten rules of your office by watching how others act in the office.

R ecall Time

Answer the following questions:

1. Before you do any work with your new company, you will be expected to fill out certain papers. One of these will be a W-4 form from the Internal Revenue Service. What information does this form request?
2. What do you understand about a policies and procedures manual? What kinds of information will this provide a new employee?
3. Every office has unwritten rules. How do you discover what these are in your new office?
4. You may have a formal orientation meeting. What sort of information will you expect to receive at such a meeting?
5. Some offices are formal and others are more informal. Who generally sets the style of an office?

You will probably become aware of your level of performance compared to others in the office.

EMPLOYER EXPECTATIONS

Expectations that your new employer will have of you include such things as a good attitude, cooperation, honesty, willingness to learn, dependability, enthusiasm, and initiative (resourcefulness). These are important components of a successful relationship with your employer. On your first day at work, begin to attempt to live up to these expectations.

The expectations listed above are attitudinal ones. Expectations related to job performance include producing high-quality work, arriving on time, and not being absent frequently. Other performance-related expectations include skillful decision making and problem solving, caring for office equipment, and safety awareness.

Quality of Work

Your employer will expect high-quality work from you. Producing good-quality work is essential to the success of your company. Whether your company provides a service or a product, customers will not return for repeat business if the goods or services provided are of low quality.

A poorly written report or a mistake in an order is an error in quality of work, and it affects the productivity of your company. Pride in your work will help create a sense of ownership in the tasks that you perform and will help you maintain a high standard. If you do quality work, your employer and your co-workers will notice and praise you for it. Likewise, if you do subquality work, your boss and co-workers will know that, too, and will not be happy about it.

Productivity

Quality of work can affect productivity throughout the company. But what does productivity mean and how is it measured? **Productivity** in the office is the total work accomplished in a given time. If you work all day long next to another typist who types thirty pages in a day and you type twenty-five, you know that your neighbor's rate of productivity is higher than yours.

Generally, being productive requires working at a steady pace and staying at the job, except for breaks, for all of the eight hours for which you are being paid. If you spend time on the telephone making personal calls or spend time visiting with other employees while you are supposed to be working, your productivity level will suffer. Bosses do not like to see people standing around chatting or talking on the telephone when they are supposed to be working. This kind of interference with your productivity can cost you your job.

Tardiness and Absenteeism

You should have signed on to your new position fully understanding what your working hours will be. Some jobs are 40 hours each week, some are 37$\frac{1}{2}$ hours each week. Whatever your schedule, your em-

What to Expect on the Job

A large company often has an employee manual with written information regarding the company's policies and expectations. Usually, it will list the company's benefits, such as vacation and sick leave, insurance, pension plans, and severance pay. Other information, such as rules regarding work behavior, is also included. The manual should detail the specific steps in handling grievances and problems, as well as information regarding performance reviews, pay raises, and promotions. Often a large company has detailed descriptions and salary ranges for each position, with progressive steps, or levels. For example, it may have three levels of secretarial positions, such as secretary I, secretary II, and secretary III. Training is sometimes more formal and extensive in a large company than in a small one. Some companies place a great deal of importance on appearance and dressing well, and sometimes this can even affect job advancement. Often, a hierarchy of reporting and procedures exists. Sometimes, it takes a longer period to get something accomplished because a request may have to go through many levels of management before it is approved.

A small company may not have an employee manual. Often, information is given informally, usually verbally, and procedures are less formal. You may not have anyone to train you, and you may have to find out how to do things by asking any number of people. More direct interaction and communication occur, and changes or requests are often acted upon quickly without having to go through many people to get approval. Small companies tend to have a more relaxed attitude about dress codes, and people are generally less formal in their communications.

Which would you prefer—the formal, clearly defined procedures and policies of a large office or the more loosely structured, informal methods of a small office? Why?

ployer will expect you to arrive on time and leave at the agreed-upon hour.

Some people always arrive a few minutes after starting time. Then, after they arrive, they spend several minutes chatting, fixing their clothing, arranging their personal belongings, and getting set for the day. Just because you're already in the building does not mean you have begun to work. Get all your organizing done before starting time.

Plan to arrive a few minutes early so you can say hello to everyone and so you won't feel rushed. Arriving five minutes earlier takes only a bit of organizing—such as setting your alarm to awaken you five minutes earlier.

Getting into the bad habit of arriving late, or even starting work late, can cause resentment from your co-workers. They have to arrive and begin on time; why shouldn't you?

Absenteeism can be a real problem for employers. It signals loss of productivity and a heavier load for the employees who are at work. Occasionally, you will have reasons that you cannot attend work. Generally, the only acceptable reason not to show up is that you are ill. If you are ill, call your immediate supervisor as early as possible and say that you have a problem and will not be able to attend work.

Regular attendance and punctuality (being on time) are attributes of dependability. It is vital to the successful functioning of an office that you be dependable and reliable, that you come to work every day, and that you always arrive on time.

Decision Making and Problem Solving

Learning when to seek advice on the job and when to make a decision yourself can be a tricky aspect of your new position. You cannot go to your boss every time a small problem requires a decision. You must devise strategies that will help you make some decisions yourself. If you don't, job advancement will be out of the question for you.

If you are puzzled by a problem, take some time to think it through. Don't be hasty and don't be rash. If the consequences of your decision will not be too dramatic, go ahead and test your decision making. The more initiative you take and the more work you get done on your own without interrupting your supervisor and co-workers with questions, the more successful you will be on the job.

Part of the process of being able to make good judgments is to be able to foresee possible outcomes. If a decision seems to be leading to a very important outcome, perhaps you should get other opinions—but if the outcome will be more or less inconsequential, make the decision yourself.

In the beginning of your new employment, you will need to ask many questions—and you will be *expected* to ask them. However, after you have become more familiar with your job, you will be expected to make more and more of the decisions related to the job.

Care of Office Equipment

A major expense of any office is the equipment. Typewriters, computer systems, photocopy machines, and calculators all come with a high price tag. Sometimes we don't realize it, but even the telephone system can be elaborate and expensive. The furnishings—desks, chairs, tables, shelves—also are expensive.

You will be expected to take care of the furniture and equipment assigned for your use. Don't eat or drink near your typewriter or computer keyboard. Dropping food into the works can cause damage to these machines. Arrange for regular maintenance and cleaning of your machines if someone else does not have that responsibility.

Treat your machines with respect. Don't drop things onto them or force parts that are supposed to release easily. Learn how to change ribbons and tapes. Treat your machines as though they were your good friends. The better you care for them, the more they will help you accomplish what you need to do.

Safety Awareness

Concern for the safety of employees is not as big an issue in an office as it is in a machine shop. Still, your company will probably have some safety rules and procedures, and you should be aware of certain things that can help ensure the safety of others in your environment.

Most large offices have procedures to follow in the event of a major disaster such as fire or earthquake. A diagram of the building's emergency exits should be posted on a wall along with some instructions about what to do in an emergency. Make yourself aware of these directions. Some offices have regular fire drills so that everyone can practice what to do. Your cooperation in these drills may later save you from injury and may even save your life.

Other little things can ensure safety in an office. For example, don't string electrical wires across floors where people are walking. Be careful about the placement of items on high shelves so that they do not tumble down on people below. Look around your office to check for safety; you may be able to think of other safety tips.

■ EMPLOYEE EXPECTATIONS

Your new employer will expect many things of you. It is reasonable for you to expect certain things from your employer, too. These include a tour of the office and introductions, training, timely paychecks, communication to keep you informed, evaluation of your work, safe working conditions, and honesty.

Tour of the Office and Introductions

You can expect that someone in the company will provide you with a tour of the office. This person will show you where materials and supplies are kept, will probably tell you who occupies which offices, and will show you the rest room and lunchroom.

At the same time that this tour is being conducted, you will probably be introduced to your co-workers. You can expect that people will be open, friendly, and helpful in welcoming you to your new office.

Training

It will be in the company's best interest to train you carefully and thoroughly. This training will probably include things about company policy and rules, and you should receive a clear statement of what is expected of you. You will likely learn who your immediate supervisor is—this is the person to whom you will be accountable.

Although you may have learned in school many of the basic skills you need to perform your new job, you will still require some training. For example, you will need to know the details about the job, what precisely your duties will be, and how you should accomplish them. Take advantage of this training, and learn as much as you can now because in a short while you will be on your own.

Timely Paychecks

If you come to work each day on time and work all the hours you are assigned, you can expect to get paid for your work. The policies and procedures manual will tell you when you can expect to be paid. For some companies, this will be every Friday; for others, it will be the first and the fifteenth days of the month. Government offices often pay only once a month, usually on the tenth of the month following the month when the money was earned. Every company has established paydays, and you can expect to be paid on those days, so you can plan accordingly.

Along with your paycheck, you can expect an accounting of the money earned and the money withheld for taxes and other items.

Communication to Keep You Informed

Your employer should keep you informed about changes in company policy, potential changes in your work load or responsibilities, and other changes in the company that might affect you. A good company has a

Each company sets its own paydays, and you can expect your employer to pay you regularly on those days.

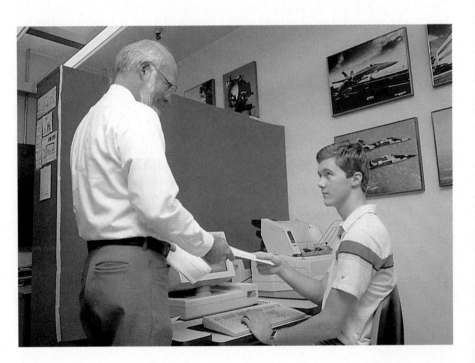

Employment Skills for Office Careers

Angela, a word processor, was the newest employee in the office. Her keyboarding skills, however, were better than anyone else's in the department. When her supervisor, Mr. Bracken, brought work into the department, he would usually give new work to those who were nearly finished with their prior assignments.

Because Angela was the most productive, she was often given big projects late in the day and would have to work late to complete them. Angela felt that Mr. Bracken was taking unfair advantage of her because she was a productive worker. She objected to this, but she did not know what to do about it.

Then Angela came up with an idea. She would simply try to avoid Mr. Bracken. Her desk was situated so that she could easily see anyone approaching the department down a long hall. So the next time she saw Mr. Bracken approaching, she quickly left her station and went to the lady's room. By doing this several times a week, she avoided several big projects that might have caused her to work late. Instead, Bob and Judy began getting these projects.

Based on what you know about Angela's approach to solving her problem, answer these questions:

1. How do you think Angela's behavior will affect her chances for promotion?
2. How do you think her practice of avoiding Mr. Bracken will affect Angela's relationships with her co-workers?
3. What would have been a better way for Angela to solve her problem?

system of communication that allows employees to feel involved and a part of the ongoing business of the company. This communication often takes place in staff meetings, but it can also be accomplished by memos, bulletins, and newsletters. You will receive a lot of information directly, by word of mouth, from either your supervisor or your co-workers. Pay attention. Some of the things you hear may directly affect your work with the company.

Evaluation of Your Work

You can expect periodic evaluations that should help you be a better employee. Having careful, thoughtful feedback from your supervisor about the quality and productivity of your work, your attitude, and how you fit into the office environment is a reasonable expectation. The evaluation is also part of the communication system of the company. You deserve to be told if you are doing an especially good job or if you are falling somewhat short in some areas.

You may discover it is very important to you to know how much your bosses appreciate what you do.

Safe Working Conditions

On-the-job safety is the responsibility of your new employers. They should be constantly monitoring the safety of the environment in which they expect you to work.

Although this is a larger concern in certain kinds of machine shops and factories than in an office, your employer should be vigilant in seeing that safety precautions are taken. Your employers should also have a plan for action in the event of an emergency.

Honesty

After you work for a few years, you may discover that honesty is probably the most important expectation you will have of your employers. Smart companies invariably have a policy of straight shooting with their employees. *Straight shooting* means direct communication about what you can expect of your employers along the lines of advancement, salary, salary raises, benefits, and so on.

If you think your employer has been unfair, you may want to discuss the problem with her. Don't approach the discussion with accusations. Simply say that you are confused about what has gone on, and you need to clarify the issues so that you can understand them. Yes, this can be risky, but you don't want to be in a situation where you are being used or manipulated. In that case, you would be happier leaving this job to seek other employment.

Companies that make promises and don't deliver have serious personnel problems and don't last long in the business world.

Be sure you know exactly the sort of business your new company is in before you agree to take the job. Some people have become involved in shady businesses through naivete (innocence) and trustfulness. If you have any doubts about the nature of the business your company is involved in, find out.

Most companies deal honestly with their employees. You need to be able to trust your employers, as they expect to be able to trust you.

■ TERMINATION OF YOUR EMPLOYMENT

On most jobs, if your training and skills match the job description, you will be happy, contented, interested, and successful. Nonetheless, most people have also experienced, at least once, being terminated from a position.

A termination might make you very unhappy if you don't clearly understand it. At the time of termination, try to get clarification. How, exactly, did your job not work out? What, exactly, should you do differently next time? Spend some time thinking about what went wrong to ensure you don't make the same mistakes again.

In many cases, you will realize that your job change will be an improvement. If you have a personality conflict with someone, or if you are in a position that is a bit difficult for you, you will be relieved that it is over.

If you are fired from your job, ask the reason for the termination. Even good, productive employees are sometimes laid off. If you lose a full-time job, you will probably be eligible for unemployment compensation while you are searching for new employment. An optimistic outlook will be helpful in looking for a new job.

Layoff

It may be that, through no fault of your own, you have been laid off. Because of economic conditions in the early nineties, many large and small employers have been downsizing—that is, reducing the size of their work forces to cut costs, hoping to maximize profits through increased productivity. Your company may be going through some difficult times, and if you were one of the last people hired, you will be one of the first to receive a layoff notice.

Being laid off is not the same as being fired. People are not laid off because of poor job performance or personality conflict or for any of the other reasons people are fired. People are laid off either because the company does not have enough work or because an employer is having financial difficulty and cannot afford to pay all the employees.

Generally, your employer will notify you in writing of your layoff and, in some cases, you will be given severance pay. **Severance pay** means money that you get because you were severed, or laid off, from a company. Your severance pay may be at the rate of one, two, or more weeks' salary. No law says an employer must give notice before a layoff or give severance pay.

Unemployment Compensation

Your employers should contribute monthly to state unemployment insurance to ensure that you can get compensation if you are dismissed from their company. To be eligible for unemployment compensation, you will have to earn a certain amount of money in the weeks and months before your claim.

Unemployment compensation is never a large sum of money. It is designed to help the unemployed over the times when no paycheck is being earned. Generally, if you are terminated from a part-time job that you hold while being a student, you will not have earned enough money to qualify for this compensation.

Unemployment compensation is administered by the state. You are eligible to receive this compensation only if you are at the same time seeking new employment.

Search for New Employment

For a short time, you will probably want to assess what went wrong with the job. However, it will be important for you to begin at once to seek other employment. Remember the adage that if you fall off a horse, you should get right back on again? This applies to employment, too.

If you have had an unhappy experience, go back to all the things you learned about how to get a job in the first place, and put all those strategies in motion so that you are not unemployed for any length of time.

Optimism

You have had an experience. Now you know more than you did before, and you have actually worked in an office. This is to your advantage.

Even though the outcome may have been less than desirable, the experience will be helpful as you look for your new job.

Be hopeful, cheerful, and optimistic. Know that you did it before, you learned a lot, and now you can do it again. Hold the thought that your new job will probably be much more suited to you, that conflicts that were part of the old job will not be there, and that your new job may be more fun, more interesting, and more gratifying.

R ecall Time

Answer the following questions:

1. Employers have many expectations of their employees, including some about attitude. What are some of them? What are some expectations that employers have about the work itself?
2. What is the difference between quality of work and productivity?
3. What are some things you need to consider when making decisions about problems on the job?
4. What are several things you can expect from your employer?
5. What does being laid off mean? How is it different from being fired?

SUMMARY

Soon, you will be making an important transition from school to regular, full-time work. Look on this change as an adventure, a new learning experience.

As a new employee, you must fill out some forms that supply your employer with certain important information. One of these forms will be a W-4 form, required by the Internal Revenue Service. The W-4 form helps your employer know how much should be withheld from each of your paychecks for taxes.

You will probably be asked to maintain a time card to determine the amount of your paycheck each pay period.

When you begin a new job, you will probably receive some sort of orientation to the company and the work you will do. This will help you understand exactly what is expected of you and what the policies and procedures are at this company. In many companies, the policies and procedures are presented in a printed document. They usually cover such topics as salaries, benefits, paydays, vacation time, overtime, probation, evaluation, termination, and grievances. Each company has its own policies and procedures to meet its unique needs.

Your orientation will probably also include introductions to other workers, a tour of the office, and some idea about the unwritten rules for the office. Unwritten rules consist of such things as how people are addressed, what kind of clothing is appropriate in this office, and the kind of speech that you are expected to use.

Your employer will have many expectations of you. Some of the expectations will concern attitude, and these include being pleasant to other workers, honest, willing to learn, dependable, cooperative, and enthusiastic. Further expectations concern the work itself. These expectations include good quality of work, high productivity, punctuality and good attendance, good judgment, good care of equipment, and awareness of safety.

You can also expect certain things from your employer. You can expect to receive adequate orientation and training, to be paid for the work you do, to be kept informed about ongoing business decisions that might affect you, to have thoughtful feedback about your work in the form of regular evaluations, and to have safe working conditions. Probably the most important expectation you might have of your new employer is honesty in what is said about work, pay, and benefits.

If you have the proper skill and training, chances are you will be successful at your new job. However, things sometimes happen on the job that are unforeseeable. You may be terminated—that is, fired—or you may get laid off. If you are fired, it will be because someone has evaluated your work as being substandard or because you have a personality conflict with someone on the job. If you are laid off, it will be because the company does not have enough work or because the company can no longer afford to pay you.

If you find yourself without a job, evaluate what happened so that it doesn't happen again. Begin at once to look for a new job, using all the strategies you used in finding this one.

During the first days and weeks on the new job, the following things will occur.

- You will fill out a W-4 form, which has information concerning withholding taxes.
- You will be shown how to keep your time card.
- You will be oriented to the way your office is run.
- You will be given a policies and procedures statement and you will need to have a clear understanding of its contents.
- You will be given training on how to do your job.
- Your employer will have certain expectations, including that you have a good attitude.
- You will be expected to be at work every day and also to arrive on time.
- You will be expected to do quality work with a reasonable rate of productivity.
- You will be expected to have regard for safety in the office.
- You will be expected to take proper care of office machines and furnishings.
- You can have certain expectations of your employers, such as that they will deal honestly with you.
- You can expect an orientation and proper training.
- You can expect a good system of communication in which your

employer keeps you informed about company matters that concern you.

■ You can expect regular and timely paychecks for the work you do, with a clear statement of money withheld.

In Conclusion . . .

When you have completed this chapter, answer the following questions:

1. *What policies and procedures do you expect to learn about during your first days on the job?*
2. *What characteristics do most employers expect of their employees?*
3. *As a new employee, what can you reasonably expect of your employer?*

Review and Application

REVIEW YOUR VOCABULARY

Match the following by writing the letter of each vocabulary word in the space to the left of its description.

_____ 1. money that an employee gets because he was laid off

_____ 2. method a company uses to allow an employee to state her side in a dispute with supervisors or other employees

_____ 3. paper that provides information about the amount of taxes you will pay

_____ 4. total work accomplished in a given time

_____ 5. period of time before permanent employment during which an employee accrues no benefits

_____ 6. small amounts of money paid to unemployed workers to help them over the times when no paycheck is being earned

_____ 7. written statement outlining the strengths and weaknesses of an employee's job performance

_____ 8. notice for an employee to leave a job

a. grievance process
b. performance evaluation
c. probation
d. productivity
e. severance pay
f. termination
g. unemployment compensation
h. W-4 form

DISCUSS AND ANALYZE AN OFFICE SITUATION

1. Ernest has been with his new company for three months. When he started the job, he was told he would receive an evaluation and would be taken off probation at the end of three months. This would give him full-time, regular employee status with all the benefits that are included. Three months have passed, and as time goes on, one week, then two, nothing has been done to evaluate Ernest's performance. He assumes he is still on probation status.

   What should Ernest do to clear up this confusion?

2. Bernardita has been hired on a new job and has been invited to attend an orientation meeting for new employees. She is grateful for the opportunity to learn what, exactly, her job will consist of. Unfortunately, she finds the orientation to be rather inadequate. In addition, when she reports to work on her first day, no one greets her, introduces her to others, or assists her in any way.

   We can expect certain things from new employers. How have Bernardita's new employers fallen short of their responsibility to her? What would you do if you were Bernardita?

PRACTICE BASIC SKILLS

Math

1. Social Security contributions are 15.3 percent of your earned money. Your employer pays 7.65 percent of that and you pay the rest. If you work forty hours in one week and earn $7.50 per hour, how much will be withheld from that paycheck for your share of the Social Security tax? How much will your employer be paying?

English

1. Some offices are formal and some more informal. Language reflects the style of an office. If you are working in a very formal office, which parts of the following conversation would not be acceptable to your employer? Assume you are talking to a customer.

   Hi, Eileen. We can fix you up with a gadget that will blow you away. I'm crazy about them and I think you'll find they're pretty neat, too. Come on over and check them out. See if you don't think they're just what you've been looking for. They should really fit the bill.

Proofreading

1. Part of your new job in the office may be typing and correcting a letter. Different companies use different formats, so you will need to determine ex-

actly how your company wants its letters set up. In the following letter, find and correct misspellings and incorrect punctuation.

Randall Russell, President
Wholesome Produce Company
1345 Class Street
Los Angeles, CA 90024

Dear Mr. Rusel:

I am writing to request an ammendment to the envoice you sent us on may 30. It seems we have ben chargd for merchandice we did not perchase and we reely don't wunt to pay for it.

I'm hopping you will be abel to cleer this up immediately. Thank you.

Yours Truely,
Leah Baker

1. Go to your local Internal Revenue Service office and ask for a W-4 form. Fill it out as you would if you were hired for a new position.
2. Visit a friend's business and ask if you might look at her policies and procedures manual. Become familiar with the types of issues covered in the document. If the business has no such document, interview your friend. Ask how she learned about the rules of the company and ask what they are.

QUIZ

*Write a **T** if the statement is true or an **F** if the statement is false.*

____ 1. Employees need to know exactly how to perform their duties before they start working because employers do not usually provide for training of new employees.

____ 2. If you smile too much in the office environment, your supervisors are likely to believe that you are not a serious employee.

____ 3. Your gross salary or wages is the amount that you take home after all deductions have been taken.

____ 4. Your employer will probably introduce you to some of your co-workers the first day on the job.

____ 5. Unwritten rules often cover such things as how you address your co-workers and how you dress on the job.

____ 6. A policy manual is usually a secret document that you won't be allowed to see until after your probation period.

____ 7. Unless you have to punch a time card, it is usually permitted to arrive at your workplace a few minutes late.

____ 8. A performance evaluation is a kind of report card.

____ 9. The quantity of work you produce is normally more important to your employer than the quality.

____ 10. You should not ask your boss to make the decision every time you have a problem.

____ 11. Employees are responsible for the care of the business machines they will be using on the job—typewriters, desks, computers, etc.

____ 12. Making the workplace safe is not a responsibility of your employer, so you must continually exercise caution to avoid injury.

(Continued on next page)

(QUIZ continued)

_____ 13. You are eligible for unemployment insurance payments if you quit your job because it doesn't suit you very well.

_____ 14. If you are terminated from a job, the best thing to do is take a month or so to regain your confidence before looking for another job.

_____ 15. If you fill out your own time card, it is fine to round off your arrival and departure times to the nearest five minutes.

Forms

When applying for temporary work, you will be asked to complete certain forms required by the federal government. One will be the Employee's Withholding Allowance Certificate or W-4 form (A) that is needed by the federal government for tax purposes. Another may be the Employment Eligibility Verification form (B) that also is required by the federal government. In addition to completing this form, each applicant must show the employment interviewer proof that the applicant is a U.S. citizen or has other verification for eligibility to work. The required documents to be shown are listed on the form.

It will be helpful to complete samples of these forms so that you will be better prepared when applying for work. On the following pages are samples of these two forms. Complete them now.

Completing a W-4 Form

As an employee, you are required by law to fill out a W-4 form to provide information about the amount of taxes you will be paying. Use the numbered instructions below to help you complete the corresponding lines of the W-4 form on the next page.

1. Type or print your name clearly. Errors in tax records can create problems that are time-consuming to correct.

2. Your Social Security number is your permanent tax identification number. All of your tax information will be referenced to it. Type or print the correct number clearly.

3. Check the appropriate box. If you are married but will receive income from which no taxes are being withheld, you may check the box for withholding at the higher single rate.

4. If you are single, have only one job, and are supporting yourself, you will probably enter "2" on this line. If you are married, you will need to complete the personal allowances worksheet. The number of allowances you claim will vary depending on whether you and your spouse both work, how much you earn, and whether you have other dependents.

5. This line is used by employees who anticipate owing more taxes. Having two jobs or being married with both spouses working might create such a situation. Seek further advice if you think this situation applies to you. The worksheet will help you determine this figure.

6. Most employees will not qualify for exemption.

7. To qualify as a full-time student, you must be enrolled at a school during any five months of the year for the number of hours that the school considers full time.

Sign and date the form. After your W-4 takes effect, you may use IRS publication 919 to see if you are having the right amount withheld. If not, you can submit a revised W-4 form to your employer.

Form W-4 (19__)

Want More Money In Your Paycheck?

If you expect to be able to take the earned income credit for 19__, you can have part of it added to your take-home pay. For details, get Form W-5 from your employer.

Purpose. Complete Form W-4 so that your employer can withhold the correct amount of Federal income tax from your pay.

Exemption From Withholding. Read line 7 of the certificate below to see if you can claim exempt status. *If exempt, complete line 7; but do not complete lines 5 and 6.* No Federal income tax will be withheld from your pay. Your exemption is good for 1 year only. It expires February 15, 19__.

Note: *You cannot claim exemption from withholding if (1) your income exceeds $600 and includes unearned income (e.g., interest and dividends), and (2) another person can*

claim you as a dependent on their tax return.

Basic Instructions. Employees who are not exempt should complete the Personal Allowances Worksheet. Additional worksheets are provided on page 2 for employees to adjust their withholding allowances based on itemized deductions, adjustments to income, or two-earner/two-job situations. Complete all worksheets that apply to your situation. The worksheets will help you figure the number of withholding allowances you are entitled to claim. However, you may claim fewer allowances than this.

Head of Household. Generally, you may claim head of household filing status on your tax return only if you are unmarried and pay more than 50% of the costs of keeping up a home for yourself and your dependent(s) or other qualifying individuals.

Nonwage Income. If you have a large amount of nonwage income, such as interest or dividends, you should consider making estimated tax payments using Form 1040-ES.

Otherwise, you may find that you owe additional tax at the end of the year.

Two Earners/Two Jobs. If you have a working spouse or more than one job, figure the total number of allowances you are entitled to claim on all jobs using worksheets from only one Form W-4. This total should be divided among all jobs. Your withholding will usually be most accurate when all allowances are claimed on the W-4 filed for the highest paying job and zero allowances are claimed for the others.

Check Your Withholding. After your W-4 takes effect, you can use Pub. 919, Is My Withholding Correct for 19__?, to see how the dollar amount you are having withheld compares to your estimated total annual tax. We recommend you get Pub. 919 especially if you used the Two Earner/Two Job Worksheet and your earnings exceed $150,000 (Single) or $200,000 (Married). Call 1-800-829-3676 to order Pub. 919. Check your telephone directory for the IRS assistance number for further help.

Personal Allowances Worksheet

A Enter "1" for **yourself** if no one else can claim you as a dependent . . . . **A** _____

B Enter "1" if: ⎧ • You are single and have only one job; or
            ⎨ • You are married, have only one job, and your spouse does not work; or   ⎬ . . **B** _____
            ⎩ • Your wages from a second job or your spouse's wages (or the total of both) are $1,000 or less. ⎭

C Enter "1" for your **spouse**. But, you may choose to enter -0- if you are married and have either a working spouse or more than one job (this may help you avoid having too little tax withheld) . . . . **C** _____

D Enter number of **dependents** (other than your spouse or yourself) whom you will claim on your tax return . . . **D** _____

E Enter "1" if you will file as **head of household** on your tax return (see conditions under **Head of Household** above) . **E** _____

F Enter "1" if you have at least $1,500 of **child or dependent care expenses** for which you plan to claim a credit . . **F** _____

G Add lines A through F and enter total here. **Note:** This amount may be different from the number of exemptions you claim on your return ▶ **G** _____

For accuracy, do all worksheets that apply. ⎧ • If you plan to **itemize or claim adjustments to income** and want to reduce your withholding, see the Deductions and Adjustments Worksheet on page 2.
⎨ • If you are **single** and have **more than one job** and your combined earnings from all jobs exceed $30,000 OR if you are **married** and have a **working spouse or more than one job,** and the combined earnings from all jobs exceed $50,000, see the Two-Earner/Two-Job Worksheet on page 2 if you want to avoid having too little tax withheld.
⎩ • If **neither** of the above situations applies, **stop here** and enter the number from line G on line 5 of Form W-4 below.

------------------------------- **Cut here and give the certificate to your employer. Keep the top portion for your records.** -------------------------------

Form **W-4**	**Employee's Withholding Allowance Certificate**	OMB No. 1545-0010
Department of the Treasury Internal Revenue Service	▶ **For Privacy Act and Paperwork Reduction Act Notice, see reverse.**	**19**__

1 Type or print your first name and middle initial	Last name		2 Your social security number

Home address (number and street or rural route)	3 ☐ Single ☐ Married ☐ Married, but withhold at higher Single rate.
	Note: *If married, but legally separated, or spouse is a nonresident alien, check the Single box.*
City or town, state, and ZIP code	4 If your last name differs from that on your social security card, check here and call 1-800-772-1213 for more information · · · · ▶ ☐

5	Total number of allowances you are claiming (from line G above or from the worksheets on page 2 if they apply) .	**5**
6	Additional amount, if any, you want withheld from each paycheck	**6** $
7	I claim exemption from withholding for 19__ and I certify that I meet **BOTH** of the following conditions for exemption:	

• Last year I had a right to a refund of **ALL** Federal income tax withheld because I had **NO** tax liability; **AND**
• This year I expect a refund of **ALL** Federal income tax withheld because I expect to have **NO** tax liability.
If you meet both conditions, enter "EXEMPT" here . . . . ▶ | **7** |

Under penalties of perjury, I certify that I am entitled to the number of withholding allowances claimed on this certificate or entitled to claim exempt status.

Employee's signature ▶ _____ Date ▶ _____ , 19__

8 Employer's name and address (Employer: Complete 8 and 10 only if sending to the IRS)	9 Office code (optional)	10 Employer identification number

Cat. No. 10220Q

(Continued on next page)

Deductions and Adjustments Worksheet

Note: *Use this worksheet only if you plan to itemize deductions or claim adjustments to income on your 19___ tax return.*

1	Enter an estimate of your 19___ itemized deductions. These include: qualifying home mortgage interest, charitable contributions, state and local taxes (but not sales taxes), medical expenses in excess of 7.5% of your income, and miscellaneous deductions. (For 19___, you may have to reduce your itemized deductions if your income is over $111,800 ($55,900 if married filing separately). Get Pub. 919 for details.)	**1** $
2	Enter: { $6,350 if married filing jointly or qualifying widow(er) $5,600 if head of household $3,800 if single $3,175 if married filing separately }	**2** $
3	**Subtract** line 2 from line 1. If line 2 is greater than line 1, enter -0-	**3** $
4	Enter an estimate of your 19___ adjustments to income. These include alimony paid and deductible IRA contributions	**4** $
5	**Add** lines 3 and 4 and enter the total	**5** $
6	Enter an estimate of your 19___ nonwage income (such as dividends or interest)	**6** $
7	**Subtract** line 6 from line 5. Enter the result, but not less than -0-	**7** $
8	**Divide** the amount on line 7 by $2,500 and enter the result here. Drop any fraction	**8**
9	Enter the number from Personal Allowances Worksheet, line G, on page 1	**9**
10	**Add** lines 8 and 9 and enter the total here. If you plan to use the Two-Earner/Two-Job Worksheet, also enter this total on line 1, below. Otherwise, **stop here** and enter this total on Form W-4, line 5, on page 1.	**10**

Two-Earner/Two-Job Worksheet

Note: *Use this worksheet only if the instructions for line G on page 1 direct you here.*

1	Enter the number from line G on page 1 (or from line 10 above if you used the Deductions and Adjustments Worksheet)	**1**
2	Find the number in **Table 1** below that applies to the **LOWEST** paying job and enter it here	**2**
3	If line 1 is **GREATER THAN OR EQUAL TO** line 2, subtract line 2 from line 1. Enter the result here (if zero, enter -0-) and on Form W-4, line 5, on page 1. **DO NOT** use the rest of this worksheet	**3**

Note: *If line 1 is **LESS THAN** line 2, enter -0- on Form W-4, line 5, on page 1. Complete lines 4–9 to calculate the additional withholding amount necessary to avoid a year-end tax bill.*

4	Enter the number from line 2 of this worksheet	**4**	
5	Enter the number from line 1 of this worksheet	**5**	
6	**Subtract** line 5 from line 4		**6**
7	Find the amount in **Table 2** below that applies to the **HIGHEST** paying job and enter it here		**7** $
8	**Multiply** line 7 by line 6 and enter the result here. This is the additional annual withholding amount needed		**8** $
9	Divide line 8 by the number of pay periods remaining in 19___. (For example, divide by 26 if you are paid every other week and you complete this form in December 19___.) Enter the result here and on Form W-4, line 6, page 1. This is the additional amount to be withheld from each paycheck		**9** $

Table 1: Two-Earner/Two-Job Worksheet

Married Filing Jointly				All Others	
If wages from **LOWEST** paying job are—	Enter on line 2 above	If wages from **LOWEST** paying job are—	Enter on line 2 above	If wages from **LOWEST** paying job are—	Enter on line 2 above
0 - $3,000	0	39,001 - 50,000	9	0 - $4,000	0
3,001 - 6,000	1	50,001 - 55,000	10	4,001 - 10,000	1
6,001 - 11,000	2	55,001 - 60,000	11	10,001 - 14,000	2
11,001 - 16,000	3	60,001 - 70,000	12	14,001 - 19,000	3
16,001 - 21,000	4	70,001 - 80,000	13	19,001 - 23,000	4
21,001 - 27,000	5	80,001 - 90,000	14	23,001 - 45,000	5
27,001 - 31,000	6	90,001 and over	15	45,001 - 60,000	6
31,001 - 34,000	7			60,001 - 70,000	7
34,001 - 39,000	8			70,001 and over	8

Table 2: Two-Earner/Two-Job Worksheet

Married Filing Jointly		All Others	
If wages from **HIGHEST** paying job are—	Enter on line 7 above	If wages from **HIGHEST** paying job are—	Enter on line 7 above
0 - $ 50,000	$370	0 - $ 30,000	$370
50,001 - 100,000	690	30,001 - 60,000	690
100,001 - 130,000	760	60,001 - 110,000	760
130,001 - 220,000	880	110,001 - 220,000	880
220,001 and over	970	220,001 and over	970

(Continued on next page)

U.S. Department of Justice
Immigration and Naturalization Service

OMB No. 1115-0136
Employment Eligibility Verification

Please read instructions carefully before completing this form. The instructions must be available during completion of this form. **ANTI-DISCRIMINATION NOTICE.** It is illegal to discriminate against work eligible individuals. Employers CANNOT specify which document(s) they will accept from an employee. The refusal to hire an individual because of a future expiration date may also constitute illegal discrimination.

Section 1. Employee Information and Verification. To be completed and signed by employee at the time employment begins

Print Name: Last	First	Middle Initial	Maiden Name

Address (Street Name and Number)	Apt. #	Date of Birth (month/day/year)

City	State	Zip Code	Social Security #

I am aware that federal law provides for imprisonment and/or fines for false statements or use of false documents in connection with the completion of this form.

I attest, under penalty of perjury, that I am (check one of the following):
- ☐ A citizen or national of the United States
- ☐ A Lawful Permanent Resident (Alien # A _____)
- ☐ An alien authorized to work until ____/____/____
  (Alien # or Admission # _____)

Employee's Signature	Date (month/day/year)

Preparer and/or Translator Certification. (To be completed and signed if Section 1 is prepared by a person other than the employee.) I attest, under penalty of perjury, that I have assisted in the completion of this form and that to the best of my knowledge the information is true and correct.

Preparer's/Translator's Signature	Print Name

Address (Street Name and Number, City, State, Zip Code)	Date (month/day/year)

Section 2. Employer Review and Verification. To be completed and signed by employer. Examine one document from List A OR examine one document from List B and one from List C as listed on the reverse of this form and record the title, number and expiration date, if any, of the document(s)

List A	OR	List B	AND	List C
Document title: _____		_____		_____
Issuing authority: _____		_____		_____
Document #: _____		_____		_____
Expiration Date (if any): ___/___/___		___/___/___		___/___/___
Document #: _____				
Expiration Date (if any): ___/___/___				

CERTIFICATION - I attest, under penalty of perjury, that I have examined the document(s) presented by the above-named employee, that the above-listed document(s) appear to be genuine and to relate to the employee named, that the employee began employment on (month/day/year) ____/____/____ **and that to the best of my knowledge the employee is eligible to work in the United States.** (State employment agencies may omit the date the employee began employment).

Signature of Employer or Authorized Representative	Print Name	Title

Business or Organization Name	Address (Street Name and Number, City, State, Zip Code)	Date (month/day/year)

Section 3. Updating and Reverification. To be completed and signed by employer

A. New Name (if applicable)	B. Date of rehire (month/day/year) (if applicable)

C. If employee's previous grant of work authorization has expired, provide the information below for the document that establishes current employment eligibility.

Document Title: _____ Document #: _____ Expiration Date (if any): ___/___/___

I attest, under penalty of perjury, that to the best of my knowledge, this employee is eligible to work in the United States, and if the employee presented document(s), the document(s) I have examined appear to be genuine and to relate to the individual.

Signature of Employer or Authorized Representative	Date (month/day/year)

Form I-9 (Rev. 11-21-91) N

(Continued on next page)

LISTS OF ACCEPTABLE DOCUMENTS

LIST A		LIST B		LIST C
Documents that Establish Both Identity and Employment Eligibility	**OR**	**Documents that Establish Identity**	**AND**	**Documents that Establish Employment Eligibility**

LIST A
Documents that Establish Both Identity and Employment Eligibility

1. U.S. Passport (unexpired or expired)

2. Certificate of U.S. Citizenship (INS Form N-560 or N-561)

3. Certificate of Naturalization (INS Form N-550 or N-570)

4. Unexpired foreign passport, with I-551 stamp or attached INS Form I-94 indicating unexpired employment authorization

5. Alien Registration Receipt Card with photograph (INS Form I-151 or I-551)

6. Unexpired Temporary Resident Card (INS Form I-688)

7. Unexpired Employment Authorization Card (INS Form I-688A)

8. Unexpired Reentry Permit (INS Form I-327)

9. Unexpired Refugee Travel Document (INS Form I-571)

10. Unexpired Employment Authorization Document issued by the INS which contains a photograph (INS Form I-688B)

OR

LIST B
Documents that Establish Identity

1. Driver's license or ID card issued by a state or outlying possession of the United States provided it contains a photograph or information such as name, date of birth, sex, height, eye color, and address

2. ID card issued by federal, state, or local government agencies or entities provided it contains a photograph or information such as name, date of birth, sex, height, eye color, and address

3. School ID card with a photograph

4. Voter's registration card

5. U.S. Military card or draft record

6. Military dependent's ID card

7. U.S. Coast Guard Merchant Mariner Card

8. Native American tribal document

9. Driver's license issued by a Canadian government authority

For persons under age 18 who are unable to present a document listed above:

10. School record or report card

11. Clinic, doctor, or hospital record

12. Day-care or nursery school record

AND

LIST C
Documents that Establish Employment Eligibility

1. U.S. social security card issued by the Social Security Administration (other than a card stating it is not valid for employment)

2. Certification of Birth Abroad issued by the Department of State (Form FS-545 or Form DS-1350)

3. Original or certified copy of a birth certificate issued by a state, county, municipal authority or outlying possession of the United States bearing an official seal

4. Native American tribal document

5. U.S. Citizen ID Card (INS Form I-197)

6. ID Card for use of Resident Citizen in the United States (INS Form I-179)

7. Unexpired employment authorization document issued by the INS (other than those listed under List A)

Illustrations of many of these documents appear in Part 8 of the Handbook for Employers (M-274)

Form I-9 (Rev. 11-21-91) N

Employer Expectations

Understanding and meeting your employer's expectations is an important part of a successful working relationship. Read the following case studies and decide what expectations are being addressed. Consider how these expectations can be met as you answer the questions that follow.

Part of Mary's responsibility in the dental office where she works is to order the supplies needed by the office staff. These orders are due every Monday morning. On several occasions, Mary has been late to work on Monday morning and has missed the supply sales representative. This means the office staff has had to do without some supplies, or Mary has needed to take time off from work to purchase them from a local store. Mary's employer is unaware of the problem.

■ How does Mary's tardiness affect the functioning of the office?

_____

_____

_____

■ Should Mary's employer be informed? If so, as a co-worker, what would you do?

_____

_____

_____

Brian worked as a patient accounts clerk in a weight loss clinic. Because he was young and appeared physically fit, his co-workers sometimes asked him for help with lifting or moving objects. One day he was asked to help move a filing cabinet. He attempted to move it without removing the drawers and severely strained his back. He missed several weeks of work and received workers' compensation. His injury resulted in considerable expense to his employer.

■ Who was responsible for Brian's injury? How could the injury have been avoided?

_____

_____

_____

(Continued on next page)

Betty and Lois are both medical transcriptionists in an orthopedic practice. Betty is a steady worker who is able to transcribe about forty pages a shift. Lois also transcribes about the same number of pages, but she takes frequent coffee breaks and makes personal phone calls during work hours. Following their performance evaluations, Betty is given a raise, but Lois is not. Lois does not understand why Betty should receive more pay since they both produce about the same quantity of work.

■ Why do you think Lois did not receive a raise?

_____

_____

_____

_____

■ If you were Lois's employer, what would you do?

_____

_____

_____

_____

The office workers at an insurance office where Ruth is employed have been instructed to cover their word processors with a dust cover at the end of each day. Ruth often forgets to do that and has been reminded several times. One weekend when Ruth left her word processor uncovered, a maintenance crew came in to paint the office. The dust from the sanding settled into the word-processor. On Monday when Ruth came to work, she tried to clean off the dust, but she found her word processor was not functioning properly. It had to be taken into the shop for cleaning and repair.

■ Who should pay for the expense of cleaning and repairing the word processor? Explain your answer.

_____

_____

_____

_____

Employment Skills for Office Careers

Employee Expectations

Knowing what is reasonable to expect from an employer and being prepared to ask for the appropriate information will help you avoid problems on the job. Read the following case studies and answer the questions to help acquaint yourself with some of these expectations.

Linda arrived for her first day on the job as an order clerk in a pharmaceutical supply company. Her supervisor greeted her, introduced her to co-workers, and began training Linda for the job. The supervisor was called out of the office to handle a problem and turned Linda's training over to Carla, a co-worker. Some of the instructions Carla gave Linda contradicted the supervisor's instructions. When Linda asked about this, Carla just shrugged and answered that no one bothered to do the work that way. It appeared that Carla's method was easier.

■ If you were Linda what would you do?

_____

_____

_____

_____

Stan, who worked part time in a physical therapy office, dropped by work to pick up his paycheck. Stan's employer had neglected to make out the checks before leaving for a conference. Stan needed his check to pay his tuition costs for the new semester at college, so he had to borrow the money to make his payment.

■ If you were Stan, what would you say to your employer?

_____

_____

_____

_____

When Karen arrived for work at the clinic, she was upset to learn that a required staff meeting was scheduled for the first hour of the morning instead of the late afternoon as usual. Karen had not been informed of the change in time and had promised one of the doctors she worked for that she would finish typing an important report by noon. She knew she would not be able to finish the report if she attended the staff meeting.

(Continued on next page)

■ If you were Karen, what would you do?

_____

_____

_____

_____

    Marie worked in a small office with poor ventilation. Sometimes fumes from the laboratories in the building came into her office. When this happened, she often went home at the end of the day with a headache. She felt uncomfortable working in this environment, but she liked her job and felt she was well paid.

■ How should Marie handle this situation?

_____

_____

_____

_____

    Leon accepted a position as an office manager for a supply house with the understanding that medical benefits would soon be made available for him. After three months on the job, the benefits were still not available. Leon had a young family and felt these benefits were essential.

■ What do you think Leon should do?

_____

_____

_____

_____

Boss for a Day

Imagine yourself as the supervisor in a business office. Write two paragraphs on what you expect from your staff, covering both work performance and personal conduct.

_____

_____

_____

_____

_____

_____

_____

_____

_____

_____

_____

_____

_____

_____

_____

_____

_____

_____

Getting Along with People

Objectives

After completing this chapter, you will be able to do the following:

1. Use human relationship skills in the office to work as a team member.
2. Be supportive of co-workers in the office.
3. Maintain a professional appearance in the office.
4. Acknowledge the good work and ideas of others.
5. Understand and deal with difficult people.
6. Accept criticism gracefully and admit your own mistakes.
7. Rid yourself of your own unhappy feelings.
8. Be assertive without being aggressive.
9. Accept assignments willingly and set priorities.
10. Keep your boss informed of your progress on your assignments.
11. Maintain high ethical standards in your office relationships.

New Office Terms

aggressive communication	hierarchy
assertive communication	human relations
assertiveness	interpersonal relations
body language	passive communication
co-workers	seniority

Before You Begin . . .

Answer the following questions that preview material covered in this chapter:

1. *What is the value of taking part in office social activities?*
2. *What is the value of maintaining positive behavior on the job?*
3. *What are some strategies you would use in dealing with difficult people?*

During your life, you will spend half your waking hours at work. Few jobs are performed by one person working alone, so you will probably work with other people in a cooperative effort. This will require good skills, good work habits, and workable strategies for dealing effectively with your co-workers.

Human relations and **interpersonal relations** are both terms meaning how people get along with one another. Good human relations makes work more enjoyable and workers more productive. Poor human relations causes unhappiness on the job, and affects the way you perform your duties. If you are unable to get along well with your co-workers, you will find it difficult to advance in your career. Some studies show that more than 80 percent of your career success depends on interpersonal skills, or your ability to work effectively with the people in your work environment.

Human relations skills, or the ability to get along well with others, benefit you in other aspects of your life, too. Begin now to practice some of the strategies and ideas that follow.

▌ TEAMWORK

Have you participated in team sports, sung in a choir, or worked with others on a committee? You have probably experienced some group activity and learned that the key to a successful team is cooperation. Each team member must fulfill his assigned role while working in concert with others.

The same sort of cooperation is required at work. Little can be accomplished if support and cooperation are missing from daily interactions. On the job, you and your team members are usually called co-workers. The word **co-workers** means people who work together in a cooperative effort.

▌ EXPECTATIONS

Your co-workers, or *team members*, will have certain implicit expectations of you. That is, they will expect you to do certain things and act in certain ways that are implied rather than directly stated.

Your co-workers will expect you to do your share of the work even though they will sometimes be willing to help you. You will be given specific assignments, and you will be expected to complete them within a reasonable time. If you don't, your co-workers will probably resent you for not doing your share.

How would you feel if the members of your household left their work for you to do? Suppose dirty dishes were always left in the sink, no one took out the garbage, and everyone left their belongings lying about the house. Would you become resentful and angry at always being stuck with other people's work? So, too, will your co-workers be unhappy if they cannot rely on you to complete your assignments. Their success depends on you finishing your work on time.

Respect Rules and Territory

In the office, certain rules are designed to ensure fair treatment for everyone. If you ignore office rules, your co-workers will probably resent you. They may feel that you think you are somehow better than they. Always follow the rules, and you will avoid a lot of problems.

People with **seniority** are those who have worked on the job a long time and have gained knowledge and skills through years of experience. They can be helpful to you in your first months on the job. Sometimes, co-workers with seniority have earned some special privileges. If so, observe their rights and treat them with respect. This will help you create good relationships with them as well as with your other co-workers.

You will be given a space, a territory, in which to accomplish the tasks you are assigned. This space may be a desk or an office, and it will usually be respected by your co-workers.

You, in turn, must respect the territory of others. Don't borrow equipment from a co-worker's space without asking permission. Don't touch personal belongings on someone's desk or behave in ways contrary to what the occupant of a space desires. For example, if an occupant does not like others eating in and around her territory, respect those wishes and don't eat there.

Be Supportive of Other Team Members

Your job will often be part of a larger operation that depends on your contribution. Thus, the success of your other team members depends upon you doing your part. So you will need to be conscientious about your part of larger projects and also try to show an interest in what others in your group are doing. Show an appreciation of how their tasks contribute to the goals that are to be accomplished.

Be Appreciative and Accepting of Others

Let your co-workers know that you believe that what they are doing is important by going out of your way to tell them so. It can be as simple as saying, "Great job, Sam." Give approval as often as possible to co-workers, and it will make you and them feel good about yourselves.

Part of approval is accepting people's differences. People come in all sizes, shapes, colors, and socioethnic backgrounds, and they may have

---

O F F I C E   T I P

Don't start making suggestions for changes in how to do things during your first few weeks in the office. Your co-workers may resent a newcomer wanting to make changes too soon. Wait until you understand the work flow and the interrelationships between other jobs in the office before making suggestions.

---

accents that you are unaccustomed to. Sometimes it is difficult but always try to be tolerant of these differences. Make people in your business environment feel comfortable, regardless of how they are different. The differences can be interesting, and you can learn a lot from people with divergent life experiences.

The United States is a country in which many ethnic groups and cultures have been assimilated to become Americans. To be an American is to be part of a unique experiment that has been going on for hundreds of years. When we shine as a country, a community, or an organization, we have not allowed intolerance, prejudice, or fear of the unfamiliar to stand in the way of progress.

You and your co-workers will get more accomplished through cooperation and teamwork while ignoring personal differences. Talent and energy directed at a common goal creates a sense of unity in the workplace.

Be Loyal

Co-workers may sometimes act in ways you don't approve of, and the company may have policies you don't like. However, don't criticize the company or gossip about your co-workers to others in the office or to outsiders. Thoughtless conversation will usually catch up with you. Be tactful, monitoring what you say. If you are not willing to say something over the public address system for all to hear, it is best to keep it to yourself. You will encounter exceptions, things you will say in private to your supervisor or to co-workers who have also become close friends. But idle chatter can backfire, be misinterpreted, and cause you problems. Loyalty—the type you expect from your family and friends—is essential to good relationships on the job.

Listen to others' requests and comments with an open mind, and they will do the same for you.

Employment Skills for Office Careers

Be Flexible

Unexpected events often bring rapid changes in the business world, so you must learn to be adaptable. Adjust to changes in the status of things as quickly as possible, without complaining. This makes it easier for your team members to adjust, too.

Take Initiative

As you learn your job, perform your tasks without waiting for someone to tell you to get started. After you have finished your own work completely and efficiently, look around to see who may need help finishing what they are doing and offer your assistance. Helping others also gives you the opportunity to learn and grow.

After you have worked on your job for a while, you may think of some new and better ways of doing certain tasks. Make suggestions to your supervisor about how you believe these tasks can be accomplished more efficiently. However, be careful that you don't sound as if you are telling your boss how to do his job.

Participate in Office Social Activities

As often as possible, attend office social activities even though doing so is sometimes inconvenient. You may not wish to spend time socially with the people you see all day at work. However, seeing your co-workers in a more relaxed frame of mind will help you to understand them as individuals.

It could be a birthday or a celebration of an important holiday. It is easy to show that you appreciate your co-workers by bringing a gift or

Office celebrations are good times to discover the human side of your co-workers and supervisors.

a card to celebrate the occasion. These are the people you spend half your waking hours with. Treating them well socially will enhance your working relationships. They will be more likely to see you as a team member if you join these celebrations and participate in the group's activities.

Office politics are sometimes tricky, and information is often passed along at social functions. You can learn a lot about your associates as well as about business decisions. Some of these things may be important to you and may affect decisions you will make about your career.

R ecall Time

Answer the following questions:

1. Julie's supervisor has informed her that the company is providing a weekend workshop on communication skills for the workplace. It is to be free of charge to all employees; however, attendance is not mandatory. Julie asks if participants will be paid overtime for attending. Upon learning that she would not be paid for her attendance, Julie tells her supervisor she is not interested.

     What conclusions do you think the supervisor will make regarding Julie's level of commitment to her job?
2. Why is gossiping with one's co-workers a harmful and nonproductive activity?
3. Carlos, one of your associates in the office, has just been given a promotion. You know that he deserved it, yet you are filled with feelings of envy. What is the most supportive thing you could say to Carlos?
4. Give an example that demonstrates the attribute of flexibility in an employee.

■ THE VALUE OF POSITIVE BEHAVIOR

In your dealings with others, think and act in a positive manner. Negative behavior stops progress, but an "I'll give it my best" approach keeps things moving along. Show enthusiasm in all your work relationships. Keep an open mind to ideas and proposals presented by others. If you feel it is necessary to disagree with a new idea, offer an alternative.

Among your friends, do you know someone who always says no to suggestions about how to spend time? Does the following sound familiar?

Rose: Shall we go to a movie?
Anders: Na.

Rose: Shall we go bowling?
Anders: Na.
Rose: How about watching the basketball game on TV?
Anders: Na, not tonight.

This can get depressing. After a while, most people choose not to be around a person like Anders. The same thing happens at work. People will seek out your company and your opinion if you have a positive enthusiastic attitude.

When you arrive at the office, greet people. And don't forget the power of a smile. It gets the day off to a positive start and makes you and everyone you smile at feel good.

Of course, not every day will have a cheerful, upbeat tone. We have all encountered personal problems or frustrations on the job that make it difficult to concentrate. But keeping your emotions under control while you're at work is a must. Outbursts of any kind detract from your job performance, make your co-workers feel uncomfortable, and may put you out of the running for advancement.

Maintain a Sense of Humor

A sense of humor doesn't require you to crack jokes constantly. That can be disruptive. However, you should be able to see the lighter side of things, have fun at work, and laugh with your co-workers.

Don't take yourself too seriously. Laugh at yourself and allow co-workers to laugh with you when you do something awkward or make a minor mistake. No one is perfect. Being able to laugh with others at things you do will help you cope with stressful situations that arise.

On the other hand, recognize that you are important to the company and to each project you work on. Don't underestimate the contribution you make or your value as a team member. You are a vital part of whatever project is under way.

In the following example, Ramona is able to maintain her sense of humor at a stressful moment:

Ms. Parkins, the president of the company, is expected in the office any minute. People are scurrying around, getting things ready for her visit. Ramona is the receptionist, and her desk is immediately inside the main entrance. She is preparing a bouquet of flowers for the front of the office and goes out to get some water. Just as Ramona reenters the office, so does Ms. Parkins. Ramona bumps into Ms. Parkins, sending water flying. Fortunately, Ms. Parkins is able to avoid most of the water, which lands on the carpet.

"I'm so sorry," Ramona says. "May I help you?" Ramona has never met Ms. Parkins, so she does not realize that their important guest has arrived. Ms. Parkins laughs. "Perhaps a paper towel. Then you can tell Mr. Black that Ms. Parkins is here."

"Oh, no, I can't believe it. I wanted things to be so nice," moans Ramona.

"Things are very nice, and the flowers are beautiful. That was quite a greeting." Ms. Parkins laughs again.

Ramona laughs, too.

Don't Be a Worrier

It is unsettling to work with people who constantly worry about things. Act with mature assurance that everything will get done on time and correctly and that disaster does not lurk around every corner. Energy spent worrying could be better spent working toward solutions.

Keep a Businesslike, Professional Attitude

Offices can get hectic with busy telephones, interruptions from supervisors, heavy work loads, and deadlines. You will find times to laugh and have some fun, but remember where you are and act appropriately.

Being businesslike means being calm, courteous, helpful, efficient, and knowledgeable. Being knowledgeable does not mean that you have to know everything, but that you know how and where to find the answers to questions you are not sure about.

Your co-workers will have confidence in you if you act in ways that project a professional attitude. Remember, too, that you are a representative of your company, and projecting a businesslike image gives the public confidence in the company.

Maintain a Professional Appearance

Even before you begin your first assignment, people are forming opinions of you. It might not seem fair, but think how you react to someone you don't know. You, like most people, make a judgment based on

Employment Skills for Office Careers

Joan is a worrier. Each day she finds something new to be concerned about. She spends a great deal of time detailing what could go wrong.

"It'll never work. It can't be done. We won't get it finished on time," she will say, frowning and looking gravely concerned.

People avoid Joan.

Jane is enthusiastic and encouraging. She is also realistic—she understands that things don't always turn out perfectly, yet she always maintains a positive attitude.

"Sure, we can do it. We have time. We can try, we'll find a way to make it work," Jane will say, smiling. Then she will set out to tackle the task and make it work.

1. Why do you think people want to spend time with Jane?
2. What could Joan do to develop a more positive attitude?

appearance. In the business setting, a well-groomed person dressed in a stylish but subtle way gives the impression of being more capable, knowledgeable, and efficient than a person who is careless about his appearance.

Some businesses have established guidelines for office attire, but most leave it to employee discretion. Don't underdress or overdress. Emulate the style of those in management positions.

Your work space should reflect your organized and neat work habits. Don't clutter it with personal items and knickknacks. If you eat at your desk, clean up immediately upon finishing.

Be aware of any nervous or unconscious habits you may have acquired through the years. Humming, whistling, muttering to yourself, drumming your fingers, snapping gum, tapping a foot—these habits can be distracting and annoying to co-workers. Practice self-control and consideration of others.

Develop a Pleasant Office Voice

What kind of voice do you respond most favorably to? Most people find that a low-pitched, well-modulated voice is easiest on the ears. It also seems warm, reassuring, and competent. In the business world, a pleasing voice is an important asset.

Since we don't hear our own voices the way others hear us, you may want to tape yourself speaking as you normally do. If it seems too high-pitched or abrasive, you can improve it through practice.

You may have had the experience of studying in the library when a loud-voiced group passed through. Those people may not have been aware that they were disturbing you. But their voices were unpleasant and out of place in that environment.

Acknowledge the Good Work and Ideas of Others

In the 1989 movie *Working Girl*, the secretary's boss stole one of her ideas and used it as though it were her own. Ultimately, the boss's scheme backfired and the movie had a happy ending with the secretary receiving the recognition she had earned.

Always give credit where credit is due. It is all right to use someone else's idea if you have her permission, but mention who thought of it.

Learn to Be a Listener

Part of showing your respect and interest in your co-workers and your supervisors is to listen to what they have to say. Hearing the sounds of someone talking is not the same as listening for the precise meaning of what is said.

In one experiment in listening, a brief recording was played for sixteen people. Four hours later, this group was asked to explain, in writing, what they had heard. Three listeners had received the message correctly, nine repeated most of what was said, and four missed the point of the message completely. Receiving a message requires some listening skills.

You can teach yourself to be a good listener. Learn to separate the significant parts of a communication from the insignificant parts. You can't remember every word that is spoken, so you need to be able to distinguish what is important to remember. Ask questions for clarification and for emphasis: "Did you mean . . .?" or "I'm sure what you're saying. Can you clarify that for me?"

A busy office contains many distractions—telephones ringing, interruptions, people coming and going. These activities can cause you to miss the main point of a message. In this environment, you will need to make a special effort to concentrate on a message.

Try to avoid planning your response while the other person is still talking. Your response may be entirely inappropriate if you have not allowed the speaker to complete his idea.

Good listening skills can improve all your interpersonal relationships, but you will find them to be especially important for success on your job.

■ DIFFICULT PEOPLE

Some people are more challenging to get along with than others. Some people are chronically (constantly) dissatisfied and have a grouchy, negative outlook. They are not pleasant to be around.

Unfortunately, you may find a few of these difficult people in your work environment. One might even be your supervisor! Consider the following example:

Alan worked with great enthusiasm on a project for his boss, Ms. Escobedo. Alan had been unhappy because he could never satisfy Ms. Escobedo. He took special care on his project, hoping he might rid himself of the general dissatisfaction he was feeling from his boss. He even handed the project in before it was due.

Ms. Escobedo called Alan into her office.

LARGE OFFICE/SMALL OFFICE: What's Your Preference?

Getting Along with People

A large office usually has many employees with many different types of personalities. Some employees may be easy to get along with and some employees may not be so easy to get along with. So if you work in a large office, you will work with many people with many different personalities. However, you usually will not work with the same one or two individuals all day. You will work with a variety of people. Many times, it is possible to avoid the individuals who are not easy for you to get along with.

In a small office, with few employees, the employees usually work closely together. They often work with the same individuals all day. A lot more interaction occurs between the same individuals day in and day out. This means that employees who work in a small office must have personalities that enable them to work closely with the same individuals on a daily basis. No matter where you work, it is important that you maintain good working relationships with your co-workers. It is especially important in a small office because you work so closely with your co-workers.

Would your personality fit best in a large or a small office? Why?

"Well, Alan," Ms. Escobedo began, frowning. "Are you certain you covered all the important points in this report? We need to be very, very sure it's accurate."

"Yes, Ms. Escobedo," Alan replied, a little timidly. "I was very careful not to leave anything out."

"And do you think it's really detailed enough?"

"I believe so, but what do you think, ma'am?"

"I suppose it's OK. But try to be a bit neater next time," Ms. Escobedo growled, as she poked at the spotless paper.

Alan was crushed. Not a word of appreciation, not a word of praise, no thank-you for completing the project early.

Some bosses, including Ms. Escobedo, don't understand the importance of positive feedback to their employees. Others think that words of praise will soften the employee and that taking a hard line promotes more and better work.

Difficult bosses pose a particularly difficult problem because you are more or less at their mercy. Sometimes, a boss is so difficult that a transfer or change of job is necessary.

You may run into some co-workers who are difficult to get along with, too.

Types of Difficult People

Some people are chronic *complainers*. They see the negative side of everything and talk about it, loudly and constantly. "I have too much to do. My back hurts. My computer is old and doesn't work well. I don't get paid enough. It's cold in here. It's hot in here. The food in the cafeteria is awful. The traffic was awful this morning. My head aches. Rhonda was really bothersome yesterday," and on and on. This type of person's ability to root out the negative is endless.

Like Alan's boss, Ms. Escobedo, some people are too demanding and are never satisfied. "Can't you do the project faster, neater, more thoroughly? Can't you do more, give more, stay later, work longer? This is not what I asked for. This was not what I said." Some co-workers act this way, too.

Many offices have *know-it-alls* who also tend to be condescending (arrogant). "Oh, I could have done it better. No, that's not what that means. You're wrong again! No, that's not the way to do it. I've done many of these projects, they're very easy to do. Oh, come on, you really don't understand this? Here, let me show you how." Few people want to know what this kind of person has to offer.

Then we have the *shirkers*. These people regularly manage to miss out on most of the work. "Oh, I'm sorry, I can't possibly stay late tonight. Here, Chris, can you do this part for me? I'm sorry I missed the meeting. Too bad, I didn't get an assignment. I'll be leaving early today, I have an appointment. Linda, can you get that phone for me? David, will you make these copies for me? Tom, will you run this errand for me?" People in the office resent shirkers because they make more work for everybody else by not doing their fair share.

Finally, we have the *criticizers*. They can be bosses or co-workers. "There you go, you've done it wrong again. Can't you do anything right? Do you really like that dress? That's some kinda tie. Your handwriting is too hard to read. Your desk is certainly messy. I liked your hair the old way." Few people want to spend time with someone who undermines their confidence all the time by criticizing.

Strategies for Dealing with Difficult People

It will be important to find strategies for dealing with both bosses and co-workers whom you find to be unusually demanding and difficult. Most strategies require that you extend yourself, that you give a good deal of energy to setting the problem right. You will receive the benefits, and your work environment will be more tolerable and more pleasant.

Learn to Be Empathetic Being empathetic means being sensitive to the feelings of others. Try to understand other people's point of view by seeing things through their eyes. You may have heard that it is good to walk a mile in someone else's moccasins before you make a judgment about her behavior. Understanding fosters tolerance. If you understand what the other person is experiencing, it is easier to tolerate difficult behavior.

Vickie Woo
Human Resources Department
Oral-B Laboratories

Q: Ms. Woo, from your experience in the business world, what advice would you give to a new entry-level office worker?

A: 1. Be flexible—don't be concerned with titles. Help out in any way to get the job/project done.

2. Make sure you are doing your job before you worry about what someone else is doing. Try to avoid office gossip. It is not productive and often comes back to "haunt" you.

3. Don't limit yourself to your job description. If you have new ideas or want to do more, let your supervisor know. She will really appreciate the input you give.

Getting to know a person better will help you understand that person. Find out what he is interested in: hobbies, studies, activities. Then discuss those interests. This will also tell you something about the person's values, which is important information to know about people with whom you work.

Learn to Read Body Language You can learn a lot about people by observing their body language. **Body language** is nonverbal communication through physical action. For example, if you are talking to someone and she is leaning a bit forward, looking intently at you, that signals that the person is involved in the conversation. On the other hand, if your companion is leaning back, looking around the room, or tapping a foot, she is probably not involved.

When you were a child you knew how to interpret the body language of your parents. Children are generally more sensitive to nonverbal cues, though they don't understand them as such. Can you remember seeing your mother or father standing in the doorway of your room, feet firmly planted, arms crossed, gaze steady and unblinking? The body language gave you that sinking feeling that you had done something wrong.

Facial expressions also tell us a good deal about another person's emotional state. Think about Mom or Dad, with feet planted and arms crossed. What was the facial expression? Some of the ways we interpret these signals are intuitive, part of what we are born with as members of the human race. We don't know quite how we came to know, but without being told we often know what people are thinking by looking at their faces. Try it. See if you can tell what a person may be thinking or feeling by the expression on her face.

John and Jim worked in the same office. They were at the same pay level but had different job descriptions. John was a clerk and Jim a mail carrier. John came to work a few minutes early each day, greeted everyone, and set to work on his daily tasks. He acted as assistant to several people, doing small clerical jobs for them. He was interested in what co-workers were doing, enthusiastic, and always willing to do more to be helpful. He saw his job as part of a larger activity and wanted to do his share to ensure the success of the overall project. He liked the people he worked with, and everyone enjoyed his company.

Jim usually arrived at work a few minutes late, often too rushed to greet people. He gave the impression that it was an imposition to come to work. For the first hour in the morning, he was grumpy when people asked him to do things. He didn't see his work as part of a larger picture. However, he completed the tasks assigned to him efficiently and on time.

One day, the president of the company, Ms. Garcia, was coming to town, and the office was in an uproar. Everyone was bustling about because they wanted things to be just right for this important visit.

A co-worker asked Jim to carry some boxes to the back room for storage. Jim promptly replied that it was not his job to carry boxes, and he had his own work to do. John, overhearing the conversation, offered to take out the boxes even though is own desk was stacked with work.

A few weeks later, a new position requiring greater responsibility and offering a higher salary opened up. Both John and Jim were qualified to fill the new position.

1. Who would you select for advancement? Why?

Observing the person, getting to know the person, and talking to the person can facilitate your dealing with, tolerating, and being patient with difficult behavior.

Make Others Feel Important Sometimes, people's objectionable behavior stems from their not feeling worthy or useful. Make it your challenge to help these people feel better and, therefore, act better. Help them feel important. Be sure you know and use their name correctly. Help them to see that their role is essential to the overall effectiveness of the work group. Smile and greet them. Invite them to lunch. Show interest in their work, and praise them for a job well done. Chances are, most people in the office will be giving them negative feedback, sometimes causing the difficult behavior to escalate. You can be pleasant to them even if no one else is.

Accept Criticism and Admit Your Mistakes Have you known someone who constantly criticized you? You can be very disarming if you simply agree with the criticism. Epictetus, a Greek philosopher some two thousand years ago, suggested, "If someone criticizes you, agree at once. Mention that if only the other person knew you better, there would be much more to criticize than that!" Remember your sense of humor. It will help you through many difficult times.

Generally, it is inappropriate for you to mention the mistakes of others. However, it will be helpful to your office relationships if you readily admit your own mistakes. Little can be gained by making excuses for

R ecall Time

Answer the following questions:

1. At a staff meeting, the office manager has just described a new plan of reorganization for the various jobs in your department. You strongly disagree with the proposal. What is the best way to communicate your thinking to the manager? What else could you offer management besides your disagreement?
2. Why is it important to maintain a sense of humor on the job? Are you sometimes able to chuckle at your own mistakes?
3. Norman decides to bring a small radio to work so that he can listen to the World Series while he works. He doesn't think anyone else will mind because all the men who work near him also like baseball. Does this show professionalism on Norman's part? Why or why not?
4. Name the four types of difficult people described in the "Types of Difficult People" section of this chapter. Choose one type and discuss some strategies for dealing with such a person.

---

what you've done. Excuses are usually transparent. You will gain more respect, and have your co-workers' sympathy as well, if you are straightforward and simply say, "Yes I did it. I made a mistake. I was wrong."

Rid Yourself of Your Own Unhappy Feelings You can do things and take attitudes that distract you, directing your focus and attention elsewhere, away from difficult encounters. These strategies can help you avoid taking someone else's upsetting behavior quite so seriously.

Recognize that the unpleasant behavior has little to do with you or what you are doing. Thus, you have not caused it. Notice that the difficult person acts poorly with other people, too, not just with you.

Understand that unpleasant behavior makes a statement about the difficult person, not about your job performance, your personality, or your basic worth as a human being. This is a hard concept to accept. If a supervisor acts angrily when dealing with you, you assume it must be something you've done. This is not necessarily true.

Even if you've made a serious error, angry behavior has more to do with the other person's state of being, feelings of worth, or personal stress and strain than it does with what you have done. Good managers rarely display anger, no matter what happens in the workplace.

Remain calm no matter how badly your associate is acting. Do you remember the attributes that made up the list of professional and businesslike attitudes? They were calm, courteous, helpful, efficient, and knowledgeable. Remain professional no matter what others in the work environment are doing.

If you feel that someone is acting inappropriately, take your time when responding to her demands. Don't respond hastily, because you are likely to say or do something you may later regret. Simply say, "I need a few minutes to gather my thoughts. Please excuse me." If you cannot leave the area, tell yourself to slow down, take some time, and not be hasty.

No matter what is going on in the environment, your first obligation is to the job you were assigned to do. Focus on that. Return to your space. A popular phrase says, "Get centered." Getting centered is focusing inward, remembering that you have personal rights and power, that you are a worthy person, and that you choose to continue with the tasks assigned you. Focus on your strengths and duties, away from the bothersome, troublesome person who is causing you discomfort. If you remember who you are, you can sail by unpleasant encounters, continuing to be efficient and effective at your job.

■ ASSERTIVENESS VERSUS AGGRESSIVENESS

Another interpersonal skill that can be effective in dealing with difficult people is assertiveness. **Assertiveness** is communicating your needs to others confidently without being aggressive. Do you freely give into others? Do you shout and bully? Or, do you state clearly and directly what your needs are? This is important. If you do not use an appropriate style of communicating, your needs are probably not going to be met.

In the workplace, where you will spend so much of your life, it is important that your needs be met. If you forever jump on people in a bullying way, people will make little attempt to please you, to do what you wish them to do. If you are always passive, giving in to what others request of you, even if it is not in your best interest or what you think is right, you will begin to be resentful and feel bad about yourself.

Let's look more closely at these two ways of communicating.

Mr. White comes into the office of his assistant, Leeann, and shouts:

"Leeann, I told you yesterday I needed this report! What have you been doing all day? Why don't I have it?"

Mr. White doesn't know that the computer malfunctioned, the secretary was ill, and Ms. Doe also asked for a complicated report. Nor does Mr. White bother to ask if Leeann had any problems he could assist her with. He just acts like a bully and yells at her.

The other hidden side of this encounter is that Mr. White's house is overflowing with out-of-town guests, and he had a flat tire on the way to work. Furthermore, his own supervisor has been loading him up with work. Mr. White feels that everything in his life is out of control, and all he can do is yell at a subordinate.

How does Leeann respond to this encounter?

"Oh, Mr. White, I'm so sorry, I tried, but you're right. I will do better next time."

Notice that Leeann does not tell Mr. White about her problems with the report. Rather, she dutifully responds that she was wrong and will attempt to be better. Both of these people will likely leave the office this evening with a headache.

The encounter would have been more satisfactory for both parties had it gone as follows:

Mr. White raps at Leeann's office door.

"Hi, Leeann. Can you give me any word on the report we talked yesterday?"

"Hi, Mr. White. I was just going to call you to apologize. It was a mess, the computer was down, and Adam was ill. Anyway, I'll have it for you by four o'clock. Will that be OK?"

"Sure, that'll be fine. I'm sorry you had problems. Next time, let me know a little sooner. Maybe I can facilitate things for you."

"Thanks for understanding. I'll have it on your desk by four o'clock."

Each person leaves the encounter getting what she or he wants, and each feels good!

The three basic methods of communication are aggressive, passive (nonassertive), and assertive.

In the first example of the encounter between Mr. White and Leeann, Mr. White behaves in an aggressive way and Leeann acts in a passive manner. Neither party gets what he or she wants or needs.

In the second example, each acts in an assertive way, letting the other know what, exactly, her or his needs are.

Aggressive communication occurs when you overstate what you want; are overbearing, bossy, and pushy; and do not consider the needs of others. People often confuse the terms *aggressive* and *assertive*, but the two styles are clearly different. Aggressiveness can be hurtful and mean, whereas assertiveness usually satisfies the needs of both individuals in an encounter.

Passive communication occurs when you do not say what you want, or if you do, you are apologetic and feel guilty. You are more likely to let others decide what is best for you and put their own needs ahead of yours.

Assertive communication occurs when you say what you want clearly and directly, without animosity, being firm yet considerate of others' needs.

Being assertive is the most effective style of communicating your needs to those in your environment. Incorporating assertiveness into all your interpersonal encounters will be helpful to you, but learning to use these skills in the workplace is especially important.

■ BOSSES AS PEOPLE

The nature of many office relationships depends on the structure of the office—how responsibilities are delegated. You will have someone to report to, your boss or supervisor. He may have a title such as office manager or administrative assistant. That person, in turn, will also have someone to report to, and so on up the ladder.

Every business has a **hierarchy**—a ranking of authority—of people who have responsibility for getting work done. On paper, you could draw a sketch of who reports to whom and it would form a kind of pyramid. That is what a hierarchy looks like and what is sometimes called an organization chart (see figure 6–1).

At the apex, or top, of the pyramid is the owner, the president of the company, or perhaps a board of directors. Along the bottom of the pyramid are people who do the everyday work of the company. In the middle ranges are the middle-management people. Notice that the people who do the everyday work, the line staff, are the foundation of the pyramid. If these people do not do their jobs, the pyramid will collapse. The company will not be successful unless every level of the pyramid is functioning properly.

Your supervisor or your boss is the person who is responsible for ensuring that you do your job. You, in turn, are responsible to that person. Although you probably have a written job description to cover your general job responsibilities, your boss will tell you more precisely what you are supposed to be doing.

Sometimes we forget that those who give us assignments, oversee and supervise our work, and evaluate what we do are people, too. Sometimes the boss seems almost "bigger than life." He has so much power in the office, is able to coordinate so much complicated activity, and seems to remain calm through it all.

In fact, to reach a high position in most offices requires a high level of skill, education, and—often—years of experience. The boss's business life can be stressful and difficult, just like yours. You can find ways to

■ FIGURE 6–1
Sample Company Organizational Chart

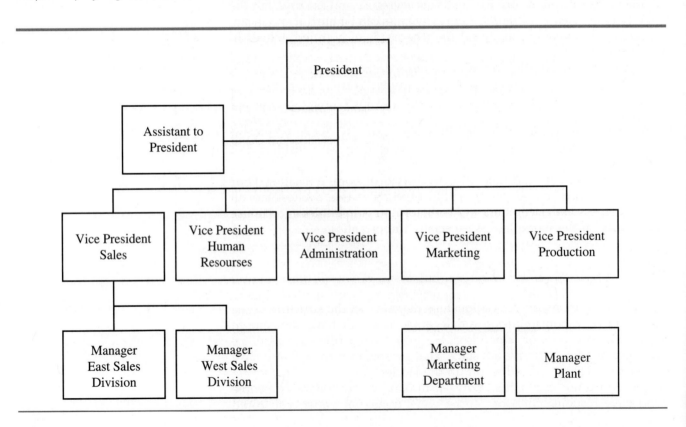

Employment Skills for Office Careers

make your supervisor's life easier, and thus make your own work easier, too. Keeping the boss happy is an excellent strategy for success in the office.

Accept Assignments Willingly

Begin by accepting work assignments with enthusiasm. You can tell your boss by your tone of voice, by what you say, and by your actions (body language) that you are happy to do the work assigned you. It is tiresome for a supervisor to feel that you are not interested in more assignments. Remember, it is the supervisor's responsibility to see that this work is done. When your supervisors make requests of you, they are simply doing their job. Make their job easier by being pleasant and accepting what they ask you to do.

Sort out, with your supervisor, which of your tasks has priority. That is, if you have more than one job, determine which you should complete first.

Know Work Priorities

Deadlines help you set priorities. A deadline is a specific time when a project must be finished. Keep a list of things you need to complete in a given time period—such as today, this week, by the first of the month. Discuss your list regularly with your supervisor. Make sure you know when things need to be done and which things are most important to your supervisor.

You may have more than one supervisor. If so, it is crucial that you know the order in which you must complete your assignments. This can be tricky. You will need clear statements from each supervisor on priorities. Some offices adopt a policy that the first work in gets done first. A *first-in, first-out policy* lessens the likelihood that someone will get upset about her requests being delayed because of someone else's requests. Even so, a higher-level supervisor may sometimes rearrange priorities.

Keep Your Boss Informed

Keep your supervisors informed about the status of things in the office, especially in their areas of responsibility. For example, if an important report has been completed while a supervisor is out of the office, inform the supervisor upon his return.

Your supervisor will also want to know how you are progressing on projects he has assigned you. If something happens that affects the outcome of a project, report it right away. Don't bother reporting petty things about interactions among co-workers. But keep communication open so important information is passed freely. Make it easy for your supervisor to get the information he needs.

Be Understanding

When dealing with supervisors don't expect things that are beyond the capabilities of human beings. Supervisors feel the same emotions and frustrations that you do. You hope your supervisor will be fair, competent, pleasant, appreciative, and honest. These are reasonable requests of someone you are expected to take orders from. Unfortunately, supervisors have bad days, too. You may need to be a bit forgiving at times. Perhaps your boss is not feeling well, or perhaps she has personal problems outside the job. You want your supervisor to be understanding, and sometimes you will have to be forgiving and understanding, too.

If you want to have a good working relationship with your supervisor, never criticize him in front of other co-workers. If you have a complaint that you feel has real merit, take it behind closed doors directly to your supervisor. Don't spread bad news about your supervisor around the office. Be loyal to your boss, remembering that supervisors are people, too.

A good way to keep your supervisors happy is by helping them look efficient and competent by being efficient and competent yourself. The more efficiently you handle your work load, and the more you accomplish, the better your supervisors look. That makes them happy, and it makes you happy, too.

Provide Solutions, Not Problems

Sometimes you will run into a problem when you are attempting to complete a task. Consider possible solutions yourself before you report the problem to your supervisor. For example, if your computer breaks down, you might call the repair service to learn whether you can get a replacement while your machine is being repaired. Or you might be able to use a co-worker's computer. When you take problems to your supervisor, bring solutions, too.

YOUR OWN ETHICAL STANDARDS

Set high ethical and behavioral standards for yourself at work. Think through what you will and will not do to get ahead.

Many situations arise in the politics and interpersonal relations in an office. Everyone in the office knows who's dependable, who's reliable, who's not to be trusted, and who will step on others' toes to get ahead. Secrets about the character of individuals who work together all day are few. Thus, it will be to your advantage to establish a standard of behavior for yourself that is honest and straightforward. Your co-workers will appreciate and respect you for it.

Use your best instincts about things that go on in the office. If you feel a situation is not right, ethically or morally, you can always make the choice not to go along. Often, not going along is a difficult choice because you must face the consequences of making that decision. It is usually easier not to make waves, and we are often admonished, "Don't rock the boat!"

Be true to yourself, your values, the things you think are important. Be the best you can be. You can make moral decisions for yourself, and you will be a better employee for doing so.

Recall Time

Answer the following questions:

1. You realize that it is impossible to complete all your projects by their deadlines. Which of the following do you do?
   a. Go to your supervisor's boss and complain that your supervisor is giving you too much work.
   b. Express your anger to your supervisor when others are present.
   c. Feel that you have failed and decide another job may be better for you.
   d. Sit down with your supervisor to discuss priorities and set realistic goals.
2. Kathy is in the middle of copying an important report, which her supervisor is to present at a meeting that day, when the machine suddenly breaks down. What steps could Kathy take to remedy the situation? In what order should they be taken?
3. Why does an employee with high ethical standards easily command the respect of co-workers?

■ SUMMARY

For companies competing in today's business world, great success is possible only when employees are content and fulfilled on the job. Where there is a true spirit of cooperation among workers who actively seek to improve their interpersonal skills, there is a happy, productive workplace. Cooperation requires that co-workers maintain a professional appearance and attitude, be loyal and tolerant of other's differences, and cultivate flexibility and the willingness to initiate projects.

Human relations is an art mastered by few. Most of us have had moments when we did things or said things that we would erase if we could. However, dwelling on the negative characteristics of ourselves and others doesn't make anyone happy and certainly doesn't increase production. Positive behavior is enthusiastic, is open-minded, is confident, and includes a sense of humor. The ability to listen to others and read their body language can enable a worker to communicate with even the most difficult people. Likewise, by graciously accepting criticism without making excuses, we invite others to communicate more openly with us.

Assertiveness is the balanced behavior between bullying (aggression) and being a victim (passivity). An assertive person communicates her needs to others effectively as well as considerately. In looking at a company's organization chart, keep in mind that all the positions, regardless of rank, are filled by human beings. Not everyone is adept at assertiveness. Furthermore, high rank does not license one to be aggressive, nor does low rank require passive behavior, and vice versa.

As a conscientious worker, practice assertiveness with your supervisor and others, accept assignments willingly, and know how to set priorities and meet deadlines. Always keep your supervisor informed of the status of your work, and if problems arise, try to provide solutions of your own if possible. Never criticize your supervisor in front of others. Be direct and speak to him personally. This is also part of having high ethical standards. A trustworthy worker is willing to swim against the tide if necessary to be true to her standards of behavior.

As an office employee, be willing to do the following:

- Be a team member and work in cooperation with others.
- Help co-workers with their work when you have time.
- Respect office rules and the territory and property of others.
- Be appreciative and supportive of co-workers.
- Participate in office social activities.
- Maintain a positive attitude and sense of humor even when the joke is on you.
- Take pride in a professional appearance and pleasant voice.
- Have empathy for difficult people and use human relations skills to reach them.
- Practice assertiveness skills in all your office relationships.
- Be honest and straightforward with your supervisor without being disrespectful.
- Learn how to set priorities for your work so that assignments are completed on time.
- Avoid compromising your moral standards even when doing so is difficult and costly.

Review and Application

REVIEW YOUR VOCABULARY

Match the following by writing the letter of each vocabulary word in the space to the left of its description.

_____ 1. nonverbal communication through physical actions

_____ 2. method of communicating your need to others confidently without being aggressive

_____ 3. terms meaning how people get along with one another

_____ 4. people who work together in a cooperative effort

_____ 5. characteristic of having worked on a job longer than others

_____ 6. way of overstating what you want, being bossy, and not considering the needs of others

_____ 7. way of not saying what you want, or being apologetic and feeling guilty

_____ 8. way of saying what you want clearly and directly, without animosity, and being firm yet considerate of others' needs

_____ 9. the ranking of authority within an organization

a. aggressive communication
b. assertive communication
c. assertiveness
d. body language
e. co-workers
f. hierarchy
g. human relations
h. interpersonal relations
i. passive communication
j. seniority

DISCUSS AND ANALYZE AN OFFICE SITUATION

1. William realizes too late that he left out an important section of a report when he prepared it for mailing to a big client. Not wanting to lose the respect of his co-workers or face his supervisor's criticism, he searches his mind for a logical and believable excuse to give them.

   How could William best gain support and approval from his co-workers?

2. Emily has decided that her boss is a hopelessly difficult person. He is always angry, nothing is ever perfect enough or on time, and he never thanks her for her work. She avoids speaking with him whenever possible and has begun complaining about him to her co-workers.

   What type of behavior is the boss demonstrating? Is Emily being assertive? What strategies might Emily employ to better this situation with her boss?

PRACTICE BASIC SKILLS

Math

1. Ginger has finally achieved a position of seniority in her office. The company has presented her with a choice of options for greater pay. She may choose a simple raise of 15 percent of her present salary, which stands at $1,600 per month, or she may opt for another plan with a base salary plus commissions.

   If she chooses the latter plan, she will receive a base salary of $1,700 per month plus 6 percent of her gross sales for the month. Currently, Ginger's monthly gross sales are averaging $4,000.

   Which plan should Ginger choose?

English

1. The following office memo needs revising. Underline examples of non-Standard English that are inappropriate in the business world.

   TO: My boss
   FROM: Gloria
   RE: Co-workers

   Ms. Banks,
   I finally have to get this off my chest. I know you are cool and will get what I mean. The jerks in my office are driving me round the bend. I'm at the breaking point. Please do something before I hit the wall.

Proofreading

1. Retype or rewrite the following paragraphs of the report, correcting all errors.

In anilyzing the profit and loss figures for last quarter ending in august we can see that the shoping center is doing well. Its important to note that sales have gone stedily up since doors open in january However We have yet to, re-view which stores are the biggest gainers.

What we can see is is that the biggest gross sales take place on week ends simply because more people are in the mall then; studies show, that people will spend simply because they are their. This is called impulse buying. Later is this report' we will address the subject of advertizing aimed at: impulse buyers.

APPLY YOUR KNOWLEDGE

1. Describe an actual experience you have had with another student or co-worker involving the subject of human or interpersonal relations. Based on what you know now, how might you have handled the situation differently?

2. You have come up with a great idea for increasing production in your office, and you are eager to share it with your supervisor. When you enter her office, you find that she has just received some bad news. Do you proceed to tell her your idea or do you decide to wait until later? Why?

3. Invite the manager of a local office to speak to your class on the subject of human relations in the workplace. Ask him to address particularly the problems faced by new employees and what is expected of them as workers.

Employment Skills for Office Careers

QUIZ

*Write a **T** if the statement is true or an **F** if the statement is false.*

_____ 1. Any time someone speaks, communication is taking place.

_____ 2. People who are chronic complainers seldom get to be supervisors.

_____ 3. Setting priorities will help you to be more efficient in your work.

_____ 4. If there are difficult people among your co-workers, the best policy is to tell your supervisor about them.

_____ 5. If you put your needs above those of someone else, you are being aggressive.

_____ 6. Listening and hearing both mean the same thing.

_____ 7. Successful women in big business usually wear little makeup and jewelry.

_____ 8. People who are flexible are willing to accept changes in their work schedule or duties without complaining.

_____ 9. Going to the office Christmas party might give your boss the idea that you are not serious about work.

_____ 10. Most employees who have initiative will soon quit to start their own businesses.

_____ 11. If you are sympathetic to your co-workers when they have problems that affect their work, you will end up being treated unfairly and working more than your share.

_____ 12. A monotone is a voice that is pleasantly lilting and upbeat.

_____ 13. Being nice to people who are difficult to deal with can help them to change.

_____ 14. People who admit their mistakes are more likely to learn from them.

_____ 15. If you always let others have their way and do not make waves, your co-workers will learn to treat you with respect.

Value of Positive Behavior

Acting in a positive manner usually brings about positive results. A positive attitude on the job will make work more pleasant. It will also help to get things done. Read the following case studies to help you think about positive behavior on the job.

> Barbara is a receptionist at a busy pediatric office. Often she must deal with many things at one time. One day she made several errors in booking appointments. That meant she would need to contact quite a few patients and change their appointments. Barbara told her office manager about the mistakes. The office manager laughed and said she had sometimes made similar mistakes. She offered to help Barbara contact the patients and make the necessary changes. She complimented Barbara on finding her errors in time to correct them.

■ If you were Barbara, how would you feel about your job? How would you feel if the office manager had been upset with you?

_____

_____

_____

> Anita worked as an admitting clerk in a small hospital. She was the first person patients had contact with when they arrived at the hospital. Anita was responsible for having the patients complete the necessary paperwork for admittance. One day while Anita was helping a patient complete the forms, her friend called to make plans to meet Anita for lunch. Anita talked to her friend about several personal concerns while the patient waited to complete the paperwork. The patient felt unhappy about the lack of attention she was being given.

■ Very often, the initial contact will determine the client's feeling about a situation. How might Anita have behaved to bring about a positive initial contact?

_____

_____

_____

■ How might Anita's behavior affect other employees who work with this patient?

_____

_____

_____

(Continued on next page)

Alan was the office manager in a very busy walk-in clinic. He had several employees who worked for him. Josie handled all the billing for the office. She was finding it difficult to keep up with the work load and made several suggestions to Alan about changes that she thought would help her accomplish her work more efficiently. Alan always acted too busy to give serious consideration to Josie's suggestions. Josie became frustrated and began looking for a new job. When Alan learned of her plans to quit, he was surprised and asked to talk with her.

■ How could Josie present her problem in a positive way to her supervisor?

_____

_____

_____

■ Do you think Josie should quit? Why or why not?

_____

_____

_____

One day at her job in a travel agency, Sara overheard her employer compliment a co-worker for doing a good job displaying some new travel brochures and posters. Sara had actually done the display, but the co-worker, who was eager for praise from the boss, accepted the compliment. Sara decided not to say anything to the boss.

■ Do you think Sara did the right thing? Explain.

_____

_____

_____

■ If you were Sara, what would you say to your co-worker?

_____

_____

Types of Communication

Communicating your needs to others is an important interpersonal skill. Communication can be aggressive, passive, or assertive. Read the following case studies and identify the kind of communication taking place. Think how you could handle the situation to communicate effectively.

Carlos is an office courier for a law firm. Several days these last two weeks he has had to work overtime to complete his unusually heavy load. When he picked up his paycheck, he noticed there was no additional pay for the overtime hours. Carlos became angry and accused his employer of taking advantage of him.

■ What kind of behavior is Carlos using? What would you do?

_____

_____

_____

Eric worked as a supervisor in the accounting department of a large community clinic. Several of the employees liked to go to lunch together. Eric felt it was important that the employees have time to socialize, but he was unhappy that these employees often returned to work a few minutes late. Even though Eric was dissatisfied with this practice, he was reluctant to speak to the employees who all seemed to enjoy working together.

■ What kind of behavior is Eric exhibiting? If you were Eric, what would you say to the employees?

_____

_____

_____

Wanda performed well in her job as a file clerk. She always completed her assigned tasks and seldom made mistakes. She hoped her supervisor would notice her good work habits and offer to teach her some of the other office jobs using the copy equipment and the computer system. Carol, a new file clerk, expressed an interest in learning these same skills. Carol let the office supervisor know she was eager to learn. In a few weeks, Carol was given a variety of tasks and trained to use the office equipment. Wanda could not understand why she was not given the same opportunity.

(Continued on next page)

■ What kind of behavior is Wanda showing? What behavior is Carol showing?

_____

_____

_____

■ Why do you think Wanda was not given the opportunity she wanted?

_____

_____

_____

Melissa was a hard-working office manager. She often worked through her lunch hour or stayed late to finish her work. There was really more work than one person could handle, but she was not willing to talk with her boss about hiring more help. Her boss did not seem to notice the long hours Melissa worked and often made unreasonable demands about deadlines. Feeling she could not please her boss, Melissa decided to quit.

■ What is Melissa's communication style? How might she effectively approach the problem?

_____

_____

_____

Paul was a medical records clerk for a doctor in a small private practice with only one other employee in the office. Paul had to arrange his lunch break with his co-worker. Paul insisted that he be allowed to have his lunch break at the same time each day so that he could use a nearby athletic club. He also insisted that he have his choice of vacation dates. He refused to compromise because he had seniority.

■ How would you describe Paul's behavior? How do you think it affects his co-worker?

_____

_____

_____

Co-worker Relationships

Getting along well with your co-workers is an important aspect of your job. Problems can and do arise between co-workers. By reading the case studies below and answering the questions, you will learn about dealing with some of these typical problems.

Gary had just been hired in his first medical transcription position, transcribing medical records for a large clinic. Gary received on-the-job training for his work. Six months later, the clinic purchased a new record keeping system. The employees received training on how to use the new system. Gary did not like the new system and found he made more errors using it. Gary decided to go back to using the original system he had learned. This caused confusion among his fellow workers when they used the records he had transcribed. His fellow workers complained to him. When he refused to change to the new method, they complained to their supervisor.

■ What do you think about Gary's attitude?

_____

_____

_____

■ What would you do if you were working with Gary?

_____

_____

_____

One day when Lori was making copies at the Xerox machine in her office, she inserted the paper tray incorrectly and the machine would not work. A co-worker saw she was having difficulty and offered to show her how to use the machine. Lori was embarrassed and said, ''I don't know what happened. It just stopped working, and the error light started flashing.'' Lori's co-worker reported the problem to the office manager. The office manager was upset and spoke harshly to the co-worker about the importance of using the office equipment properly. Lori did not say anything to either the office manager or her co-worker.

(Continued on next page)

■ How do you think Lori's behavior will affect her co-worker?

_____

_____

_____

■ What would you have done in Lori's situation?

_____

_____

_____

Renee was excited to have her first job as a receptionist in a busy ophthalmology office. She wanted to make a good impression. At night, before the office closed, the receptionists and other clerical workers were expected to clean up the waiting room. They straightened magazines, watered plants, and put out fresh coffee supplies. The workers usually took turns doing these tasks. Renee often stayed and did the work even when it was not her turn. Some of her co-workers appreciated her help. Others were annoyed at her attempts to "look good." Renee felt confused about what she should do.

■ If you were Renee, how would you handle your willingness to do extra work and your relationship with your co-workers at the ophthalmology office?

_____

_____

_____

One day at lunch, Justin was complaining to a co-worker about their boss, Mr. Miles. Justin called the boss uncomplimentary names and said he thought Mr. Miles was incompetent. The co-worker did not say anything. She was a friend of Mr. Miles and sometimes socialized with him outside of work. The next time she spoke with Mr. Miles, she told him about the incident. Justin was fired.

■ Was it fair that Justin was fired? Why or why not?

_____

_____

_____

Handling Difficult People

Getting along with people is an important part of most jobs. You will encounter many kinds of people at work. Some of them may be difficult. It is important that you have good relationships with your co-workers and other people you encounter. Think about how you could handle the following situations.

Peter is one of several computer programmers in a large hospital. He does not make good use of his time, frequently taking breaks or making personal phone calls. On busy days he often is unable to finish all his work and so asks the other programmers to help him out. He never offers to help any of his co-workers in return.

■ If you worked with Peter, what would you do?

_____

_____

_____

Colleen worked as an office assistant in a dental office. She did not have many regular assigned duties. She was to be available to help the other office personnel with a variety of tasks. She worked for several employees and was never sure how to prioritize her work. It was difficult for her to know if her work was satisfactory or appreciated. Colleen began to feel dissatisfied with her job and became disinterested in her work. Her attitude became unpleasant.

■ Suggest some things Colleen's co-workers might do to improve the situation.

_____

_____

_____

Bill performed well in his new job as research clerk. He learned the information systems quickly and was able to locate most information that was requested. After a few months, he was given a position supervising other employees doing the same kind of work. He was very critical of the other employees and became irritated when they were unable to find the information they needed. He complained about their lack of skill and seldom offered any praise. The atmosphere in the office became strained and stressful.

(Continued on next page)

■ Why do you think Bill behaved this way?

_____

_____

_____

■ If you were Bill's supervisor, what would you do?

_____

_____

_____

Joan was a clerk-typist for an insurance office. One day while she was gathering insurance information from a customer, her supervisor interrupted her and angrily berated her for not completing some work she had been given to do.

■ If you were Joan, how would you respond?

_____

_____

_____

Paul asked his boss if he could leave work a half hour early that day to allow himself time to get to a special concert. He offered to make up the time by working later the next day. Hesitatingly, the boss gave Paul permission, but Paul could tell by her body language that she was not pleased.

■ If you were Paul, what would you do? Why?

_____

_____

_____

Employer-Employee Relations

Both the employer and employee can expect certain things of each other. When these expectations are not met, problems often arise. By reading the cases below and answering the questions that follow each one, you will learn more about dealing with employer-employee problems.

Lacy worked as an office manager in a doctor's office. In Lacy's desk was a small cardboard box containing about five to ten dollars in "petty cash" supplied by the doctor for overdue postage or inexpensive office items. One day Lacy used all the money to pay for some office supplies and a soft drink for herself. She neglected to let the doctor know she was out of petty cash. A few days later, mail arrived with postage due. Lacy did not have the money to pay the postage, so the mail was returned for delivery the next day. When Lacy told the doctor, the doctor was unhappy. She had been waiting for that mail.

■ What should Lacy have done to avoid this problem?

_____

_____

_____

_____

_____

■ What would you do if you were the doctor and you found out that part of the money had been used for personal expenses?

_____

_____

_____

_____

_____

Marcy was an assistant to the admissions clerk at Saint Francis hospital. She did not really enjoy her work and felt she was underpaid and overworked. When her supervisor did not have enough work for her to do, the nurses asked her to help with some of their housekeeping tasks. She felt this was not her responsibility and resented the nurses telling her what to do. Marcy often called in sick, even when she was not. Sometimes she waited until the last minute before her shift was to start to call in sick. This did not give the hospital an opportunity to replace her with a substitute.

(Continued on next page)

■ If you were Marcy's supervisor, what would you do about her?

_____

_____

_____

_____

■ When the usual time period for a raise came, would you give it to Marcy or hold it back? Why?

_____

_____

_____

_____

Joe had a part-time job after school at a pediatrician's office. Joe's job was to enter information into the computer for billing purposes. Joe was good at working on computers, but this work was repetitious and Joe quickly became bored. Joe was very fond of children, so he spent a considerable amount of time visiting with and entertaining the patients. The children liked playing with Joe. Unfortunately, this slowed down Joe's work at the computer. The pediatrician noticed how much time Joe spent away from the computer and suggested that he talk less and work more. Joe felt insulted, became very upset, and quit his job.

■ If you were Joe, what would you have done? Why?

_____

_____

_____

_____

While she attends community college, Yolanda works part time as a salesperson at a medical supply business. Her job is to fill phone orders. Yolanda's employer had promised her that as part of her job, she would receive computer training. She was looking forward to this and felt it would be valuable training for her. But the supply house had been very busy, and the employer had not gotten around to the training. There always seemed to be something more pressing. Yolanda had been working there for over three months and felt frustrated.

(Continued on next page)

■ Was the employer being fair to Yolanda? Why or why not?

_____

_____

_____

_____

_____

■ Should Yolanda say something to her employer? What would you do?

_____

_____

_____

_____

Kate took a job as an administrative assistant in an engineering office. One night, she was working late. Everyone had left except one of the engineers. He came into her office, chatted briefly, and asked her for a date. She turned him down. The next month when she received her employee evaluations, she received a very poor report from that engineer. The rest of her evaluations were satisfactory or better.

■ What would you do if you were Kate?

_____

_____

_____

_____

Difficult People—Part of Life

Strategies for dealing with difficult people should be among your office skills. Here are three situations you may encounter. Write your strategies.

1. A person with whom you must work closely is a chronic complainer. The morale of your department would improve if this person would just be part of the team.

   _____

   _____

   _____

   _____

2. Your supervisor's preoccupation with personal problems is creating an atmosphere of tension and confusion. Staff members are reluctant, for obvious reasons, to say anything.

   _____

   _____

   _____

   _____

3. A person you must speak with frequently on the phone is always rude and impatient.

   _____

   _____

   _____

   _____

Aggressive, Passive, Assertive Responses

Become familiar with the distinctions between aggressive, passive, and assertive responses by writing three responses to each of the following setups.

1. Your boss informs you shortly before you would be leaving for home that she needs you to stay an extra hour. Working overtime would make you late for a long-planned special occasion that evening.

_____

_____

_____

_____

_____

_____

_____

2. A co-worker takes credit for an idea of yours that really impressed your supervisor.

_____

_____

_____

_____

_____

_____

_____

Agree or Disagree? Why?

1. Someone who needs a pat on the back for a job well done is insecure.

_____

_____

_____

_____

_____

2. As long as you do your job right, your appearance is irrelevant.

_____

_____

_____

_____

_____

3. If someone finds your voice unpleasant, that's his problem. You can't help how you sound.

_____

_____

_____

_____

_____

(Continued on next page)

4. When you arrive and when you leave the office doesn't matter as long as you get your work done.

_____

_____

_____

_____

_____

_____

5. Never, ever let anyone in the office know you have personal problems.

_____

_____

_____

_____

_____

_____

Employment Skills for Office Careers

Moving Ahead toward Your Career Goal

After completing this chapter, you will be able to do the following:

1. Improve your chances of achieving success by dressing for success.
2. Understand and learn from your work evaluation.
3. Earn pay raises and promotions.

New Office Terms

constructive criticism
remuneration

Before You Begin . . .

Answer the following questions that preview material covered in this chapter:

1. What is the name of a guide on how to dress for success?
2. What is the most important status symbol of men's attire?
3. What is the main purpose of an evaluation?
4. What are six questions you should ask yourself before you ask for a raise?

After you have worked at your new office job for several weeks, you will likely know all your co-workers and their roles in the office and understand your own job. You should also understand the office rules and procedures and follow them. You will then be on your way toward gaining the reputation of being a good, reliable, competent worker.

What's next? If you're interested in looking ahead to your future, you can do some things to enhance your success and ensure your advancement toward your ultimate career goal.

Dress and appearance, image, attitude, evaluation of progress, assessment of changing career and personal needs, participation in career-related activities, and education will all be important considerations in your quest for higher achievement.

When you begin working full time, you will want to progress toward your ultimate career goal. Doing so will depend greatly upon whether you are making progress on your current job. Your employer will provide a written evaluation of your work on a regular schedule. If you are performing well, you will probably earn some salary increases and perhaps even a promotion. As you move toward your career goal, you may want to take advantage of some further education and training.

■ YOUR PROGRESS ON THE JOB

You are responsible for completing your work assignments to the best of your ability. Reasonable expectations of your employer include satisfactory quality of work, productivity, punctuality and attendance, and care of office equipment. If you are meeting these expectations and you have a good attitude toward your work and your co-workers, you have a good start toward success on your career path.

Your progress will also depend on your appearance. Research has shown that dressing like the successful men or women in your office will boost your own success. You can do this and still dress especially for you and your job.

Dressing for Success

The image you express through your appearance on the job—your grooming and how you dress—is a serious consideration. The way you look makes a statement about how you see yourself, how you see your

250   Employment Skills for Office Careers

Margaret has been on her new office job for about twelve weeks. She likes the job very much and eagerly continues to learn as much as she can about it. Her supervisor considers Margaret an excellent employee because of her enthusiasm and her willingness to take on new responsibilities.

Though Margaret tries to do her best in all areas of her employment, she has a problem with grooming. She does not realize it, but the clothes she wears are inappropriate in an office setting. She wears skirts that are faddishly short, boots with fringes, blouses with silver decorations and tassels, and other kinds of clothes that are appropriate for a rock concert but not for an office.

Margaret is called in by her supervisor for her three-month evaluation. Her supervisor praises her for her excellent working habits, her punctuality, and her dependability.

Then the supervisor asks Margaret about her career goals and asks what her plans are for the future. Margaret responds that she eagerly looks forward to advancement and more responsibility. She says that someday she would like to be a supervisor herself.

The supervisor looks surprised. He tells Margaret that he had no idea she had these kinds of ambitions. He thought she was more a fun-loving person than a serious career-minded woman. He explains that he arrived at these conclusions strictly from the way she dressed, not from her job performance.

Margaret is very surprised and a little hurt. However, her attitude about the job is so good that she wants to change her image as quickly as possible.

1. What would you do if you were Margaret?

---

job, and how you feel about advancement. With the correct information and with some effort, everyone can look good.

Dressing for success begins with cleanliness but also requires that you be neat and attractive—which is what grooming is all about. Several aspects to grooming of which you should be aware are general health, hairstyles, skin care and makeup, shaving, and antiperspirant.

General Health People who exercise regularly, get sufficient sleep, eat properly, and do not have excessive social lives tend also to look better. Nothing is like the glow of good health and vigor to help you look your best.

Regular exercise means some aerobic-type exercise—running, biking, dancing, walking, or swimming—that is done for at least one-half hour at least three times each week.

Sufficient sleep for most people means six to eight hours of sleep each night. Individual sleep requirements differ, and you may need more or less sleep than the average.

A proper diet consists of minimum servings each day from the five food groups: six servings of grain products; three vegetables; two fruits; two servings of meat, poultry, or fish; and two of milk, cheese, or yogurt. The healthiest people consume a diet containing many fruits and vegetables. There is no real reason to have sugar products in your diet at all, and excessive amounts of fats and oils can seriously impair your health and your good looks. It is important to avoid eating too many of the wrong foods if you want to avoid becoming overweight and unhealthy.

Be aware of your appearance in the office at all times. Take a couple of minutes, two or three times a day, for a *short* grooming break. Sometimes, in a busy office, you forget to freshen your makeup or straighten your hair. Especially when you are expecting a new client or an important guest in the office, take the time out to make certain your look fresh.

Remember, you are a representative of your business and your looks will help assure outsiders that they are doing business with a good company.

Sometimes it's difficult when you are working full time to take time to eat properly. In American society, we tend to eat on the run, so we often turn to junk foods. However, eating the right foods will give you more energy on the job and help you look your best.

It's easy to socialize too much on the weekends when you have worked hard all week. But it's difficult to return to work on Monday with a clear head and a healthy glow if you have been excessive with your socializing. Don't let the way you spend your leisure time adversely affect your health or your performance at work.

When you attend to your health, you take a large step toward looking your best on the job.

Hairstyles You will find many acceptable ways to wear your hair. The key is to have hair that is neatly trimmed and brushed and never too faddish. Hairstylists can help you determine what sort of hairstyle best suits your facial features, what will be the most becoming, and what will be easy to care for. It is important to have a hairstyle that you can take care of yourself without having to fuss with it too much. You will be very busy, and saving time will be important to you.

Men on the job must carefully consider how they wear their hair. Older men who may be supervising new employees will have ideas about how men's hair should look. If you expect to get ahead in your business, you will have to cater to the older men's opinions. It makes good business sense to go along on this. Later on, you will have opportunities to take stands on much more important issues.

Skin Care and Makeup Some climates are very hard on the skin. You may need to apply a moisturizer each day on your hands, arms, and face—so that you do not have a dry, scaly appearance.

Women might want to seek a consultant to help them decide what colors and amounts of makeup to wear. Makeup that is poorly applied can detract from your looks in serious ways, but a carefully planned use of makeup can greatly enhance your appearance and give you a well-groomed, professional look.

Shaving Men do have a choice about whether to be clean shaven. Men who decide they want a beard or mustache should begin their growth at vacation time because showing up at the office with a stubble looks careless and unkempt.

Be sure to trim your mustache or beard regularly and to shave your neck and uncovered parts of your face daily.

Antiperspirant It is important for good grooming that you control body odor and wetness with a good antiperspirant. Perspiring can begin immediately after a bath or shower, so it is a good grooming practice to apply antiperspirant regularly after bathing.

Women's Wardrobes and Work Success

Some interesting research has related how people dress and how successful they are at work. People dress differently in different parts of the country, the most conservative area being the Northeast, and the most casual the West, especially California. Different industries also have different dress customs—law offices, for instance, tend to be much more formal places than insurance or real estate offices. For these reasons, it is important to notice what others in the office are wearing. Although many employers claim not to have a dress code, pay attention to what the most successful, highest-paid people in your office wear. If you hope to advance to supervisory status, it is important to dress like a supervisor, not like an entry-level employee.

Generally, women who wear solid colors rather than prints or bright patterns are perceived, rightly or wrongly, to be more serious. Although standards of business dress for women are changing, skirted dark-colored suits with pale blouses are still seen as more businesslike clothing than dresses. More women are wearing good dresses, often with jackets, and in some offices women in management positions are beginning to wear elegant trouser suits styled much like men's, but, again, it is essential to pay close attention to what the standard is in your own office because of the wide variation in what is acceptable. Being conservative is the safest policy, especially at the beginning.

Your hairstyle and dress should be complemented by tasteful accessories. Shoes should be midheeled or low-heeled. Save the spike heels or cowboy boots for evening wear. Wear simple jewelry—no clunky bracelets or dangling earrings. Keep rings to a minimum, and avoid large stones or elaborate designs that draw attention to your hands. Flashy jewelry and strong perfume may attract attention, but it won't be the kind of attention that leads to success in the office! If you work in an office where you meet the public, remember that you represent the company to them, and looking neat and well groomed reflects well not just on you but on the company.

Men's Wardrobes and Work Success

John T. Malloy's New Dress for Success (Warner Books, New York, 1988) tells men all about how to dress in various settings. Extensive research was conducted to arrive at the opinions espoused by the book. The clear message is "Use clothing as a tool."

When you begin your employment in a new industry, one of the first things you might do is research how people dress in that industry. Do this systematically by observing several male industry executives and keeping notes on what they wear. The most important observations will come from your own office. From your notes, eliminate the most conservative as well as the most innovative dress, and you will come up with an appropriate range of clothing for yourself.

Men's clothing may vary from sport shirts and slacks to formal suits, depending both on what part of the country you live in and what type of business you work for. Whether informal or formal, however, attire should be conservative in style. Dark colors (navy, dark brown, gray) are best for slacks, sport coats and suits, with contrasting light-colored shirts. Cotton or cotton-blend shirts that are not too fitted are best, and you should stay clear of shiny or partially transparent fabrics. Socks

Your grooming and dress reflects the way you see yourself. If you want to become a success, you must dress like those who are already successful.

should be dark and should complement trouser color (if you're color-blind, stick to black and charcoal), and shoes should be dark-colored leather.

Ties are the most important status symbol of your attire. Whether or not you wear a tie directly affects how you are perceived in terms of social status. In one experiment, men who wore ties to restaurants were allowed to pay for their dinner by check when they explained to the management that they had left their cash and credit cards at home. Men who were not wearing ties were refused the same courtesy.

In another experiment conducted in several New York restaurants, men who were not wearing ties were assigned the worst house seating. Men with ties were given the more desirable tables.

In yet another experiment, men who did not wear ties to job interviews were much less likely to get a job.

The point is, employers and customers alike will take you more seriously if you wear a tie. A tie is a symbol of your respectability. Wearing a tie cannot make you a success in business, but it can help.

Other clothing accessories are important, too. Most leather belts are all right, but be careful that the buckle is small and not a large metal decoration. Wear a thin, simple watch—no deep-sea-diving sports watches—and no other jewelry with the exception of a plain wedding band. Do not wear tiepins, tie clips, or tie bars—and wear a lapel pin only if it has a significant meaning for you. If you wear cuff links, use only small, simple ones. Only older men tend to wear a handkerchief in the breast pocket, and then only with a conservative suit. Wear no matching handkerchief-and-tie sets.

You will create your own fashion statement, adopted in part from what you've learned about your industry and what is comfortable and appropriate for you. Good clothing and a hairstyle that makes you look successful also will help you feel confident that you will be successful!

Dressing Especially for You and Your Job

Special jobs have special outfits. Some jobs even require that you wear a uniform, such as those in the front office of a hotel or in a doctor's office. Wearing a uniform removes all the questions about what to wear on the job. However, you still have other considerations about your clothing, including taking care of your clothes.

Take Proper Care of Your Clothes Whether you have the latest and most expensive clothing or you wear the same uniform day after day, your clothes should be immaculate—always clean and well pressed. When you take off your clothes at the end of the day, hang or fold them neatly to avoid unnecessary and unsightly wrinkling. Most articles of clothing have a tag attached that describes the proper care of the garment. Follow those instructions, and your clothes will last much longer and look much better.

Plan Your Wardrobe Carefully Clothing can be expensive. When you first begin to work, you can't expect to complete your wardrobe all at once. Choose high-quality, well-made clothing. Use mix-and-match combinations so that you will appear to have a variety of attractive, interesting outfits. For men, gray slacks with navy blazers and two or three good shirts are a good beginning. For women, a couple of dark skirts with several good blouses or sweaters of different colors or career dresses with coordinating jackets will start you off.

Fad clothing does not belong in a place of business, as it is expensive and it goes out of style rapidly. You will do better to spend your wardrobe money on basics that will last you a long while.

Wear What Looks Good on You Look around the office to see what other people are wearing. However, each of us has a unique look, a unique style all our own. When you are deciding what to buy and what to wear, be sure the styles you choose, choose you. In other words, wear clothing that is most becoming to you. Someone else may be able to wear a certain style that you admire, but it may not be right for you. Enhance your own looks with clothes that match your features, hair and skin colors, and personality.

If you incorporate the ideas about dress, image, and grooming into your plan for career advancement, you will probably notice that looking good makes you feel confident and sure about yourself.

R ecall Time

Answer the following questions:

1. What are several issues you will want to consider as you look toward advancement in your career?

2. What are several ideas to consider when thinking about good grooming? Discuss these.
3. Caring for your health can be important in how you look. What do you need to do to make sure you remain healthy and vigorous?
4. Why is it important for men to carefully consider what hairstyle they will choose?
5. Some basic colors are best for clothing for both men and women in the office setting. What are these colors? Discuss several other tips about how to dress on the job.

JOB EVALUATIONS

For as long as you have been a student, you have received regular reports from your teachers about your progress. You are probably not surprised to learn that an important part of your work experience will also be your regular evaluations.

You need to know how your work is being received. Even if you are feeling good about what you've accomplished, you will feel more comfortable when you know what your supervisor thinks about your work. You will learn this through the process of evaluation—the purpose of which is to inform you about how your supervisor views your work.

The Process

Someone in your office is responsible for overseeing your work. That person—your boss or direct supervisor—will constantly evaluate your work in an informal way. Your supervisor will notice things about your attitude, your performance, and your work habits nearly every day. That is your supervisor's job.

In some small offices, job performance evaluations are done informally, at a small meeting or over lunch, with no forms or records of any sort.

Most offices, though, have a formal evaluation process that is standardized for the protection of the employer as well as the employee. That is, if all employees are evaluated with regularity on the same form for the record, no employee can complain about unfair treatment in the evaluation process. Furthermore, a standard format and process helps an evaluator to be more precise in these evaluations.

Before your supervisor sets your evaluation meeting, he will fill out a form that is designed to record your progress. A sample evaluation form is shown in figure 7–1.

Every company designs its own form for evaluation according to its own needs. Generally, a list of categories is on the left side of the page and ratings are on the right side. It is common to have number ratings, with higher numbers indicating excellent performance and lower numbers indicating poor performance. The rating scale might be from

■ FIGURE 7-1
Sample Performance Evaluation Form

PERFORMANCE EVALUATION FOR EMPLOYEES

Evaluation Report:
_____1st Probationary
_____Final Probationary
_____Annual
_____Special Request

Employed _____

Date Issued _____

Date Due _____

Employee Status
_____ Initial Probationary
_____ Permanent

_____ Permanent in prob. assign.
_____ Temporary

Report for _____ to _____

FULL NAME (LAST NAME FIRST)   SOCIAL SECURITY NO.

POSITION TITLE   DEPARTMENT

Exceeds Work Performance Standards ⟶
Meets Work Performance Standards ⟶
Below Work Performance Standards ⟶

If "Below Work Performance Standards" is checked, please give your reasons for this rating and indicate suggestions made to the employee on how to improve.

SUGGESTIONS OR COMMENTS MADE BY IMMEDIATE SUPERVISOR

1. QUALITY OF WORK 1. ☐ ☐ ☐
   a. Job Knowledge a. ☐ ☐ ☐
   b. Accuracy b. ☐ ☐ ☐
   c. Neatness c. ☐ ☐ ☐
   d. Thoroughness d. ☐ ☐ ☐

2. QUANTITY OF WORK 2. ☐ ☐ ☐
   a. Volume of output a. ☐ ☐ ☐
   b. Meeting schedules b. ☐ ☐ ☐

3. WORK HABITS AND ATTITUDES 3. ☐ ☐ ☐
   a. Dependability a. ☐ ☐ ☐
   b. Punctuality b. ☐ ☐ ☐
   c. Orderliness c. ☐ ☐ ☐
   d. Compliance with instructions, rules and regulations d. ☐ ☐ ☐
   e. Ability to work without immediate supervision e. ☐ ☐ ☐
   f. Safety practices f. ☐ ☐ ☐

4. PERSONAL QUALITIES 4. ☐ ☐ ☐
   a. Judgment a. ☐ ☐ ☐
   b. Initiative b. ☐ ☐ ☐
   c. Adaptability to emergencies and new situations c. ☐ ☐ ☐

5. INTERPERSONAL RELATIONS 5. ☐ ☐ ☐
   a. Employee contacts a. ☐ ☐ ☐
   b. Public contacts b. ☐ ☐ ☐

6. SUPERVISORY ABILITY (if applicable) 6. ☐ ☐ ☐
   a. Leadership a. ☐ ☐ ☐
   b. Fairness & impartiality b. ☐ ☐ ☐
   c. Decision making c. ☐ ☐ ☐
   d. Training & instructing d. ☐ ☐ ☐
   e. Planning & assigning e. ☐ ☐ ☐
   f. Supervisory control f. ☐ ☐ ☐
   g. Evaluating performance g. ☐ ☐ ☐
   h. Productivity h. ☐ ☐ ☐

7. OVERALL WORK PERFORMANCE 7. ☐ ☐ ☐

Recommendation by Supervisor:
☑ Recommend continued employment
☐ Retain in position subject to further evaluation
☐ Recommend termination
☐ Recommend disciplinary action

My signature below is an acknowledgment that I have seen and discussed this evaluation, but does not necessarily imply agreement with the conclusions of the supervisor.

_____   _____
Signature of Employee   Date

_____
Signature of Immediate Supervisor

_____   _____
Title   Date

_____
Signature of Department head to whom immediate supervisor is responsible.

_____   _____
Title   Date

five to one or from ten to one. From these numbers, an overall job performance rating can be calculated.

Some categories found on these forms are attitude toward job, attitude toward co-workers, attendance, tardiness, ability to follow directions, willingness to take initiative, ability to make good judgments, productivity, quality of work, dependability, personal grooming, ability to get along well with others, and willingness to improve through education and information about the job. Many possible categories exist, and these can be broken down in smaller subcategories if a company feels it needs that kind of information about individual employees.

When you arrive at the office for your evaluation meeting, the form will be explained to you and your ratings will be carefully discussed. Generally, you will be asked to sign the evaluation. This does not indicate that you agree with the evaluation, only that you received it. Your evaluation will go into your permanent records with your company, and you will be given a copy for your own records.

The Purpose

The main purpose of the evaluation is to inform both the employer and the employee about the employee's job performance. The information gathered by the job performance evaluation may be utilized in a number of different ways.

You will probably begin your new job on probation, a period during which you can be fired without cause. At the end of three to six months, you will be given an evaluation to ascertain how you are doing and to upgrade your position to that of a full-time, regular employee. Therefore, one use of the evaluation is for advancement.

Another use is to determine if a pay raise is in order and if so, how much. Most employers understand that good performance should be rewarded. It helps the morale of the workers to gain recognition of this sort when they are doing a good job.

The evaluation may also be used when new positions open up to discern who among the employees may be best suited to fill them. Especially in the case of advancement, the evaluation plays a big role in the selection process. The evaluation may make it clear that an employee would be better suited to work in another department at another type of job. In this case, a transfer may be ordered.

The most important benefit the evaluation offers the employee is discovering how well he is performing and what can be done to improve performance. This is part of the ongoing education along your path toward your career goal. Sometimes evaluations can be hurtful, but mostly they will be given in the spirit of **constructive criticism**—suggestions that will help you do your job better—and you should receive them as such.

During the evaluation meeting, you will have the opportunity to ask questions or to air any problems you may be having. Don't bring up petty difficulties with co-workers. Your supervisor will not be impressed if he is forced to spend time in that sort of discussion. Rather, bring up issues about work that have been confusing to you. For ex-

When you are evaluated on your work performance, the form will be explained and your rating will be discussed with you.

ample, you might want to know how to determine whose work and which work should take priority or how to improve some skill with which you are having problems. Take this time to solve difficult, important problems that can help raise your level of competence.

Take the information you learn from your evaluation and immediately put it to work in your best interests. If you plan to do that, you will learn to view the evaluation process as a benefit that is important to your development.

■ SALARY INCREASES AND PROMOTIONS

When you began your job with your new company, you agreed on a rate of pay. That is the best time to inquire about procedures for salary increases so that you will know when to expect them. If you are serious about your ultimate career goal, you should also inquire about the possibilities for advancement and promotion. Do you have a future with this company?

No matter how satisfying your job, you will want to know that your employers appreciate you. The most concrete way employers can express appreciation is through a raise in pay.

Remuneration (compensation, or pay) comes in many other forms. These include the benefits that accrue for you as you are employed. For example, you could go from earning one week's paid vacation to earning two weeks' paid vacation—a nice benefit, indeed.

As you look to the future, you will set goals that will lead to satisfying your future employment needs. These goals will probably include earning increases in pay and may include earning promotions, too. A pro-

Davis came to work in the office of a new company. He is younger than most of the other office workers, and he is a little shy. He does his work meticulously. His attitude is excellent because he continually seeks more information about how to do his job more effectively. He is eager to advance and to take on more responsibility.

His supervisor, Ms. Jordan, knows Davis is a good worker, but she mistakes his shyness for snobbery and unfriendliness. She is not pleased by what she views as an attitude problem.

It is time for Davis's end-of-probation interview, so Ms. Jordan calls him into her office for an evaluation. She has filled out an evaluation form and explains it carefully to Davis. Davis's ratings are very high on all categories except getting along with co-workers.

Davis is puzzled by this and asks Ms. Jordan what it means. As they spend time together chatting, Davis explains to Ms. Jordan that he has a problem with being shy, and it becomes clear to Ms. Jordan that what she has perceived as standoffishness is indeed shyness.

Ms. Jordan is sympathetic to Davis's problem and gives him several ways to overcome the difficulty. She assures him that with time—and as he feels more secure with his work—the shyness will diminish.

1. What did Ms. Jordan learn about Davis during his end-of-probation interview?
2. Will Davis's evaluation and end-of-probation interview prove helpful to him?

motion is another way your employer indicates satisfaction with your work.

You can increase your opportunities for raises and promotions in several ways. Appearance and dress are only part of what you can do to further your career.

Types of Compensation

Several forms of compensation are available, depending on the type of job you have. You may work in the office of a restaurant, in a real estate office, or in some other type of business. Different types of businesses compensate their employees in different ways, including wages, salaries, pay for work accomplished, bonuses, and benefits.

Wages People who work in offices often receive a set hourly wage. The amount you will be paid is determined by multiplying the number of hours worked by the agreed-upon hourly wage. Generally, your workweek will consist of forty hours. If you work more than forty hours, you are working overtime, and you will be paid one-and-a-half times your hourly wage for each hour of overtime you work.

Salaries Many office workers—usually those with supervisory responsibilities—receive a set salary instead of an hourly wage. Thus, no matter how many hours they work, they receive the same salary. A salaried worker may receive his check each week, every other week, or each month. Paydays are different for different companies and depend on what is most efficient for a company.

Pay for Work Accomplished Some people are paid by the piece for work they do. For example, a typist or word processor may get paid by the completed page. Therefore, no consideration is made for how long it took to do the work—only that the work has been completed. When the work is turned in, the worker is paid. Generally, no benefits of any kind are associated with this pay arrangement.

Bonuses A bonus is extra money rewarded or gifted to employees. It can be a special holiday gift, or it may be a gift given because a job was well done. Sometimes, if a company has an especially good season or year, the employer decides to share some of the profits with the employees. Bonuses are an excellent way to boost employee morale!

Benefits Recall that benefits are the extra expenses your employer is responsible for, such as various kinds of insurance, Social Security, and so on. Benefits also include vacations and sick leave. Any or all of these benefits can be increased, which increases your total compensation from a company.

Evaluation of Your Employment Needs: Goal Setting

You will move ahead toward your ultimate career goal faster by setting some career path goals. These might include frequency of raises, guidelines for what you want to achieve regarding advancement and promotion, and what you want to accomplish concerning productivity or training on the job.

Have an idea where you want to be in one year and in five years. Often, potential employers will ask, "What do you expect to be doing in five years?" Knowing this not only helps you answer an employer's question, but also helps guide you toward your ultimate career and lifestyle goals.

Even though your salary range is adequate for a beginning worker, you may have changing obligations that require you to make more money. For example, you may get married or you may decide you want to save money to further your education, so your expenses increase. All these changing life situations will require that you upgrade your salary and, perhaps, your responsibility on the job.

From time to time, take a look at your life circumstances. If you are still relatively free of obligations, perhaps you will not need a raise in pay or a promotion for a while. But things change. Be aware of your own changes so that you can bring about adjustments on the job to meet your changing financial needs.

Increases in Compensation

In some companies, automatic pay raises are given at certain intervals, perhaps at six months or at one year. Often these raises are attached to a good performance evaluation. Salary increases are also related to the kind of job performed. For example, the engineers in a company may

Office politics are a reality, so try to be aware of how they work in your office. If you are interested in advancing, learn who listens to whom and which alliances are important. Sometimes, in an office, one person will be another's mentor, or informal sponsor. Find out about these relationships because this information can be helpful in your chances for promotion. Don't spy on people or be a busybody, but educate yourself on who relies on whom and how things get done. Your advancement in the company can be assisted by your understanding of these things.

get more frequent and higher raises than the office workers. Generally, an industry standard of pay exists for different types of jobs.

Not all companies have a standard procedure for awarding pay increases. In companies that do not, it is up to the employer to decide when a pay raise should be granted, and in some cases the employer waits for a request for a raise from the employee. In case it becomes necessary to request a raise, you will feel more comfortable doing so if you follow the suggestions given below.

Is It Time to Request a Pay Raise? If you think it is time to ask for a raise, you must ask yourself some things:

1. Have I been on the job a sufficient length of time to warrant asking for a raise?
2. Have I learned my job well and become very efficient, and is my productivity adequate?
3. Do I have good relationships with the other employees?
4. Have I been able to make some crucial decisions and judgments that positively affected my work? In other words, have I acted independently when it was appropriate to do so?
5. Have I had good evaluations and other feedback about my work from my supervisor and other co-workers?
6. Does the company seem to be in good condition financially? Can the company afford to pay more now, or would it be better to wait a few weeks until things improve?

With the exception of question 6, asking yourself these questions can help you prepare yourself for requesting a raise. If the answer to any of your questions is no, take some time to improve that area before you go to your boss seeking a raise.

How Do I Ask for a Raise? If you have decided that the timing is right and that you have, in fact, earned a raise, request an appointment with your supervisor to ask for a raise. This may be kind of scary, but you will be able to do it. In some companies, if you don't ask, you will stay at the same level of pay for longer than necessary.

First, ask your supervisor what workers must do to get a raise. Your supervisor may then list the requirements for a higher rate of pay. If you have accomplished all those things, tell her so—and say that you hope to receive your raise right away.

If, on the other hand, your supervisor tells you the company has no set standard to follow, that it has no rules for granting raises, then you must simply state your case. List your good points, and talk with confidence about why you deserve a raise. Be respectful—as you always should be—to your boss. Show that you believe you have earned a raise, and you want your superior's thoughts on the matter.

If you are denied, accept the decision—and ask what your supervisor wants you to improve in order to earn a raise. Take this direction seriously, and begin at once to work on the areas that need improvement so that your raise will be forthcoming at your next request.

Russ Whiteford
SEE-YOP
Stanford University

Q: Mr. Whiteford, from your experiences would you give some hints for students who wish to "move up the ladder" from an entry-level clerical position.

A: Learn as much as possible and take on extra assignments for the experience even if they are not most glamorous. Look ahead at what you need to learn for the next step up the ladder. Try not to stay in one job too long.

I can remember one clerical worker who started as a receptionist, advanced to an interviewer and then to a personnel analyst. It took initiative to get the necessary education and training to take on extra assignments and assertiveness to pursue the opportunities.

It is also important to dress appropriately for the job and the company or department's environment. In addition, act "professionally" under all circumstances.

Finally, if you don't know, ask—don't "wing it."

Promotions

By now, you probably know what attributes make a good employee. You have read about a pleasant attitude, the ability to get along with co-workers, good work habits, enthusiasm and willingness to learn, and the willingness to take responsibility for your job and decisions related to it. In this chapter you have read about appropriate attire and grooming. If you put into practice all the ideas discussed in this book, you will be a perfect employee. Your bosses will eagerly and regularly promote you along your career path.

Sounds easy, doesn't it? However, you will probably need to consider one more element. You learned about setting goals to guide you toward your ultimate career and life-style goals. The only missing element is your determination.

As you move along your career path, you will need to demonstrate that you are eager and willing to take on new responsibilities and learn new things. Sometimes, you will need to exercise a degree of assertiveness. Often, you will need to demonstrate initiative, taking on a little more than you are asked to do. It's like wearing a sign that says, "I want to get ahead, I want to succeed, I want to do well." Don't be obnoxious and overdo it, but make it clear that you are serious about your job and your career.

Your bosses will be looking for this attitude. They will be looking for people to advance who, along with excellent job performance evaluations, are eager to do so. Be aware of when promotions become available and how to apply for them.

When Do Promotions Become Available? Opportunities for promotions become available for two reasons. The first is when an employee who has greater responsibility than you vacates her position. The second is when the company creates a new position providing greater responsibility than your present position.

In growing companies, new positions are created fairly often. If, in your initial interview, you asked whether promotions would be possible, your boss already knows you are interested. Your good evaluations and your attitude can help your employer make a promotion decision in your favor.

How Do I Apply for a Promotion? Your company may make decisions about promotions without input from eligible employees. Some companies, however, advertise that a position is available and that they are seeking someone from within the company to fill it.

If you are seriously interested in promotion, stay alert to changes in the office. Know when someone is vacating a position that might interest you.

Before you actively seek promotion, ask yourself the questions that were outlined earlier about asking for a raise. Make certain you are ready before you ask to be included in the selection process. Then, let your supervisor know that you are interested and that you eagerly seek more responsibility and opportunity.

If a formal selection process is used, prepare your application as carefully as you would when applying for a new job.

When Promotion within Your Company Is Not Available Sometimes it seems the only way to move up in your career is to move on— that is, to leave your present employer and look for work elsewhere. This is an important decision to make, and there are several things you should take into consideration before taking this step.

If you have been offered a job with another company, it is important to be sure that it really is a step up for you. It may offer higher pay, but what about fringe benefits and chances for further promotions? Are you certain the company is financially sound and will still be in business in a few years time? Does the company promote from within or recruit outsiders to fill supervisory positions? Visit the office and try to get a feel for what working there might be like—is the atmosphere one in which you could be productive? Are your potential co-workers people you feel you could work well with? Add up the advantages and disadvantages carefully before deciding to take the new position. And remember, it's never wise to quit one job without assurances that the new one is yours.

If you finally do decide to quit your current job and move on, it is important to follow the procedures set down in your company. It is necessary to notify your supervisor, and often the personnel office, if you work in a large company. Give plenty of notice—at least two weeks, or a month if you are paid monthly. The best policy is to give written notice. This kind of courtesy will help ensure that your current employer thinks well of you and will give a good recommendation to any future employers.

R ecall Time

Answer the following questions:

1. What are the main purposes for conducting a job performance evaluation? List the categories that might be rated on an evaluation form.
2. What does your employer pay for you that are considered benefits?
3. What are several things you might want to ask yourself if you were going to ask your boss for a raise or for a promotion?

■ SUMMARY

After you have become successful on your first real job, what is next?

One way you tell your employer that you are ready to do more is by your appearance—which signals many things about you. It is important to look like the person you want to become.

Attending to your health is a major step toward looking well. Exercise, proper eating habits, sufficient sleep, and a reasonable social life are the keys to that healthy, attractive glow.

You also want to be clean, neat, and businesslike. Though faddish clothes are fun for leisure time, if worn to work they make a statement that you do not take your job seriously.

Much research has been conducted that demonstrates which clothing helps achieve a successful career. For women, this includes skirted suits of blue, gray, or beige, with a contrasting blouse, neutral-colored hose, and plain-colored pumps.

Men should wear suits or slacks and sports coats of blue, gray, or brown with a shirt in a contrasting color. Research shows that when you wear a necktie, others perceive you as respectable and responsible.

When planning your wardrobe, select clothing that isn't too expensive and that will last. Taking good care of your clothes helps them last so that over time you can increase the variety of things you have to wear—and you will always look good.

As you look toward advancement, you will find that your regular job performance evaluations provide valuable information. These evaluations are conducted by your supervisor, and generally he will use a standardized form and procedures so that every employee is treated the same.

At the time of your employment, you may have discussed salary increases. After you have been on the job for a while and you have been doing a good job, you may want to ask for a raise. In some companies, raises are connected with the performance evaluation and are given on a regular basis without a request from the employee. In other companies, you may have to ask your supervisor for a raise.

Setting employment goals will help you determine when you need a pay raise, how rapidly you wish to advance, and what additional training you will need.

When positions become available in your company, check your career goals to see if the positions advance you in the direction you want to take. You may have to formally apply for a new job, or your bosses may select someone on the basis of her job performance evaluations.

When you begin to think about your career path and how to best achieve your goals, you will want to consider the following:

- Do everything you know to do to be successful in the position you now hold.
- Meet the expectations of your employers regarding attitude, productivity, and good work habits.
- Be careful about your grooming. Keep yourself clean and neat, with your hair properly combed. Make sure your makeup is right.
- Choose your wardrobe carefully to reflect how you feel about advancement and taking on more responsibility. Avoid faddish clothes.
- If you are a man, always wear a necktie to important meetings and every day to work if it is appropriate.
- Understand the purpose of your job evaluations and make them useful to yourself.
- Know how and when to ask for a raise.
- Know how to ask for a promotion.
- Know when a job change is the best option.

In Conclusion . . .

When you have completed this chapter, answer the following questions:

1. *What is the name of a guide on how to dress for success?*
2. *What is the most important status symbol of men's attire?*
3. *What is the main purpose of an evaluation?*
4. *What are six questions you should ask yourself before you ask for a raise?*

Review and Application

REVIEW YOUR VOCABULARY

Match the following by writing the letter of each vocabulary word in the space to the left of its description.

____ 1. suggestions that will help you do your job better

____ 2. compensation, or pay

   a. constructive criticism

   b. remuneration

DISCUSS AND ANALYZE AN OFFICE SITUATION

1. Garth has done a fine job in his new position. He is respected as a man who has a good attitude, is always willing to take on more responsibility, is reliable, and is capable. A new position has opened up in his department that requires more responsibility and offers a better salary. Garth's supervisor has offered him the position. Garth doesn't know whether to accept the offer because he has not really thought through what he wants to accomplish in the long run.

   Garth has not taken a fundamental planning step. What is it? What would you do if you were Garth?

2. Rosemary has been on the job for several months and she has never had an evaluation. She approaches her supervisor and asks if it isn't time to have the evaluation and, hopefully, a salary increase. At the evaluation meeting, Rosemary's supervisor gives her an evaluation that is not too favorable and denies her request for a pay raise. Rosemary is surprised and hurt by her supervisor's evaluation. She thought she was doing whatever was requested of her.

   How can Rosemary use this evaluation to her advantage?

PRACTICE BASIC SKILLS

Math

1. A person can be remunerated for the work she does in several ways. When agreeing to a certain type of pay, you should be aware of what you might be making if you were under another type of pay. For example, compare the following:

   - *Job 1.* You work forty hours per week at $6 per hour and you expect to work five overtime hours each week at $9 per hour.
   - *Job 2.* You work the same number of regular and overtime hours as in job 1, but you are offered a flat salary of $300 per week.

   Assuming the two jobs are exactly alike except for the method of payment, which job will you take?

English

1. When your supervisor evaluates your work, he will notice whether you use formal or informal language. In business settings, informal language is not appropriate. Read the paragraph below, then rewrite it in formal, Standard English.

   I'm bummed. I really don't know what I want to do. This job's alright, I guess. I make enough to buy CD's and stuff, but I'm, like, in a rut. I could do some classes, hit some parties, and just hang out til I get a plan.

Proofreading

1. In your office job, you may have occasion to proofread a letter or a report that a supervisor hands you to type. See if you can find the mistakes in the paragraph below.

   We are happy to announce that our knew line of clothing is out. We hope you wil join us at our fall sho where our new lien will be shown. The springe fashions wil be off particular interst to you becaus the stiles are fresh, cool, and exciting.

The shwo will be heald on Mondy, Juli 23rd at 3:00 P.M. at the Coral Room of the Blue Lagoon Hotel. Please let us know if you entend to atend. make your resergvations by callin 714-259-3109.

APPLY YOUR KNOWLEDGE

1. Think about what you want to accomplish in the next five years. Write a comprehensive goal statement that includes specific steps in a specific time frame.
2. Take a trip to a clothing store. Keep in mind the kinds of statements you want to make with what you wear. Take a notebook and make notes about things you see that you would like to buy. If you bought all the clothing items that you feel would make up an appropriate wardrobe, what would the items be? How much would the items cost?

---

*Write a **T** if the statement is true or an **F** if the statement is false.*

_____ 1. If you dress like the top management in your office, others may think you are trying to get special treatment, and you will probably suffer for it.

_____ 2. Most executives prefer that their secretaries have long fingernails and makeup that is noticeably glamorous.

_____ 3. Most people need between eight and ten hours of sleep a night to perform at their best.

_____ 4. Eating a candy bar at your afternoon coffee break can give you the boost you need to make it through the day.

_____ 5. Getting plenty of aerobic exercise will influence the way you look on the job.

_____ 6. If your style of hair and dress stands out from that of the rest of the people in the office, it's likely that it isn't appropriate.

_____ 7. Men in office work do not have to be clean shaven to fit into the office environment.

_____ 8. Being clean and smelling fresh are important only if you will be continually meeting the public—as a receptionist, for example.

_____ 9. The most appropriate office wear for women is a skirted suit in a neutral color with a contrasting blouse.

_____ 10. The most important status symbol of male clothing is wearing well-made shoes.

_____ 11. Employees are not normally given job evaluations unless there is something seriously wrong with their performance.

_____ 12. A pay raise is the most concrete way an employer can let you know that your work is appreciated.

(Continued on next page)

_____ 13. Taking initiative and being eager to get ahead are likely to make your supervisor uncomfortable and not likely to lead to a promotion.

_____ 14. You should certainly ask for a raise if you have been on the job six months and have not yet received one.

Dressing for Success

It is important to present a good appearance—not only in your interview—but also after you have been hired. The case studies below illustrate how your appearance can affect your success on the job.

Maria and James both work in the medical records office of a community hospital. James often comes to work in jeans and a somewhat wrinkled shirt. Maria always looks neat, clean, and professional. Both Maria and James are good workers, and they get along well with the other employees.

■ If appearance is the only way Maria and James differ, and you as the employer have to cut down your medical records staff by one, which one would you let go? Explain your answer.

_____

_____

_____

_____

_____

Rita does data entry three days a week in the back room of a doctor's office. Rita's hair is dyed black and sticks up in spikes in the front. Her face is made pale by her makeup, with bold black eyeliner applied heavily around her eyes. She wears mostly black, with heavy metal jewelry around her neck and wrists. There is an opening for a full-time receptionist, and Rita has hinted to her employer that she would like to be considered. But her employer has hired someone from outside.

■ If you were the employer, would you have considered Rita? Explain your answer.

_____

_____

_____

_____

_____

(Continued on next page)

Ray works in a district office of a large high-tech medical products manufacturing company. Ray spends a lot of time on the phone with customers but almost never sees them in person. So he feels it is acceptable for him to dress rather casually at the office. But the office manager is being promoted, and the company will need to replace him. Ray would like to get the job, so he decides to start dressing the part. He begins to wear a jacket and tie every day.

■ Do you think Ray's change in dress will affect his chances at getting the new job?

_____

_____

_____

_____

■ Who is Ray really dressing for? Do you agree or disagree with his decision?

_____

_____

_____

_____

Carla works as a receptionist in an ophthalmologist's office. Carla typically arrives at work barely in the nick of time and always in a rush. She looks as if she got dressed at the last minute, without much thought or time spent on her outfit, hair, or makeup. She obviously does not put much effort into her appearance for work.

■ If you were Carla's employer, what do you think you might assume about how serious or enthusiastic Carla was about her job?

_____

_____

_____

_____

_____

Winning a Raise or a Promotion

Your career goals will include raises and promotions to advance you in your work. Read the following case studies and answer the questions to help you identify the attributes and skills you need to develop to receive these raises and promotions.

Martha received a notice of an increase in her rent, so she decided to ask her office manager for a raise. As soon as Martha arrived for work the next day, she approached the manager and told her she needed a raise.

■ If you were in Martha's place, how would you have approached asking for a raise?

_____

_____

_____

During his job interview, Roger felt uncomfortable asking about pay and raises. He was eager to get the job at the hospital and did not want to offend the interviewer. He had now worked as an admitting clerk for six months and felt he had earned a raise. His boss seemed pleased with his work, but Roger had not received any formal evaluation.

■ Suggest some things Roger could do to initiate an opportunity to discuss a raise.

_____

_____

_____

Carol was an efficient receptionist who worked hard and rarely socialized with the rest of the staff. She was surprised to learn of a new position that had been created and filled for setting up a computer appointment system. Carol had some expertise in that area and would have liked the job.

■ Why do you think Carol was not considered for the position?

_____

_____

_____

Job Evaluations

Formal job evaluation forms are standard tools used by many employers. Read the completed evaluation form below and then answer the questions that follow.

PERFORMANCE EVALUATION FOR EMPLOYEES

Evaluation Report:
✓ 1st Probationary
___ Final Probationary
___ Annual
___ Special Request

Employed __4-7-94__
Date Issued __6-24-94__
Date Due __7-8-94__

Employee Status
___ Initial Probationary
___ Permanent
Report for __4-7-94__ to __6-24-94__

___ Permanent in prob. assign.
___ Temporary

536-42-8051

FULL NAME (LAST NAME FIRST)

SOCIAL SECURITY NO.

POSITION TITLE

Pathology Lab

DEPARTMENT

Exceeds Work Performance Standards
Meets Work Performance Standards
Below Work Performance Standards

If "Below Work Performance Standards" is checked, please give your reasons for this rating and indicate suggestions made to the employee on how to improve.

SUGGESTIONS OR COMMENTS MADE BY IMMEDIATE SUPERVISOR

1. QUALITY OF WORK
a. Job Knowledge
b. Accuracy
c. Neatness
d. Thoroughness

2. QUANTITY OF WORK
a. Volume of output
b. Meeting schedules

Carol's typing speed is particularly valuable.

3. WORK HABITS AND ATTITUDES
a. Dependability
b. Punctuality
c. Orderliness
d. Compliance with instructions, rules and regulations
e. Ability to work without immediate supervision
f. Safety practices

Carol is often a few minutes late to work or takes an extra few minutes on breaks or at lunch. I have asked her to be more punctual.

4. PERSONAL QUALITIES
a. Judgment
b. Initiative
c. Adaptability to emergencies and new situations

5. INTERPERSONAL RELATIONS
a. Employee contacts
b. Public contacts

Carol considers questions from patients an interference with her assigned work. She prefers working away from the public.

6. SUPERVISORY ABILITY (if applicable)
a. Leadership
b. Fairness & impartiality
c. Decision making
d. Training & instructing
e. Planning & assigning
f. Supervisory control
g. Evaluating performance
h. Productivity

7. OVERALL WORK PERFORMANCE

Recommendation by Supervisor:
✓ Recommend continued employment
☐ Retain in position subject to further evaluation
☐ Recommend termination
☐ Recommend disciplinary action

My signature below is an acknowledgment that I have seen and discussed this evaluation, but does not necessarily imply agreement with the conclusions of the supervisor.

Carol Greene   6-24-94
Signature of Employee   Date

Elena Holden
Signature of Immediate Supervisor
office manager 6-24-94
Title   Date

Signature of Department head to whom immediate supervisor is responsible.

Title   Date

1. What kind of evaluation report is this particular evaluation? _____

2. How many probationary evaluations does this company require? _____

3. How frequently are evaluations given after the probationary period? _____

4. What is the employment status of Carol Greene? _____

5. What is Carol Greene's position with this company? _____

6. In which area did Carol receive the highest evaluation? Lowest? _____

7. Carol's supervisor is very pleased with the quantity of work she completes. Do you think the supervisor is justified in giving Carol low marks for punctuality if she is able to complete more work than the average employee? Explain your answer.

   _____

   _____

8. Looking at this evaluation, would you consider Carol for a receptionist position in a busy office? Why or why not?

   _____

   _____

9. If you were Carol, what questions would you ask the evaluator?

   _____

   _____

10. If you received this evaluation, would you feel justified in asking for a raise based on this evaluation? Tell why or why not.

    _____

    _____

11. Assume you are the evaluator. Give a response to Carol's request for a raise.

    _____

    _____

    _____

The Goal Line

Define and clarify your career goals by writing them down, first in list form, then expanded to complete sentences. Remember: some of the most successful people changed their goals when an unexpected opportunity presented itself. So allow for flexibility and alternate routes to the goal line.

_____

_____

_____

_____

_____

_____

_____

_____

_____

_____

_____

_____

_____

_____

_____

_____

_____

_____

_____

_____

Role Models

Choose a successful businessperson and gather enough information about that person to write a one-page biography.

_____

_____

_____

_____

_____

_____

_____

_____

_____

_____

_____

_____

_____

_____

_____

_____

_____

_____

_____

_____

It Doesn't Hurt to Practice

In the course of your career, opportunities for advancement may present themselves. Write a convincing paragraph to an imaginary supervisor stating why you should be considered for promotions.

_____

_____

_____

_____

_____

_____

_____

_____

_____

_____

_____

_____

_____

_____

_____

_____

_____

_____

_____

_____

Glossary

A

Aggressive communication An exchange of information that occurs when a person overstates what he wants and is overbearing, bossy, and pushy, not at all considering the needs of others.

Aptitude The potential for learning a skill.

Assertive communication An exchange of information that occurs when a person states what she wants clearly and directly, without animosity, being firm yet considerate of others' needs.

Assertiveness A method of communicating one's needs to others confidently without being aggressive.

B

Back-office jobs Positions that involve little or no contact with the public.

Body language Nonverbal communication through physical action.

C

Civil service jobs Government positions with federal, state, county, and city agencies.

Constructive criticism Suggestions that will help employees do their job better.

Cover letter A letter that always accompanies a resume and that simply states how an applicant learned about a particular job and why she is especially interested in that job.

Co-workers People who work together in a cooperative effort.

D

Dictionary of Occupational Titles (DOT) A. U.S. Department of Labor publication that includes descriptions of more than twenty thousand jobs.

Direct calling Contacting employers by telephone or in person when you don't know whether they have any job openings.

E

Employment Development Department (EDD) A state department that handles unemployment.

Employment in services A subgroup within the service-producing sector, expected to be the fastest-growing industry division in the 1990s. Examples include legal services and business services.

Employment tests Instruments used to determine an applicant's qualifications for a particular job. Examples include skills and aptitude tests, psychological tests, and general abilities tests.

Esteem The degree to which people value themselves and others. Part of a person's self-concept.

Extrovert A person who has an outgoing personality.

F

Flextime A system for allowing workers to set their own times for beginning and finishing work within a range of available hours.

Fringe benefits The extra payments or services, in addition to a salary or wage, that people get from their employer.

Full-time work schedule A plan under which employees work a standard forty-hour week.

G

Grievance process The method a company uses to allow employees to state their side in disputes with supervisors or other employees.

Guide for Occupational Exploration (GOE) A U.S. Department of Labor publication that organizes jobs into twelve interest areas and further divides those areas into work groups and subgroups.

H

Hierarchy The ranking of authority within an organization.

Human relations How people get along with one another. Also called interpersonal relations.

I

Interest survey An instrument that lists statements describing a variety of activities. Sometimes called an interest inventory or interest test.

Interpersonal relations Same as **Human relations.**

Introvert A person with a quiet personality.

J–K

Job lead card An index card on which a job seeker records all relevant information about an available job.

Job sharing An arrangement in which two people divide responsibility for a single job.

L–M

Letter of application A sales letter in which an applicant describes all his qualifications and tries to convince an employer that he is the best person for a particular job.

Letter of inquiry A letter asking whether a specified type of job is available.

Life-style goal The way a person wants to live in the future.

N

Negative attitude A bad mental position characterized by low self-esteem and a tendency to blame others for one's own shortcomings. Workers with a *negative attitude* are unpleasant, are indifferent, rarely smile, and constantly complain.

Networking Obtaining job leads from friends, family members, neighbors, and acquaintances.

O

Occupational Outlook Handbook (OOH) A U.S. Department of Labor publication that includes detailed information on the skills required for more than two hundred occupations and is updated every two years.

P–Q

Passive communication The exchange of information that occurs when people do not say what they want, or if they do, they are apologetic and feel guilty.

Performance evaluation A written statement outlining the strengths and weaknesses of an employee's job performance.

Personality The outward reflection of a person's inner self, apparent in how that person looks, speaks, and acts.

Positive affirmation A pep-talk you give yourself in the form of a repetitive phrase or phrases such as "I'm smart, I'm prepared, I can do this."

Positive attitude A good mental position characterized by a high level of self-esteem and respect for other people's views. Workers with a *positive attitude* are pleasant to be around, have many interests, smile easily and rarely complain.

Private employment agencies Organizations that are not supported by taxes and that charge a fee for finding people jobs.

Probation A period of time after hiring but before permanent employment during which a worker accrues no benefits.

Productivity The total work accomplished in a given time.

Public employment agencies Organizations that provide job referral service free of charge because they are supported by taxes and operated by the federal or state government.

R

Remuneration Compensation, or pay, for doing a job. *Remuneration* may include benefits as well as a salary, a wage, or a payment for work accomplished.

Replacement needs Needs to fill job openings because people leave occupations.

Resume A form, usually one or two pages in length, that organizes all the facts about an applicant related to the job he wants.

Reverse chronological order Date order beginning with the most recent date and working backward in time.

S

Self-actualization A psychological term that means individual potential fully realized. It means that you have become what you have aspired to become. You are your best possible self.

Self-concept How people feel about themselves.

Self-talk All the negative and positive thoughts people have about themselves.

Seniority The status of having worked on a job a long time and having gained knowledge and skills through years of experience.

Service-producing industries Businesses that exist to provide an intangible product, or service, to the public. Examples include the banking, insurance, health care, and education industries.

Severance pay Money that a person gets because she was severed, or laid off, from a company.

Standard English The correct style of speaking and writing that people learn in school and use to communicate in business.

T

Temporary office workers Employees who work for a few days or a few weeks at one company until a job is completed.

Termination A request for an employee to leave a job.

U

Unemployment compensation A small amount of money, administered by the state, that is paid to unemployed workers to help them over the times when no paycheck is being earned.

V

Values The things a person believes to be true, important, desirable, and worthwhile, such as honesty, integrity, family, friends, industry, and success.

W–Z

W-4 form A document that all workers in the United States are legally required to fill out and that provides certain information about the amount of taxes a worker will pay.

Work Any useful activity or purposeful, creative endeavor.

Work ethic The idea that everyone should do her share and make a contribution to society through working.

Work values Values that define needs people expect to fulfill through work.

Index

employer, 176–179
of team members, 206–207
Extrovert, 75

F

Flextime, 79
Franklin, Benjamin, 6
Fringe benefits, 77–78, 172–174, 261
Full-time work schedule, 40
Future job openings, prospects for, 40

G

Gates, Bill, 5
General office clerk, occupational
outlook, 41
Goal setting:
career choice and, 83
life-style and, 83
Grievance process, 174
Guide for Occupational Exploration (U.S.
Department of Labor), 81

H

Health insurance, as benefit, 78
Helmstetter, Shad, 15
Hierarchy, 221
Honesty:
from employer, 182
work and, 12
Hospital unit clerk, 49
Human relations:
aggressiveness and, 221
assertiveness and, 220–221
bosses and, 221–223
defined, 206
difficult people and, 214–216
ethical standards and, 224
positive behavior and, 210
team members and, 206
Human resource department, *See*
Personnel department

I

Information clerk, occupational
outlook, 41

Information services, and career
opportunities, 41
Intellectual stimulation, 7
Interests, and career choice, 74
Interpersonal relations, 206
Interview, job. *See* Jobs, interviewing
for,
Introvert, 75

J, K

Job(s). *See also* Careers; specific job
titles
applying for, 118
classification of, 40, 42
dressing for, 212–213, 250–251,
252–256
employee expectations in, 179–182
employer expectations in, 176–179
first days at, 168
interviewing for, 129
lead card for, 112
leads for, 113, 117
looking for, 110
outlook for, 40–41, 81
sharing of, 47
*John T. Malloy's New Dress for
Success*, 253

L

Layoff, 183
Learning, work and, 13
Letters:
of application, 119
of inquiry, 118
Life-style:
career choice and, 70
goals for, 73
Listening skills, 214
Lopez, Molly, 11
Lumbert, Jeanne, 132

M

Malloy, John T., 253
Mead, Margaret, 5
Medical records clerk, 49
Meehan, Paula Kent, 5
Mozart, Wolfgang, 6

N

National Aeronautics and Space
Administration (NASA), 7
Negative attitude, 9, 15
Networking, 114
Nonverbal communication, in job
interview, 135

O

Occupational Outlook Handbook (U.S.
Department of Labor), 40, 42, 81
Occupations. *See* Careers; Jobs; Work.
Office:
careers in, 40
safety in, 181
Office equipment, care of, 178
Office technology, advances in, 40

P

Passive communication, 221
Pauling, Linus, 5
Pay raise. *See* Compensation
People. *See also* Human relations
bosses as, 221–223
difficult, 214–215
Performance evaluation, 174, 256–259
Peripheral equipment operator,
occupational outlook, 50–51
Personal attributes, 72
Personal conduct:
off the job, 14
work and, 13
Personal data sheet. *See also*
Resume, 121
Personal problems, and job
performance, 14
Personality, career choice and, 75
Personality tests, for employment, 128
Personnel department, 117, 173
Policies and procedures manual,
172–173
Positive affirmation, 15
Positive attitude, 10, 15
Positive behavior, value of, 210
Preferences, and career choice, 70–71
Private employment agency, 116
Probation, 174

Problem solving, employer
    expectations and, 178
Productivity, 176
Profit-sharing plans, 77
Promotion, 83, 263–264
Prospects for future job openings, 40
Psychological tests, for
    employment, 128
Public employment agency, 116

Q

Quality of work, 176

R

*Random House Dictionary of the English
    Language,* 4
Receptionist, 41, 50
    occupational outlook, 41
Remuneration, 259. *See also*
    Compensation.
Replacement needs, 40
Reprographics clerk, 51
Responsibility:
    accepting, 7
    on the job, 7
Resume, 119
Retirement plan, 77
Reverse chronological order, 123, 125
Ride, Sally, 5

S

Salary. *See* Compensation.
Secretary, occupational outlook, 41

Self-actualization, 16
Self-concept, 4, 15
Self-confidence, 16
Self-fulfilling prophecy, 15
Self-talk, 15
Self-Talk Solution, The (Helmstetter), 15
Seniority, 207
Service-producing industries, 41–42
Severance pay, 183
Skills:
    career choice and, 74
    clerical, 42–48
Smoking, and work, 131
Social Security tax, 170
Standard English, and applying for
    jobs, 120
Stress, on-the-job, 77

T

Tardiness, 176
Taxes, withheld, 170
Tax forms, 168
Team members, 206
Teamwork, 206
Telecommunications, and career
    opportunities, 70
Temporary work, 78–79
    office, 45
Termination, 182
Time card, 170
Training, on-the-job, 127, 179
Typist, occupational outlook, 41

U

Unemployment compensation, 183
Unions, 78, 172

Unwritten rules of an office, 175
U.S. Department of Labor, Bureau of
    Labor Statistics, 40, 70

V

Values, 16, 73
    career choice and, 73

W, X, Y, Z

W-4 form, 169
Walters, Barbara, 5
Wardrobe, for work, 212–213,
    250–251, 252–256
Whiteford, Russ, 263
Withholdings, 170
Word processors, occupational
    outlook, 41
Work. *See also* Careers; Jobs
    attitudes toward, 4
    defined, 4
    employee expectations and,
        179–182
    employer expectations and,
        176–179
    at home, 79
    motivations for, 5
    responsibilities to, 7, 11
    temporary, 45, 78–79
Work ethic, 8
Work schedule, 45
Work values, 73
Working conditions, 43, 45, 57, 77,
    181–182
Working Girl, 213

Photo Credits